THE FUTURE DIRECTIONS OF EMPLOYEE RELATIONS

MONOGRAPH AND RESEARCH SERIES

Editing and Production
Jane Abelson Wildhorn
Sharon O. Geltner

Manuscript Preparation
Margaret Zamorano
Calvin Blake
Jeannine Schummer

Sales and Distribution
Kathleen Y. Greene
Michael Marinacci

THE FUTURE DIRECTIONS OF EMPLOYEE RELATIONS

Edited by
Eric G. Flamholtz
with
Felicitas Hinman

CENTER FOR
HUMAN RESOURCE MANAGEMENT

INSTITUTE OF INDUSTRIAL RELATIONS
UNIVERSITY OF CALIFORNIA, LOS ANGELES

Institute of Industrial Relations
Publications
University of California, Los Angeles 90024

© 1985 by the Regents of the University of California
All rights reserved
Printed in the United States of America

ISBN 0-89215-132-3

Foreword

The Institute of Industrial Relations, UCLA, is pleased to present **The Future Directions of Employee Relations,** the forty-fifth volume in its Monograph and Research Series.

The papers in this collection reflect the research findings and views of leading scholars who participated in an invitational conference held at UCLA in June 1984. The conference was commissioned by International Business Machines Corporation (IBM) and organized by the Institute's Center for Human Resource Management and the UCLA Graduate School of Management. The papers, which touch on a variety of important aspects of human resource management and the broader employee relations context, seek to identify and explore those emerging issues which will be particularly significant in the coming years.

Viewpoints expressed are those of the contributors to this volume and are not necessarily those of the Institute of Industrial Relations or of the University of California.

> Daniel J.B. Mitchell, Director
> Institute of Industrial Relations
> University of California, Los Angeles

Preface

During the past decade it has become increasingly clear that the areas of human resource management and industrial relations are undergoing a period of profound change. Fundamental changes are taking place in many, if not all, aspects of the employment relationship.

It is also increasingly clear that the most progressive and sophisticated business organizations attempt to stay ahead of environmental changes. This can be accomplished in a variety of ways, but one of the most valuable is to tap into the knowledge of a pool of experts in a given field.

International Business Machines Corporation (IBM) has long been a recognized leader in the area of personnel management. The Center for Human Resource Management, part of the UCLA Institute of Industrial Relations, was asked by the Employee Relations Department of IBM to organize a two-day conference on the future directions of employee relations in the United States. This conference was held at UCLA on June 13-14, 1984.

The intent of the Future Directions of Employee Relations Conference was to explore emerging issues and trends in the area of human resource management and employee relations affecting U.S. business and industry. In my capacity as Assistant Director for the Center for Human Resource Management at the UCLA Institute of Industrial Relations, it was my responsibility to invite a select group of scholars and practitioners to present papers at the conference. Although the audience contained the members of the professional staff of one corporation, there was no attempt to assess the implications of the emerging trends and issues in human resource management and employee relations for that company; rather, the papers and discussion were more generic in nature. Accordingly, we anticipate that others will find them of interest.

This volume is based on the papers presented at the conference by the invited participants. We are grateful to IBM for providing the funding for the conference which produced the papers contained in this monograph. It must be noted that the views expressed in these papers are those of the individual authors and, of course, are not necessarily those of IBM. Funding for the publication of the monograph per se was provided by the UCLA Institute of Industrial Relations.

I hope the reader will find the papers of interest and value.

Eric G. Flamholtz

Acknowledgments

The editors would like to thank the following individuals for their contributions to the production of this volume: Victoria Martinez, Kay Mason, Yvonne Randle, Ann Sprowls, Jane Wildhorn, Sharon Geltner, Margaret Zamorano, Calvin Blake, and Michael Marinacci.

Contributors

Benjamin Aaron
    Professor, School of Law, University of California, Los Angeles

Reginald H. Alleyne, Jr.
    Professor, School of Law, University of California, Los Angeles

Maria Lombardi Bullen
    Assistant Professor, School of Accountancy, Georgia State University

J. Curtis Counts
    Management Consultant, Los Angeles

Eric G. Flamholtz
    Assistant Director for Center for Human Resource Management, UCLA Institute of Industrial Relations; Professor, Graduate School of Management, University of California, Los Angeles

Robert J. Flanagan
>   Professor, Graduate School of Business,
>   Stanford University

Sanford M. Jacoby
>   Associate Professor, Graduate School of
>   Management, University of California,
>   Los Angeles

Larry J. Kimbell
>   Professor, Graduate School of Management,
>   University of California, Los Angeles

Daniel J.B. Mitchell
>   Director, UCLA Institute of Industrial
>   Relations; Professor, Graduate School of
>   Management, University of California,
>   Los Angeles

William Ouchi
>   Professor, Graduate School of Management,
>   University of California, Los Angeles

Yvonne Randle
>   Research Assistant, Center for Human
>   Resource Management, UCLA Institute of
>   Industrial Relations

Caren Siehl
>   Professor, Graduate School of Business
>   Administration, University of Southern
>   California

Lloyd Ulman
>   Professor of Economics and Industrial
>   Relations, University of California,
>   Berkeley

Contents

Foreword v

Preface vii

Acknowledgments ix

Contributors xi

1   **Introduction and Overview**
    Eric G. Flamholtz and
       Yvonne Randle 1

2   **Environmental Pressure and Union-Management Cooperation: Historical Evidence from the United States, 1920-1965**
    Sanford M. Jacoby 7

3   **Some International Crosscurrents in Labor Relations**
    Lloyd Ulman 47

4   **Some Informal Remarks on the M-Form Society**
    William Ouchi 107

5	Corporate Culture: Managing the Magnetic Force Caren Siehl	145
6	Human Resource Accounting: An Overview Eric G. Flamholtz, Yvonne Randle and Maria Lombardi Bullen	167
7	The Contemporary Scene in Labor- Management Relations J. Curtis Counts	203
8	Industrial Policy: A Critical Review of Several Suggestions Larry J. Kimbell	221
9	Illusory Shrinkage of Employer Discretion to Discipline Reginald H. Alleyne, Jr.	267
10	Trends in Labor Relations Law: Past and Future Benjamin Aaron	297
11	Labor Compensation and Labor Costs Robert J. Flanagan	329
12	Labor Relations Over the Past Five Years: Implications for the Future Daniel J.B. Mitchell	359

Eric G. Flamholtz and Yvonne Randle

1

Introduction and Overview

Currently, organizations are faced with a number of environmental changes which will have profound effects on employee relations. These include, but are not limited to, the change from an industrial to a service economy, changes in the nature and composition of the work force, changes in the nature of union membership, changes in labor law and industrial policy, and changes in the nature of ideas about managing people. In order to meet the challenges of the future, organizations will need to understand these trends and their implications for labor-management relations.

This book brings together the latest research findings and thinking of a number of leading scholars and practitioners who explore the changing industrial relations scene from various perspectives. The chapters that follow are grouped into three main subject areas which reflect these different perspectives. The first grouping (Chapters 2 and 3) looks at labor-management relations historically. In Chapter 2, Sanford Jacoby provides an historical analysis of union-management relations. He describes three waves of union-management cooperation: the 1920s, the Second World War, and the third wave of cooperation which began in the mid-1950s. From his analysis of these three "waves" of union-management cooperation, Jacoby suggests that peaks in union-management cooperation occur when: (1) environmental pressure is relatively high; (2) the perceived benefits of union-management cooperation outweigh the perceived costs; and (3) environmental pressure is high, but not so high that neither management nor unions are interested in cooperating with one another.

In Chapter 3, Lloyd Ulman compares the history of labor relations in the United States with developments in Europe. He describes a number of forces which have contributed to the divergent development of trade unionism and collective bargaining in Europe and the United States. These include the absence of radical politics and unionism, represented by the absence of a major Socialist or Communist party in the United States; the higher incidence of hostility towards unions which exists among employers in the United States; and the tendency, among American unions, for their bargaining power to be stronger than their organizing power. The author points out, however, that while the United States and Europe currently have divergent labor relations policies, the experience of unions in Europe in recent years closely parallels events which previously occurred in the United States. Thus he speculates that labor relations policies in Europe and the United States may be converging.

The second grouping of papers (Chapters 4 through 8) discusses current issues in employee relations and is divided into two subgroups. Chapters 4 through 6 deal with current concerns in the area of human resource management. Topics include the implications of corporate organizational style, the nature of corporate culture and how to manage it, and the importance of accounting for investments in human resources. Chapters 7 and 8 deal specifically with current labor relations issues in the United States, including the industrial policy debate.

Drawing upon his research on Japanese organizations, in Chapter 4 William Ouchi describes how M-Form (multidivisional) organizations offer a competitive edge through achieving a balance between teamwork and competition. He describes how the creation of M-Form organizations have contributed to the success of Japanese firms as well as to increasing the prosperity of the American city, Minneapolis.

Caren Siehl, in Chapter 5, examines the nature of corporate culture, the importance of corporate culture to managers and to organizations, and finally, how corporate culture can be managed in order to increase individual commitment to the organization. She suggests that one of the critical tasks of organizational leaders is to create and maintain a set of shared values. Further, she stresses that in creating these values, managers must learn which means are appropriate for the company's particular situation.

In Chapter 6, Eric Flamholtz, Yvonne Randle, and Maria Lombardi Bullen argue that, given the changing nature of the economy from industrial to service-based, there is an increasing need to account for investments in human resources, and they present an introduction to the uses, methods, and concepts of human resource accounting. They suggest that information provided by systems of human resource accounting can help management make better and more rational decisions with regard to human resources. While few organizations currently possess the technology necessary to implement a well-developed human resource accounting system, the authors contend there will be a need for such systems in the future as organizations begin to recognize the significance of their investments in human resources.

In Chapter 7, J. Curtis Counts describes the effects which a number of changes - in the nature of work, the composition of the work force, labor-management policies, union membership, and the regulatory environment - have had on current labor-management relations. He contends that the future success of labor-management negotiations will depend on the development and use of nontraditional solutions to bargaining problems as well as on recognizing the need for continuous rather than crisis-oriented negotiations.

Chapter 8 focuses on the current industrial policy debate. Larry Kimbell critically reviews the arguments of three major contributors to this debate. The arguments discussed are: (1) the de-industrialization thesis, as developed by Barry Bluestone and Bennett Harrison; (2) the need for new government credit market interventions, as developed by investment banker Felix G. Rohatyn; and (3) the Japanese-cooperative-paradigm thesis, as developed by William Ouchi. Kimbell concludes that while each argument has its merits, each suffers from flaws which policymakers should understand and scrutinize.

The final chapters of this book deal with certain environmental trends which are affecting employee relations, particularly those having to do with labor law, compensation, and the economy.

In his paper on employment at will (Chapter 9), Reginald Alleyne suggests that the trend away from employment at will may not be realized. To support this contention, he reviews three "encroachments" on employer discretion to discipline with impunity: the National Labor Relations Act, Title VII of the Civil Rights Act, and Common Law related to wrongful discharge. He concludes that, based on the effects of these encroachments, the long-standing practice of permitting American employers wide discretion in disciplining employees is far from obsolete.

In Chapter 10, Benjamin Aaron points out how the National Labor Relations Act has affected labor relations since 1977 and how it will continue to affect them into the 1980s. On the basis of his review of a number of recent legislative, court, and NLRB decisions, he concludes that changes in labor-management relations are likely to continue to be influenced by policy decisions and that current government policy, if continued, will have severe effects on all workers.

Robert J. Flanagan, in Chapter 11, looks at the growth of compensation and labor costs during the 1970s and early 1980s and describes how this growth affects organizations and workers. He also discusses how the structure of compensation has changed in terms of the union-nonunion gap and the proportion of compensation accounted for by fringe benefits.

He concludes with an examination of wage inflation and its control during the past twenty years as well as possibilities for the future and the effect of income policies on this growth.

In the final chapter, Daniel J.B. Mitchell describes the causes and implications of union wage concessions during the period 1979-1983 and discusses the implication that these concessions have for the future. He suggests that economic conditions are the cause for the wage concessions made since 1979. While these concessions have contained some new features, including job and security guarantees and encouragement for workers to participate in decisions affecting them, Mitchell suggests that some of these ideas may be detrimental to labor relations. He concludes that the economy, rather than policy decisions, will continue to have profound effects on unionization and union negotiations in the future.

Sanford M. Jacoby

2

Environmental Pressure and Union-Management Cooperation: Historical Evidence from the United States, 1920-1965

Introduction

Under normal circumstances, labor and management limit their relationship to the formal, adversarial procedures of collective bargaining and contract administration. Matters related to technological change and the improvement of productivity typically are not discussed; these are considered management's prerogatives. However, there have been several periods during the last sixty years when a number of unions and managements put aside their normal way of doing things in order to work together to improve productivity and reduce unit costs. Such union-management cooperation occurs outside of the bargaining procedure and involves the union in matters that were previously controlled and decided upon by management. (Hence the recent spate of "concession bargaining" was not in itself an instance of union-management cooperation, although it often was accompanied by that kind of cooperation, as when the parties agreed to jointly establish quality of worklife programs, quality circles, labor-management production committees, or plant rescue operations.)

There have been numerous experiments in union-management cooperation during the past decade. Academic observers, the business press, and even the parties themselves have viewed these as evidence that the American system of adversarial industrial relations has reached an unprecedented turning point. It still is too early to say whether a lasting change has taken place, although there is cause for skepticism. In any event, it is interesting to note that this is not the first time that the United States has witnessed joint efforts to improve productivity. Rather, this actually is the fourth wave of interest in union-management cooperation, the others having occurred during the 1920s, World War II, and the late 1950s.

In this chapter these earlier instances of union-management cooperation are examined to see what light they may shed on the current wave of cooperative experiments. The basic insight derived from this historical analysis is that union-management cooperation is a fragile phenomenon that flourishes best in an environment of economic adversity, although hard times alone do not guarantee that cooperation will occur; they are a necessary, but not sufficient condition. The parties also must be willing to shed their traditional adversarial stance, something that they are not always willing to do, even under economic duress or external compulsion from government, as occurred during World War II.

The 1920s[1]

The 1920s have often been characterized as a "golden decade," but the period's economic prosperity was unevenly distributed. Although new industries like motor vehicle and electrical machinery manufacturing performed well, older industries such as the railroads, textiles, and steel showed signs of economic maturity and stagnation. The latter represent the type of industries in which the decade's five major experiments in union-management cooperation took place. Although the experiments differed in their timing, scope, and objectives, they had many features in common. Before looking at these common features, it is helpful to give a brief sketch of each experiment.

The Cleveland Garment Industry: Beginning in 1919, this experiment involved an agreement between the city's garment manufacturers and the garment workers' union (ILGWU) to jointly determine production standards and methods by using time study techniques.

Amalgamated Clothing Workers: In its various markets, the clothing workers' union (ACWA) worked with employers to set production standards, conduct market studies, and organize production; this began in 1921.

Baltimore and Ohio Railroad: In 1923, the seven unions representing craft workers on the B&O

---

[1]This section is a summary of previous research reported in Sanford M. Jacoby, "Union-Management Cooperation in the United States: Lessons from the 1920s," **Industrial and Labor Relations Review,** 37 (October 1983), 18-33.

adopted a system for discussing with management how to improve working conditions and methods; this took place outside of regular bargaining channels.

Philadelphia Hosiery Industry: The hosiery workers' union (FFHW) conducted its own studies of market trends and in-plant production standards; made efforts to eliminate waste in unionized factories; and worked with employers to otherwise improve the productivity of unionized workers.

Pequot Mills: Beginning in 1927, the Naumkeag Steam Cotton Company (Salem, Massachusetts) and the union that represented its employees (UTW) agreed to conduct joint production standard studies, and the union promised to help market the firm's products.

Common Features

The parties involved in these experiments became interested in cooperation not because they were convinced of its virtues, but because they were faced with dire economic circumstances: a continuation of normal, adversarial bargaining could have proved fatal to either or both of the parties. A common element in the five experiments was stiff and growing competition from nonunion producers. After World War I, production in such industries as garments, textiles, and hosiery started to shift to nonunion establishments located in rural areas. In addition, after major strikes in 1919 and 1922, the B&O began to move its repair work to nonunion shops.

A second common feature was that, except for the railroads, the experiments took place in industries that were highly competitive. The clothing, textile, and hosiery industries had numerous producers, low profits, and high mortality rates. (The average lifespan of a clothing firm then was under five years.) Those firms that didn't go bankrupt or relocate to nonunion sites presumably were too weak to resist any union demands that would have raised their unit labor costs. Thus, unions in these industries helped stave off membership losses by restraining their demands and by cooperating with employers to improve productivity. But it was not a foregone conclusion that a union would pursue this cooperative path. In the coal mining industry, the unions followed the alternative policy of insisting on high wage increases, a stance that led to the partial destruction of the mineworkers' union in the late 1920s. Similarly, many employers faced with intensified competition or stagnation did not choose to have the unions assist them. Non-unionized firms preferred to face their troubles alone, as in the steel industry. These firms had other options, such as government protection and the formation of noncompetitive trade associations. When union-management cooperation occurred, it was either because the employer was too weak to resist the union or philosophically predisposed to cooperate.

Hence a third common feature of the decade's experiments was that they occurred in firms that were owned and managed by some of the most liberal men of their day. "Golden Rule" Nash, Earl Dean Howard, Morris A. Black, and Daniel Willard were quite sympathetic to unions, especially those that demonstrated their conservatism and maturity. These employers also realized that union-management cooperation helped to ease what might have been quite violent or radical reactions to employment declines and cuts in the effort wage. Cooperation gave some legitimacy to what might otherwise have been viewed as rapaciousness or greed on the employer's part.

Common Problems

Despite the belief that union-management cooperation would open new channels for nonadversarial communication, this didn't always occur. In several of the experiments, issues that were supposed to be decided outside of normal channels found their way into collective bargaining sessions and thereby became the basis for haggling and disputation. For example, the B&O plan was designed to separate issues for joint consultation from collective bargaining topics, but this distinction rarely held in practice. Because the B&O's cooperation plan lacked any formula for measuring or sharing productivity gains that came about as a result of cooperation, the question of gainsharing repeatedly cropped up during regular bargaining sessions.

Another difficulty encountered in each of the experiments was employee suspicion of cooperation, and distrust of their union leaders' involvement in joint productivity efforts with the employer. This hardly was surprising, given that all of the plans had been introduced in a top-down fashion and often entailed wage cuts and layoffs. Also, none of the plans provided for employee participation. Yet, contemporary observers like Sumner Slichter thought that membership opposition was to some degree inevitable, and that only professional union leaders had the foresight and maturity necessary to understand the employer's production problems and the ability to communicate these problems to the membership.

Nevertheless, as the 1920s turned into the Great Depression, union leaders had an increasingly difficult time trying to convince their membership of the virtues of cooperation. Rank-and-file opposition grew intense, especially when union leaders were linked to impending layoffs and deep wage cuts. By 1933, the unions no longer could secure their members' consent to further distress in already tragic situations. As a result, most of the cooperative experiments came to an end.

The Second World War[2]

In 1940, America began shifting to a war economy. In May of that year, President Roosevelt announced the establishment of a seven-member National Defense Advisory Commission, which was to help plan the production of a vast quantity of defense material. In recognition of the crucial role that organized labor would play in the defense effort, Roosevelt appointed Sidney Hillman, president of the Clothing Workers, to the Commission. Later that year the NDAC was dissolved and a new agency, the Office of Production Management (OPM), took its place. Hillman was named codirector of the new agency

---

[2]This section summarizes research previously reported in Sanford M. Jacoby, "Union-Management Cooperation in the United States During the Second World War," in Melvyn Dubovsky (ed.), **Technological Change and Workers' Movements** (Beverly Hills: Sage Publications Inc., 1985).

along with William Knudsen of General Motors. But organized labor, despite this unprecedented appointment, was dissatisfied with its influence in the war planning effort. The powerful unions that made up the new Congress of Industrial Organizations (CIO) wanted labor to play a much greater role in organizing and directing the nation's war production efforts.

In particular, they wanted the government to implement a proposal that Philip Murray, of the new Steelworkers' Union, had announced in the fall of 1940. Known as the Murray Plan, the proposal called for the creation of industry councils in each basic defense industry, to be composed of equal numbers of management and union representatives. These councils would have the power to coordinate defense production facilities, allocate raw materials and contracts, and promote industrial peace through collective bargaining. The councils would be given the discretion to organize regional and local machinery to secure the full participation in the war effort of local management, labor, and other groups in the community.

Although the plan led to a few tentative experiments by the OPM, it never was enacted, largely because of stiff opposition from industry. But CIO union leaders persistently agitated for the Murray Plan, applying pressure to the OPM and its successor agency, the War Production Board (WPB). In response to this, the head of the WPB, Donald Nelson, in 1942 announced that his agency was launching a major drive to increase the production of war materiel, and that the unions would be involved. Nelson's proposal called for the voluntary establishment of joint labor-management committees to increase production in war plants. Union leaders were quick to endorse the proposal, hoping that these committees would be a first installment of the Murray Plan, and that at the very least the committees would give the unions some participation in decisions that previously had been management's prerogative.

Thus the wartime experiments in union-management cooperation began under very different circumstances than had those of the 1920s, although both were a response to external pressure. During the 1920s, an increase in non-union competition and a prolonged decline in profitability facilitated a softening of adversarial postures. But neither the firms nor the unions that practiced cooperation during the war were faced with imminent shrinkage of markets or membership. Instead, the pressure to cooperate came from the government and, indirectly, from the unions, who pursued the experiments not as a survival tactic, but as a way to extend their influence over corporate and industrial production decisions. The government supported the experiments to ensure that adversarialism would not impede war production and also to check the unions' efforts to enact the Murray Plan.

The Committees at Work

Although the WPB's records showed over 5,000 labor-management committees in existence in 1945, only about 3,000 actually functioned at any given time. (Four out of five of these committees were found in unionized firms.) Half of the 3,000 committees limited their activity to patriotic functions and publicity, including blood drives and sales of war bonds.

Another one-third of the active committees had plantwide subcommittees to discuss matters such as absenteeism, health and safety, and employee transportation. Finally, about 500 committees conducted the above activities in addition to discussing production-related issues like work quality, material conservation, plant lighting and layout, tool and equipment care, and production schedules. So, no more than 15 percent of the active committees cooperated with management on matters that were outside the traditional scope of labor-management relations.

Some large plants had production subcommittees in each shop in addition to plantwide labor-management committees. These met regularly to discuss employee suggestions about such matters as waste reduction, material flow, and equipment placement and maintenance. Management vigilantly guarded its rights by insisting, in line with government policy, that the committees steer clear of bargaining and grievance issues. At some firms, members of the union's bargaining committee were not allowed to serve on the labor-management committee.

Although the record is mixed, some of the committees that dealt with production problems successfully improved productivity. Most managers were pleased with the operation of employee suggestion systems, and they thought that relations with the union had improved as a result of the work of the committees. But the committees also had numerous problems.

As during the 1920s, the most difficult issue faced by the committees was how to divide the gains produced by cooperation. Unions were unhappy with the size of the reward received for their suggestions; they were anxious to establish procedures to deal with any job elimination that came about as a result of committee work; and they were desirous of establishing some tangible way to prove to the employees that cooperation with management was beneficial. Without this, union leaders easily could be accused of having gone "soft."

Problems emanated from management as well. Management's strong defense of its prerogatives was a barrier to labor-management cooperation on production issues. Farsighted managers realized that any concessions made in this area during the war could come back to haunt them when the war was over. This fear of giving up too much during wartime explains why the largest firms in such basic industries as steel and autos usually refused to allow any committees in their plants. General Motors, out of 115 plants, had labor-management committees in only eighteen of them.

Postwar Decline

The committees quickly disappeared at the end of the war. Three years after the war, less than 10 percent of the 3,000 committees active in 1945 were still functioning; by 1950, they had become a rarity. The end of the war removed the rationale for many of the committees' activities, such as bond sales and blood drives, and this helps to explain their rapid demise. But a more important reason for the disappearance of the labor-management committees was management's determination to prevent any further union inroads into the realm that management considered its domain. During the war, the unions had for the first time begun to bargain over such matters as production standards, job evaluations, promotion procedures, and a host of other issues that previously had been management's sole prerogative to determine.

As a result, the immediate postwar period saw employers concerned as never before with defining and protecting their rights. Management rights clauses were for the first time widely inserted into collective bargaining agreements. At the historic President's National Labor-Management Conference, held in November, 1945, a subcommittee representing employers issued a report on "Management's Right to Manage," which outlined the areas in which unions should not be allowed to encroach. These included: the location of the business; the determination of plant layout and equipment, of processes, techniques, and methods of manufacture and distribution; the determination of financial policies; the determination of the management organization of each producing unit; and the determination of job content. The list left little room for the issues that labor-management committees had discussed during the war.

The committees that survived the war tended to be those that dealt strictly with noncontroversial, "integrative" issues like plant safety, sanitation, and accident prevention. Of a group of twenty committees studied in the early 1950s, only one discussed production problems, a ratio supported by the figures in Table 1. These safety committees typically met on a monthly basis to recommend safety rules and practices, to propose actions to eliminate hazards, and, less frequently, to conduct in-plant safety inspections. The committees care-

TABLE 1

HISTORICAL DATA ON LABOR-MANAGEMENT COMMITTEES*

Year	Safety Committee	Productivity Committee	Productivity and Sales Committee
1954	22%	0.3% (est.)	1.9%
1964		4.8	7.0
1974	28	5.9	

*Proportion of major collective bargaining agreement provisions for labor-management committee.

Sources: **Collective Bargaining Clauses: Labor-Management, Safety Production, and Industry Stabilization Committees,** U.S. Bureau of Labor Statistics, Bulletin No. 1201 (Washington, D.C., 1956); **Management Rights and Union-Management Cooperation,** U.S. Bureau of Labor Statistics, Bulletin No. 1425-5 (Washington, D.C., 1966); **Characteristics of Major Collective Bargaining Agreements, July 1, 1974,** U.S. Bureau of Labor Statistics, Bulletin No. 1888 (Washington, D.C., 1975).

fully steered away from areas of managerial prerogative, thus ensuring their viability. As one study noted, "By avoiding the controversial issues touching upon questions of managerial functions and the sharing of the fruits of increased production, these committees appeared to have improved their chances of survival."[3]

In short, the unions accepted the terms set by management after the war. For the next fifteen years they pushed where they found the least resistance, which led to significant gains for union members in wages, benefits, and employment security. The postwar claim that unions were challenging management's right to manage turned out to be somewhat of an exaggeration. By the mid-1950s, the CIO had discarded its visions of industrial democracy in favor of a philosophy that portrayed labor's exclusion from decision making not as a necessity but as a virtue of American unionism. Academic observers were quick to champion these virtues and pronounce that Selig Perlman was right after all: that American unions were basically "job conscious" and uninterested in plant decision making. The data bore this out. A 1955 study of forty Illinois unions found that none participated in decisions that touched on areas not directly related to the

---

[3] Ernest Dale, "Union-Management Cooperation," in Arthur Kornhauser (ed.), **Industrial Conflict** (New York, 1954), 364-368; Frank S. McElroy and Alexander Moros, "Joint Production Committees, January 1948," **Monthly Labor Review,** 67 (August 1948), 123; Frederick H. Harbison and John R. Coleman, "Working Harmony in Eighteen Companies," in Clinton S. Golden (ed.), **Causes of Industrial Peace Under Collective Bargaining** (New York, 1955), 339-344.

worker's job, such as equipment layout, plant location, materials sourcing, product prices, and accounting practices.[4]

The Third Wave of Cooperation

In the mid-1950s, industrial relations seemed to be in a happy equilibrium: Managements had accepted unionism and were moving into a "mature" relationship with unions; unions had grown to respect management's basic prerogatives and its desire for long periods of uninterrupted (i.e., strike-free) production. Everywhere there were signs of successful bargaining and quid pro quos. In particular, the unions agreed to sign three-year contracts containing management's rights and management security clauses in return for receiving hefty wage increases and, in many instances, automatic cost-of-living protection as well. But beneath the surface there lurked numerous problems. These became increasingly noticeable with the onset, in 1957, of a prolonged period of economic recession and high unemployment (Table 2).

Structural Shifts

At the end of World War II, the United States emerged as the world's preeminent power. Europe and Japan lay in ruins and presented no challenge to American industry in the world market. Indeed, in order to rebuild their economies Europe and Japan required an enormous

---

[4]Milton Derber, W.E. Chalmers, and Milton Edelman, "Union Participation in Plant Decision-Making," **Industrial and Labor Relations Review**, 15 (October 1961), 83-101.

TABLE 2

UNEMPLOYMENT AND GROWTH RATES IN THE UNITED STATES 1948-1967

Civilian Unemployment Rates[a]

Year	Rate	Year	Rate
1948	3.8	1958	6.8
1949	5.9	1959	5.5
1950	5.3	1960	5.5
1951	3.3	1961	6.7
1952	3.0	1962	5.5
1953	2.9	1963	5.7
1954	5.5	1964	5.2
1955	4.4	1965	4.5
1956	4.1	1966	3.8
1957	4.3	1967	3.8

Average Annual Change in Real GNP[b]

Period	Rate
1948-1956	4.1
1957-1961	2.5
1962-1967	4.9

Sources: ([a]) **Handbook of Labor Statistics- Reference Edition,** U.S. Bureau of Labor Statistics, Bulletin No. 1865 (Washington, D.C., 1975), 145; ([b]) **Economic Report of the President, 1980** (Washington, D.C. 1980), 205.

influx of American products and technology. In the domestic market there also was a voracious demand for goods, especially consumer durables, which was the result of consumers cashing in what they had been forced to save during the war. It was the best of times: the dollar was high, inflation was low, and aggregate demand was strong and steady.[5]

But good things usually do not last forever and this was becoming apparent during the late 1950s. For one thing, European nations and Japan were by then well on their way to restoring their industrial capacity. Given their relatively low labor costs and favorable exchange rates, these nations were beginning to penetrate both the domestic and international markets where American manufacturers held sway. For example, by 1960 imports held a firm and growing share of the domestic U.S. market for such products as automobiles (6 percent), steel (5 percent), and electrical products (2 percent).[6] Moreover, as in the case of Japanese steel, competitor nations now had more modern equipment and plants than American producers.

---

[5]Harold G. Vatter, **The U.S. Economy in the 1950's** (New York, 1963).

[6]U.S. International Trade Commission, **Automotive Trade Statistics, 1964-1979,** Publication No. 1102 (Washington, D.C., 1980), 2; U.S. Department of Commerce, Bureau of Economic Analysis, **Business Statistics, 1979** (Washington, D.C., 1980), 134-137; U.S. Department of Commerce, Bureau of the Census, **U.S. Commodity Exports and Imports as Related to Output, 1960 and 1959,** Series ES2, No. 3 (Washington, D.C., 1962), 29-30. Electrical products includes radio, phonograph, and television apparatus and other components.

Another problem was that by the late 1950s, for the first time in twenty years, domestic demand was on its own, in the sense that it no longer was being fueled by massive deficit financing (1941-45), liquidation of wartime savings (1946-48), or spending on the war in Korea (1950-53). Without this extra fiscal and monetary stimulus, the economy began to falter. The Eisenhower administration's policy of balanced budgets and restrained growth in the money supply also contributed to macroeconomic malaise, resulting in a five-year period of stagnation stretching from 1957 to 1962.[7]

In this environment, American companies felt that they had to reduce their labor costs and accelerate the modernization of their facilities in order to remain competitive. Unit labor costs had risen sharply since the war (Table 3) and employers wanted to bring compensation into line with what they perceived to be their ability to pay. To accomplish this, unionized employers began to stress the necessity of placing restraints on postwar innovations like pattern bargaining and cost-of-living escalators, both of which were thought to have driven wedges between a company's wage levels and its ability to pay. Thus American management, in the late 1950s, was beginning to feel that it had paid too high a price for industrial peace and stability, and that changes were in order in what had come to be regarded as customary pay practices.[8]

---

[7]Richard N. Cooper, "The Competitive Position of the United States," in Seymour Harris (ed.), **The Dollar in Crisis** (New York, 1961), 137-164.

[8]George H. Hildebrand, "The New Economic En-

TABLE 3

CHANGE IN NONFARM UNIT LABOR COSTS, 1948-1972

	Total (%)	Annual Average (%)
1948-1952	17.5	3.5
1953-1957	10.6	2.1
1958-1962	4.4	0.9
1963-1967	8.6	1.7
1968-1972	20.9	4.7

Source: **Economic Report of the President, 1980** (Washington, D.C., 1980), 247.

The other route to improving industry's cost structure was to modernize operations wherever possible. At the time it was widely believed that we were on the verge of a new technological revolution based on automated production processes and computer controls. There appeared a spate of books, articles, and reports describing both the wonders and the horrors of the new technology. Although there was some overstatement of automation's transformative effects, as well as a tendency to exaggerate the amount of new technology available for immediate use, employers nevertheless believed that there was something "out there" that could help them remain competitive, or regain a competitive edge.[9] But during and after World War II, many unions had established work rules and other practices that gave them considerable power to regulate the pace and the effects of technological change. Consequently, before the new technology could be used, employers felt that they had to wrest control of the shop floor away from their unionized workers.

---

vironment of the United States and Its Meaning," **Industrial and Labor Relations Review,** 16 (July 1963), 523-538.

[9]James R. Bright, **Automation and Management** (Cambridge, 1958); Eugene S. Schwartz and Theodore O. Prenting, "Automation in the Fabricating Industries," in **The Outlook for Technological Change and Employment,** National Commission on Technology, Automation, and Economic Progress, Appendix Volume 1 of **Technology and the American Economy: The Report of the Commission** (Washington, D.C., 1966), 291-362; Robert L. Aronson, "Automation: Challenge to Collective Bargaining?" in Harold W. Davey et al. (eds.), **New Dimensions in Collective Bargaining** (New York, 1959).

The late 1950s were a seemingly auspicious time for managements to attempt the realization of these objectives. Union bargaining power was relatively weak as a result of the economy's slow growth and accompanying high unemployment rates between 1957 and 1963 (Table 2). Beyond this cyclical effect the unions were confronted by some unfavorable secular trends, notably that union membership as a proportion of the labor force had begun to slip after 1953, its postwar peak.[10] In part this reflected the fact that manufacturing employment, except for a brief rise during the Korean War, was growing much more slowly than overall employment. (This was a phenomenon that ultimately was responsible for the contemporary perception of rising "structural" unemployment.)[11]

One way in which the unions might have dealt with these problems would have been to expand their representation among manufacturing workers, the group most favorably inclined to-

---

[10]Following are data on union membership as proportion of nonagricultural employment:

1947	33.7	1960	31.4
1954	34.7	1962	29.8
1956	33.4	1964	28.9
1958	33.2		

Source: **Handbook of Labor Statistics, Reference Edition,** 389.

[11]Following are data on average annual changes in manufacturing employment:

1947-1950	-1.9%	1956-1959	-3.3%
1950-1953	15.0	1959-1962	1.0
1953-1956	-1.7	1962-1965	7.2

Source: **Ibid.,** 105.

wards unionism. But it was getting harder and harder to make organizing gains in that sector, as illustrated by the declining union "win" rates in Table 4. Unlike the 1930s and 1940s, the unions now met with greater indifference or hostility when they attempted to organize industrial workers, in part because many of these workers were found in areas (e.g., the South) where unionism never had been very favorably regarded.

The other alternative would have been for unions to push into new areas such as the burgeoning service industries and white-collar occupations. Unions in the late 1950s were becoming aware that their continued growth would depend on making organizational gains in these areas,[12] but they had not yet devised a successful strategy for doing so (Table 5).

But although union strength was beginning to ebb, it had by no means disappeared. Some unions were determined to preserve their work rules and employment base, while others were willing to give these up only in return for substantial job security programs funded by management. In other words, if employers decided to go on the offensive, the unions were ready to strike, this in spite of their slowing organizational momentum and, in part, because of it.

The "Hard Line"

Beginning in 1958, a number of dramatic and bitter strikes occurred in which evidence could be seen of a new, tough management posi-

---

[12]Jack Barbash, "Union Response to the 'Hard Line,'" **Industrial Relations** (October 1961), 25-38.

TABLE 4

TRENDS IN REPRESENTATION ELECTIONS, 1936-1957

	Percent Won by Unions	Percent of Votes Cast for Unions
1936-1945	82.6	81.1
1945-1956	72.8	75.1
1954-1957	65.2	68.1

Source: Lloyd Ulman, "Unionism and Collective Bargaining in the Modern Period," in Seymour Harris (ed.), **American Economic History** (New York, 1961), 425.

TABLE 5

UNION GAINS IN NEW ORGANIZATION CAMPAIGNS,
1951-1959

	Percent Won By Unions	
	1951	1959
Manufacturing	68	62
Wholesale, retail	20	21
Services	2	4
Other	10	13

Source: Joseph Krislov, "New Organizing by Unions During the 1950s," **Monthly Labor Review,** 83 (September 1960), 922-924.

tion. The disputes took place in a variety of industries, but they had in common union demands for greater job security in the face of an employer hard line on reducing labor costs and removing limits on management's technological and allocative flexibility. Examples of these disputes included:

- The United Glass and Ceramic Workers struck for 134 days in 1958 against Pittsburgh Plate and Glass in response to the company's attempt to reduce labor costs and to change work rules.[13]

- The United Steelworkers conducted a 116-day national steel strike in 1959 to obtain higher wages and greater employment security; the companies were determined to gain more operating efficiency and flexibility, in part by changing local working rules (Section 2-B of the contract).[14]

- Wilson took a three-month strike in 1959 by the United Packinghouse Workers in order to limit COLA clauses and preserve its rights in the area of introducing labor-saving technology. A 52-day strike took place at another meatpacker, Swift, over the same issues.[15]

---

[13] Benson Soffer and Irwin L. Herrnstadt, "Recent Labor Disputes Over 'Restrictive' Practices and 'Inflationary' Wage Increases," **Journal of Business,** 34 (October 1961), 453-470.

[14] Edward R. Livernash et al., **Collective Bargaining in the Steel Industry: A Study of the Public Interest and the Role of Government** (Westport, Conn., 1976 [1961]).

[15] **Monthly Labor Review,** 81-84 (1958-1961), various issues.

- The International Longshoremen's Association (ILA) in 1959 struck ports on the East and Gulf coasts in response to employer efforts to reduce manning levels and introduce mechanized loading equipment and cargo containerization. (The strike was cut short by a Taft-Hartley injunction.)[16]

- The International Union of Electrical, Radio and Machine Workers (IUE) in 1960 struck fifty General Electric plants for three weeks when GE refused to negotiate over its "firm but fair" final offer on wages and issues related to technological change.[17]

In addition to these protracted disputes, there were other signs of management's hard line. First, employers in several industries began to explore and engage in new cooperative activities designed to coordinate their labor relations strategies and strengthen their bargaining power. The airlines signed mutual assistance pacts (MAPs), which essentially provided strike insurance for a carrier singled out by the unions. In the automobile industry, the major producers began to consult with each other prior to national negotiations in 1958 and 1961 as part of an effort to present a more

---

[16]Ibid., various issues; Joseph H. Ball, **The Government-Subsidized Union Monopoly** (Washington, D.C., 1966).

[17]James Kuhn, "Electrical Products," in Gerald G. Somers (ed.), **Collective Bargaining: Contemporary American Experience** (Madison, 1980), 209-262; Herbert Northrup, **Boulwarism: the Labor Relations Policies of the General Electric Company** (Ann Arbor, 1964).

united front to the union.[18] Second, as after World War II, there was now another wave of employer interest in the legal, philosophical, and practical issues surrounding managerial prerogatives and management rights clauses.[19] Finally, a growing number of companies after 1957 began to pursue a strategy of transferring their operations to nonunion workers, either through subcontracting or, more significantly, through decentralization and the construction of smaller facilities in geographic areas that were relatively impervious to unionism, such as rural areas in the South.[20]

---

[18]Frank C. Pierson, "Recent Employer Alliances in Perspective, **Industrial Relations,** 1 (October 1961), 40-55; Mark L. Kahn, "Mutual Strike Aid in the Airlines," **Monthly Labor Review,** 83 (June 1960); 589-591; William H. McPherson, "Bargaining Cooperation Among Auto Managements," **Ibid.,** 592-594.

[19]Jules Justin, "How to Preserve Management Rights under the Labor Contract," **Labor Law Journal,** 11 (March 1960), 189-215; George W. Torrence, **Management's Right to Manage** (Washington, D.C., 1961).

[20]Margaret K. Chandler, **Management Rights and Union Interests** (New York, 1964), 27-60; Herbert Northrup, "Management's 'New Look' in Labor Relations," **Industrial Relations,** 1 (October 1961), 22; Thomas A. Kochan and Peter Cappelli, "The Transformation of the Industrial Relations and Personnel Function," in Paul Osterman (ed.), **Internal Labor Markets** (Cambridge, 1984), 133-162.

Actually, the acceleration in the shift of manufacturing employment to the South began somewhat earlier. General Electric, for example, began building in the early 1950s satellite or 'dual' plants to provide it with parts in case a strike occurred at a sole supplying plant. The following are rates of

Union-Management Cooperation

Yet, despite some bitter strikes, the late 1950s also saw a number of companies and unions taking a less adversarial approach to their problems, especially problems involving technological change and employment security. Very often the parties involved came from the same industries where others were fighting costly battles in order to win their objectives. As in the 1920s, competitive pressure was a necessary but not a sufficient condition for union-management cooperation; it could, so to speak, lead the horses to water but not make them drink.

Those who chose to imbibe differed in several respects from those who took a traditional, adversarial stance. For one thing, cooperating companies tended to be smaller than others in the industry. While the giant national steel companies were slugging it out with the steelworkers, the union entered into an innovative agreement with Kaiser Steel on issues related to technological change. Similarly, although the "Big Three" auto companies and the UAW came close to blows in 1961, American Motors worked out a separate agreement with the union that entailed a cooperative approach to

---

change in the proportion of total manufacturing employment located in the South (comprising the South Atlantic, East South Central, and West South Central regions):

| 1939-1947 | -7.9% | 1952-1957 | 6.7% |
| 1947-1952 | 2.1 | 1957-1962 | 7.9 |

Source: **U.S. Statistical Abstract,** various years, 1947-1964.

modernization and other issues. Because of their small size, these companies may have had higher operating costs than their larger competitors and, therefore, a greater incentive to secure the unions' assistance in breaking out of the industry's labor cost structure.

In addition to size, the outlook and orientation of the parties also mattered. Armour, a meatpacking company that devised a cooperative solution to its automation problems, had a somewhat more enlightened management than Swift or Wilson. On the other side, the West Coast longshoremen's union, the ILWU, was led by men who had a more realistic view of the future and greater ability to communicate that view to their members than the leaders of the longshoremen's union on the East Coast, the ILA. In brief, some of the major cooperative agreements of the period included the following:

American Motors: In 1961, the UAW and the company negotiated a jointly administered profit-sharing plan that would be used to fund employee security programs like pensions and supplemental unemployment benefits (SUBs). The idea behind the plan was to share any of the productivity gains arising from improvements in technology, and in this respect it was similar to, although less explicit than, a Scanlon plan. In addition to profit sharing, the agreement called for the UAW's leaders and American's managers to periodically meet away from the bargaining table to discuss their "philosophies" and "views." This was intended to facilitate a cooperative, problem-solving approach to bargaining.[21]

---

[21] Edward L. Cushman, "The American Motors-UAW Progress Sharing Agreement," **14th Annual Pro-**

Armour: After it closed six of its obsolescent plants, Armour signed an agreement in 1959 with the meatcutters and packinghouse workers to set up a tripartite "Automation Committee" to study, discuss, and recommend solutions to problems arising from technological change. These problems included the provision of retraining and job assistance to workers displaced by plant closures, as well as arranging transfers for them to other Armour plants. The company funded the committee at a cost of about $100,000 per year. Some of the committee's success was attributed to the high caliber of its neutral members, including Clark Kerr, the impartial chairman, and George P. Shultz.[22]

Kaiser Steel: During the 1959 national steel strike, Kaiser broke away from the other steel companies and signed a separate agreement with the steelworkers. The agreement established a tripartite committee charged with finding ways of modernizing the company while at the same time protecting the job security of the employees. The committee, which included George W. Taylor and John T. Dunlop as neutrals, in 1962

---

ceedings of the **Industrial Relations Research Association, New York, December 1961** (Madison, 1962), 315-324. On Scanlon plans, see Frederick G. Lesieur, **The Scanlon Plan: A Frontier in Labor-Management Cooperation** (Cambridge, 1958).

[22]Harold E. Brooks, "The Armour Automation Committee Experience," in **21st Annual Proceedings of the Industrial Relations Research Association, December 1968** (Madison, 1969), 137-143; Jack Stieber, "Work Rules and Practices in Mass Production Industries," in **14th Annual IRRA Proceedings,** 399-412; Edwin Young, "The Armour Experience: A Case Study in Plant Shutdown," in Gerald G. Somers et al. (eds.), **Adjusting to Technological Change** (New York, 1963), 144-158.

announced a "Long Range Sharing Plan." Like the plan at American Motors, it was a gain-sharing plan that, although it was not explicitly tied to technological innovation, nevertheless was intended to distribute gains from modernization and automation.[23]

West Coast Longshoring: The well-known Mechanization and Modernization (M&M) agreement was developed in anticipation of rapid containerization of cargo handling on the West Coast. Although the M&M agreement was signed in 1960, it was the fruit of three years of informal talks and negotiations between the employers and the union. Instead of a prolonged gain-sharing plan, the employers in the Pacific Maritime Association worked out a one-shot deal with the union. It provided that unionized longshoremen would receive $29 million in the form of a guaranteed annual wage plan and vested early retirement rights. In return, the ILWU agreed to give up many of its restrictive work rules and manning regulations, thus clearing the way for containerization. Employers preferred this arrangement because they despaired of ever being able to accurately measure the continuing productivity gains arising from the agreement.[24]

---

[23] Gerard E. Balsley, "The Kaiser Steel-United Steelworkers of America Long-Range Sharing Plan," in **16th Annual Proceedings of the Industrial Relations Research Association, Boston, December 1963** (Madison, 1964), 48-59; Charles C. Killingsworth, "Cooperative Approaches to Problems of Technological Change," in Somers (ed.), **Adjusting**, 61-94; James A. Henderson et al., **Creative Collective Bargaining** (Englewood Cliffs, 1965), Chap. 8.

[24] Paul T. Hartman, **Collective Bargaining and**

There also were a number of cases in which unions and management formed plant-level production committees similar to those created during the 1920s and World War II. The committees were viewed as a way to bolster productivity, reduce costs, and make workers less resistant to process innovations. They became increasingly popular after 1957, although the numbers involved were quite small (Table 1). These new production committees were scattered across the industrial landscape, ranging from a small metal products company to a group of potteries. Although conclusive data are lacking, it seems that they were prevalent in firms and industries facing immediate and severe competition and were not a response to problems arising from prospective technological change. As in earlier periods, the committees were limited to making recommendations about matters such as waste elimination, improving methods of production, and rewarding workers for ideas that would improve efficiency. They were not allowed to engage in collective bargaining or contract administration.[25]

Productivity: The Longshore Mechanization Agreement (Berkeley: University of California, 1969); Lincoln Fairley, **Facing Mechanization: The West Coast Longshore Plan** (Los Angeles: UCLA Institute of Industrial Relations, 1979); Wayne L. Horvitz, "The ILWU-PMA Mechanization and Modernization Agreement," in **16th Annual IRRA Proceedings,** 22-33; Charles C. Killingsworth, "The Modernization of West Coast Longshore Work Rules," **Industrial and Labor Relations Review,** 15 (April 1962), 295-306.

[25]**Management Rights and Union-Management Cooperation,** U.S. Bureau of Labor Statistics, Bulletin No. 1425-5 (Washington, D.C., 1966), 25 ff.

Thus the 1957-1962 period saw both management "hardening" as well as union-management cooperation. Although it is difficult to evaluate the costs and benefits arising from this particular series of cooperative experiments, it is clear that the parties in several of the experiments avoided or minimized costly labor disputes by eschewing an adversarial approach. Moreover, a number of the companies that took a hard line later discovered that they had failed to realize their labor relations objectives despite having weathered some lengthy and costly strikes. Pittsburgh Plate and Glass, for instance, only was able to get rid of a few of the work rules it considered undesirable. Similarly, the East Coast shipping employers did not significantly shrink the vast number of union work rules nor did they reach any agreement with the union concerning how labor costs would be affected by technological change. Swift and Wilson defeated union proposals to establish Armour-type automation committees, but only by agreeing to a costly wage and benefits package. The steel companies also signed an expensive agreement and were unable to get the steelworkers to give up their local working conditions clause.[26]

---

[26]Yet even though managements didn't get everything they sought, labor costs grew rather slowly during this period. Nonfarm unit labor costs rose less than 1 percent each year between 1958 and 1962, down from 2.1 percent during th 1953-1957 period (see Table 3). Also, median wage changes in the union sector were less than those in the nonunion sector from 1959 through 1966. See George Ruben, "Observations of Wage Developments in Manufacturing during 1959-1978," **Current Wage Developments,** 33 (May 1981), 47-59.

But during the course of the 1959 steel strike, management decided that it needed to improve its future relationship with the union. It proposed to the steelworkers that two joint committees be created after the strike: one would deal with the local working conditions issue; the other would meet regularly but informally to discuss each side's concerns, thus improving the likelihood of a strike-free settlement when negotiations next rolled around. The union eagerly accepted the proposal. Like management, it wanted to avoid future strikes because they brought unfavorable publicity and government intervention, and also opened the market to imports. During the period between the signings of the 1960 and the 1962 agreements, the informal bargaining group (known as the Human Relations Research Committee) met over 200 times to thrash out such thorny issues as overtime and subcontracting. In 1962 and again in 1965, the committee was credited with having allowed the parties to reach a strike-free agreement.[27]

But union-management cooperation has its perils, not the least of which is the possibility that union leaders will be accused of

---

[27]**Final Report to the President: The 1959 Labor Dispute in the Steel Industry,** Submitted by the Board of Inquiry under Executive Order 10843 (January 6, 1960), 59, Appendix E, 2 (mimeo); Benson Soffer, "Improving Labor Relations in the Steel Industry," **Labor Law Journal,** 12 (February 1961), 147-153; Richard Betheil, "The ENA in Perspective: The Transformation of Collective Bargaining in the Basic Steel Industry," **Review of Radical Political Economics,** 10 (Summer 1978), 1-24; Jack Stieber, "Steel," in Gerald G. Somers (ed.), **Collective Bargaining,** 151-208; Livernash et al., **Collective Bargaining in Steel,** 97-117.

having sold out the rank-and-file's interests by being soft (cooperative) rather than tough (adversarial) with management. Indeed, in the heated 1964-65 campaign for the presidency of the steelworkers union, the union's incumbent president, David J. McDonald, was attacked for having been an active member of the Human Relations Research Committee. I.W. Abel, the insurgent who later won the election, criticized the idea of union-management cooperation on the grounds that, "The union can't serve two masters - the companies can well take care of themselves. The union's leadership must look after the interests of the membership."[28]

In 1965, many of the problems that had loomed so large during the late 1950s and early 1960s seemed to be magically disappearing. The unemployment rate was on its way down, manufacturing employment was rising sharply, and the proportion of the labor force in unions, which had fallen from 1956 to 1961, halted its decline and actually rose slightly between 1963 and 1968. A stimulative fiscal policy, including hefty spending on the Vietnam War and social programs, gave the economy its rosy, Keynesian glow. Few worried anymore about foreign competition, plant closures, automation, or structural unemployment. As a result, bargaining in most places returned to its adversarial norm. The number of labor-management production committees stopped growing (Table 1), as did interest in other forms of union-management cooperation. Management's hard line became softer, and unit labor costs turned sharply upward in 1966.

---

[28] Quoted in Betheil, "The ENA," 12.

But, as we know, the bubble burst in the mid-1970s. As in the late 1950s, there again were signs of a change in the bargaining and economic climate. Once powerful industries like steel, motor vehicles, and rubber tires began to suffer from intensified international competition. Strong unions in construction, trucking, and coal mining were threatened by domestic nonunion production. Social critics dusted off their tomes from the 1950s and again began to worry about automation, plant closures, and the decline of unionism. Amidst this déjà vu, ideas about union-management cooperation that had been dormant for well over a decade again were in the air, accompanied as before by a hardening management line on technological change and labor costs.[29]

Conclusion

The preceding historical analysis provides a number of insights concerning union-management cooperation. First, environmental pressure - either economic or that arising from government intervention - has been a necessary condition for union-management cooperation to occur in the past. Otherwise the parties were content to remain in their traditional, adversarial roles, with management in charge of production and the union bargaining for a larger share of the fruits of production. This may

---

[29]For a similar analysis, albeit in a slightly different vein, see Charles C. Killingsworth, "The Fall and Rise of the Idea of Structural Unemployment," **31st Annual Proceedings of the Industrial Relations Research Association, New York, December 1978** (Madison, 1979), 1-13.

seem like an obvious point, but it is one that researchers with a behavioral orientation have tended to overlook. Such economic pressures may arise from the growth of nonunion competition, either domestic or international, or from substitute products based on a new technology.

Second, once these external pressures have created an incentive for union-management cooperation, the parties will only adopt it if the perceived benefits from doing so outweigh the perceived costs. Here there is a role for behavioral interventions that change these perceptions, although historical analysis suggests that adversarialism is deeply rooted in the American industrial relations system, along with the belief on both sides that it is (only) management's job to improve productivity. Favorable union attitudes are likely to be the result of having strong, forward-looking union leaders who are trusted by the membership (e.g., the clothing workers in the 1920s or the ILWU in the 1950s). However, union leaders will be wary of cooperation because it may distance them from the membership or leave them open to factional charges that they have lost their militance. Favorable management attitudes will depend on the existence of alternatives to cooperation, such as shifting operations to nonunion facilities, closing down facilities, or seeking tariff and other protection from the government.

Third, although external economic pressure provides an incentive for union-management cooperation, there may only be an intermediate range in which this pressure provides an incentive for cooperation. If as during the 1930s, stress increases to the point where it appears unlikely that changes in labor productivity will greatly benefit sales, both sides may lose interest in cooperation. This is also the point at which there is likely to be a high degree of factionalism in a union. On the other hand, if external pressure moves back down to lower levels, as after World War II or during the mid-1960s, the parties are likely to shift back to their traditional positions.

Today we are witnessing union-management cooperation's fourth wave, and as before it is a response to unfavorable economic conditions in a number of industries, and to the growth of domestic nonunion competition. To some extent these pressures represent a return to the situation that provoked interest in union-management cooperation in the late 1950s.

It is difficult to predict how long-lived and deep-rooted the present wave of cooperation will prove to be, although there is little reason to believe that economic conditions in most segments of manufacturing will soon move either to the hyper-prosperity of the late 1960s or to the wretchedness of the early 1930s. But it is interesting to note that in the automobile industry, which is just beginning to come out of a deep slump and where labor and management have been strongly committed to a quality-of-work-life program, strong criticism recently has been voiced of the union's involvement in the program. Similarly, now that Chrysler is getting back on its feet, management is not as enthusiastic as during the late 1970s about having a union representative on its board of directors.[30] Thus cooperative experiments can change the parties' attitudes toward each other, but our historical analysis suggests that this result depends to a great extent on external, economic factors.

---

[30]"Why the UAW May Go Back to Old-Style Bargaining," **Business Week** (12 March 1984), 98-100; "Labor's Voice on Corporate Boards: Good or Bad?" **Business Week** (7 May 1984), 151-153. Also see Harry C. Katz, Thomas A. Kochan, and Kenneth R. Gobeille, "Industrial Relations Performance, Economic Performance, and QWL Programs: An Interplant Analysis," **Industrial and Labor Relations Review,** 37 (October 1983), 3-17.

Lloyd Ulman

3

Some International Crosscurrents in Labor Relations

Unionism and collective bargaining seem to have been experiencing greater difficulty remaining as viable and stable institutions in the United States than in most other advanced industrial democracies. Will the United States become the only advanced economic democracy without a significant union establishment? If not, will it become the first advanced economic democracy without a significant union establishment? Or neither of the above? These are interesting questions, so it will be worth waiting some decades for answers. Meanwhile, the questions invite speculation, which in this paper is divided into three (unequal) parts: first, a characterization of differing critical opinions about the economic performance of unions in this country and abroad; second, divergent patterns of institutional developments in the prewar past; and third, some postwar convergences and their limits.

Performance and Reactions

American unions and employers have developed highly institutionalized, sophisticated, and otherwise "mature" systems of collective bargaining and have established significantly higher levels of wages, benefits, and job security, as well as "industrial democracy" and "jurisprudence," than would have prevailed in the absence of collective bargaining. It might be expected that union efforts and achievements in raising pay and improving other conditions of employment would have attracted more members; union organizers have certainly proceeded on that assumption, and one study has produced econometric evidence suggesting that the lower the pay of an employee in a firm, the more likely he or she is to vote for a union.[1] Yet in the postwar period the union success rate in NLRB certification elections has declined sharply since the mid-1950s, and a recent analysis shows that this decline, together with the decline in the fraction of nonunion employees involved in certification elections, has accounted for more of the decline in the growth rate of union membership after the mid-1950s than have adverse economic factors.[2] (That growth rate itself has, of course, been negative, as total union membership declined from nearly 35 percent of nonagricultural employment in the mid-1950s to under 25 percent by the end of the 1970s, although membership remained

---

[1] H.S. Farber and D.H. Sake, "Why Workers Want Unions: The Role of Relative Wages and Job Characteristics," **Journal of Political Economy** (April 1980), pp. 349-369.

[2] W. T. Dickens and J.S. Leonard, **Accounting for the Decline in Union Membership,** National Bureau of Economic Research, Inc., Working Paper No. 1275 (Cambridge, MA, February 1984).

largely unchanged in absolute terms[3] and increased strongly in both absolute and relative terms in the government sector.) Effective employer resistance, both direct and indirect (i.e., emulating negotiated gains sufficiently to take the wind out of union sails), has accounted for a good part of the failure of union organizing and electoral efforts,[4] but the unions have not escaped blame for contributing to low pay and poor conditions among unorganized workers when a combination of bargaining success and organizing failure allegedly contributed to segmentation of labor markets into "protected" and "secondary" sectors.

Meanwhile, American unions have also been blamed for creating or exacerbating some of the same adverse economic conditions which have been contributing to their organizational decline. Depending on whether the critic happens to be a neoclassical conservative or a Keynesian liberal, unionism has helped to make either equilibrium (and therefore actual) levels of unemployment higher or tradeoffs between inflation and unemployment more unfavorable. The latter diagnosis has supported incomes policies as a remedy which would enable the economy to maintain lower levels of unemployment

---

[3] G.S. Bain and R. Price, **Profiles of Union Growth: A Comparative Statistical Portrait of Eight Countries** (Oxford: Blackwell, 1980), pp. 88-89, 98-100.

[4] W.T. Dickens, "The Effect of Company Campaigns on Certification Elections: 'Law and Reality' Once Again," **Industrial and Labor Relations Review** (July 1983) pp. 560-575.

and inflation by subjecting bargaining institutions to either official or self-imposed restraint. The natural rate diagnosis points to demand deflation as the only feasible way to avoid increasing inflation, thereby paying for free collective bargaining with higher levels of unemployment. Both diagnoses would support alteration of the legal parameters of collective bargaining so as to reduce the potential bargaining power of unions and hence the degree of monopoly in the economy. On the other hand, the increased organizational weakness of the unions in the United States has not been imputed to them for economic righteousness. It is standard monetarist-competitive doctrine that an increase in the degree of unionization, which is taken to indicate an increase in the degree of monopoly power in the labor markets of the economy, results in a rise in the average real wage and hence in the rates of both unemployment and inflation. Yet, decreasing unionization has so far not been cited and documented as a factor which has tended to retard inflation and unemployment, even in stagflationary periods.

In Europe, on the other hand, the unions have tended to fare better in the postwar period. There has been no general pattern of pronounced relative decline in membership; on the contrary, Bain and Price report an upward trend in union growth after the late 1960s (to the mid-1970s) in four of the five European countries examined in their statistical study, and in all five countries the levels of "union density" substantially exceeded those in the United States from the late 1940s on.[5] Real

---

[5] See Figure 1. The source is Bain and Price,

Figure 1

Union Density 1950-1976: Sweden, Great Britain, Germany, and United States

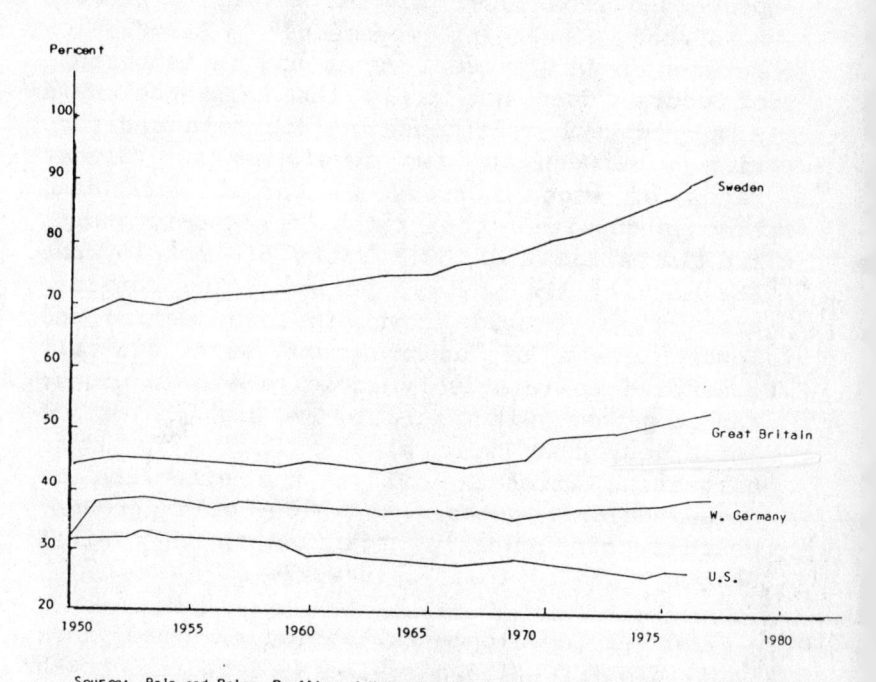

Source: Bain and Price, **Profiles of Union Growth,** Oxford: Basil Blackwell Ltd., 1980.

Note: Density is defined as number of union members divided by number of potential union members. The definition of union member and potential union member varies by country.

wages also grew more rapidly in Europe and Japan than in the United States in the 1960s and 1970s; this relative growth in wages (unlike the relative growth in union density) proceeded from lower initial levels to produce a strong converging movement.[6] Association between growth in real wages and in membership of course does not imply the existence of a simple causal relationship - in either direction - between the two developments. Higher rates of wage increase in Europe were also associated with higher rates of economic growth and inflation and lower rates of unemployment for most of the postwar period. The combination of more rapid growth in labor demand and lower levels of unemployment were directly conducive to relatively rapid growth in wages; and together with relatively high rates of inflation, they were also conducive to union bargaining strength and to the extension of organization - notably to white-collar groups, which remained weakly organized in the United States - and to lower-paid workers.

Other developments, however, were less favorable for union bargainers. Economic growth rates began to slow down in most European coun-

---

op. cit., p. 163. The European countries included are Great Britain, West Germany, Sweden, Denmark, and Norway. Union density in the latter peaked in the mid-1960s (pp. 158-159).

[6]Labor productivity in manufacturing rose less rapidly in the United States between 1973 and 1979 (J.D. Sachs, "Wages, Profits, and Macroeconomic Adjustment: A Comparative Study," **Brooking Papers on Economic Activity,** 2 [1979], p.258, Table 1).

tries after the mid-1960s; international competition intensified; strongly adverse movements in the terms of trade resulted first from increased prices of imported raw materials in the boom of 1972-73 and then especially from the oil price shocks in 1973-74 and 1979; government transfer payments and associated payroll taxes rose rapidly. These developments tended to reduce what the Scandinavians (led by Odd Aukrust) called the "room" for wage increases which would have maintained the existing distribution of income between wages and nonlabor income. But European unionists, an increasing proportion of whom were younger, better educated, and less haunted than their predecessors by memories of prewar unemployment or hyperinflation, were less disposed to accept a halt or even a slowdown in the progress to which they had become accustomed since the early 1950s. Their impatience and disaffection were demonstrated by a series of grass roots strikes which swept across most of Europe in the late 1960s and early 1970s. In any event, real wages rose sharply in Europe between 1969 and 1973 and did not decelerate markedly until the second half of the 1970s. Meanwhile, unemployment rates in Europe rose to sharply higher levels in the mid-1970s and remained there, while unemployment declined markedly from higher levels in the United States and approached the EEC rate in 1979 (see Figure 2). By the 1980s unemployment as well as wages seem to have been converging on American levels.

Collective bargaining became a target of criticism in Europe even before it gave evidence of difficulty in accommodating wage settlements to the constraining forces referred to above, so that wage increases overflowed their

Figure 2

Unemployment in the United States, the European Economic Community, and Japan

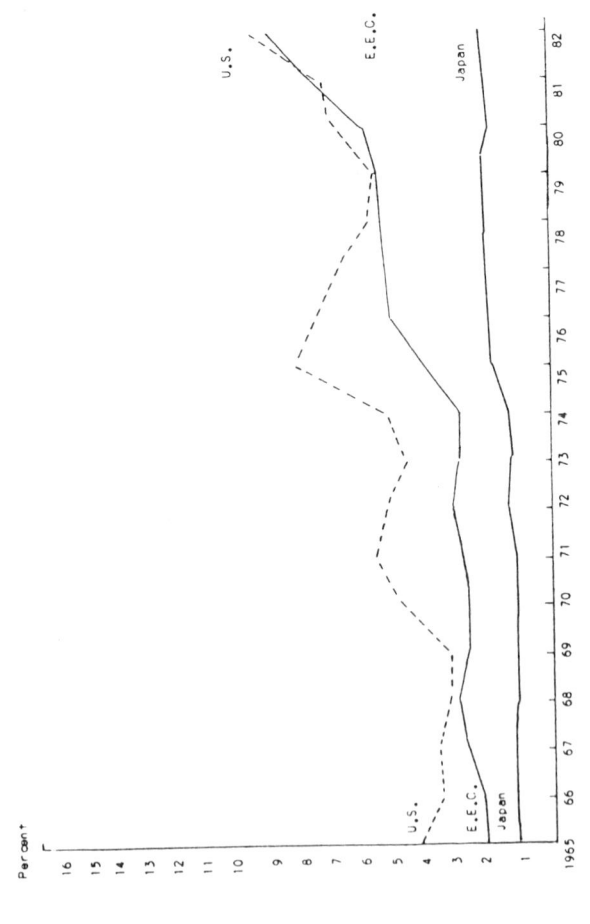

Note: The E.E.C. countries include West Germany, France, Italy, United Kingdom, Belgium, Netherlands, Luxembourg, Ireland, and Denmark

Source: OECD Economic Outlook

allotted room and helped to squeeze profits. In economies more exposed to international trade, it was plausible to believe that negotiated increases in money wages would be translated into increases in real wages when exchange rates were fixed or "managed" and when negotiated increases were not uniform and simultaneous across countries. Wage settlements could threaten the competitiveness of a country's export or import-competing industries and/or levels of profitability and internal price stability. And even before unemployment began its steep ascent in the second half of the 1970s, some Europeans had come to the belief that collective bargaining was exerting a demand-side influence on a growing structural component of unemployment by raising wages relative to the cost of (mainly imported) capital goods, which induced substitution of capital for labor and gave rise to "capital shortage" unemployment.[7] Lately there has been a tendency (articulated strongly by Herbert Giersch), first, to attribute the greater growth of unemployment in Europe than in the United States since the early 1970s to the greater inertia or momentum of real wages in Europe and, second, to attribute the latter to certain peculiar features of collective bargaining in the United States - i.e., the relative prevalence of overlapping, multiyear contracts with incomplete indexation - which tend to make money wages less responsive and real wages more responsive to changes in mone-

---

[7]Cf. R.J. Flanagan, D. Soskice, and L. Ulman, **Unionism, Economic Stabilization, and Incomes Policies: European Experience** (Washington, D.C.: Brookings, 1983), pp. 90-99.

tary policy in that country than in Europe.[8]

Since this is inferentially the kindest word yet put in for American collective bargaining by the economics profession, it should perhaps be accepted with appropriate gratitude for the variety which it provides. Yet it is difficult to attribute distinctive wage performance primarily to perculiarities in contractual form in a country in which less than a quarter of the relevant population is organized. The greater flexibility of real wages in the United States reflected a largely nonunion economy (although one is left with the sticky task of explaining sticky money wages in the absence of explicit contractual restraints in nonunion firms). This is caricatured in Figure 3, where the shoe is partially put on the other foot: wage behavior in the most heavily unionized segment of U.S. manufacturing (at least 60 percent organized) is compared with wage behavior in all manufacturing in the other countries as well as with the less unionized segment of American manufacturing. The movement of real wages in the more heavily organized American group, which contains industries that have been increasingly exposed to external competitive pressures, appears somewhat more European than the rest, but it was still negative in the period 1973-82. The bar representing changes in productivity in the (total) U.S. manufacturing sector is shorter than corresponding bars in the other countries;

---

[8]Sachs, **op. cit**; also "Real Wages and Unemployment in the OECD Countries," **Brookings Papers on Economic Activity,** 1 (1983), pp. 255-289, and critical comments by R.J. Gordon and others, pp. 290-304.

Figure 3

Average Annual Percent Change in Hourly Earnings and Productivity in Manufacturing, 1973-1982

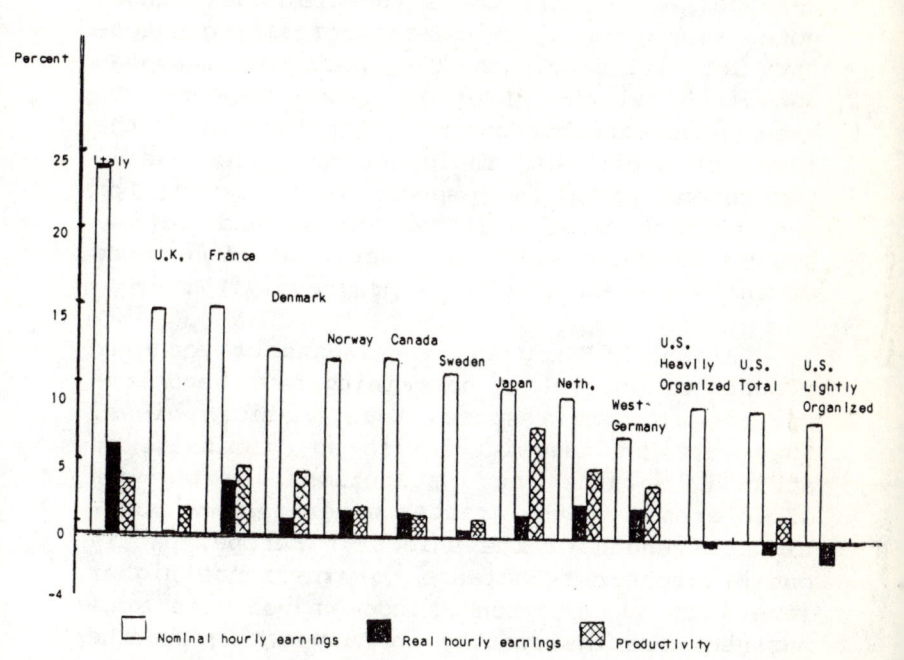

Note: Lightly organized U.S. industries are lumber, furniture, machinery, electrical machinery, instruments, leather, textiles, apparel, printing, chemicals, and rubber. Heavily organized U.S. industries are stone, primary metal, fabricated metal, transportation, food, paper, tobacco, and petroleum. The lightly and heavily organized totals are weighted by industry size. Lightly organized industries have <60% union coverage and heavily organized industries have >60% union coverage.

Source: Freeman and Medoff, "New Estimates of Private Sector Unionism," ILRR, Vol. 32, No. 2 (January 1979). OECD, Main Economic Indicators (earnings, CPI); ILO, Yearbook of Annual Statistics (earnings, CPI); BLS, Monthly Labor Review (U.S. industry earnings); Neef and Capdevielle, "International Comparisons of Productivity and Labor Costs," Monthly Labor Review (December 1980); Capdevielle, Alvarez, and Cooper, "International Trends in Productivity and Labor Costs," Monthly Labor Review (December 1982).

hence the more rapid growth of real wages in other countries during the 1970s may reflect a relative rise in capital-labor ratios abroad, as Daniel J.B. Mitchell's recent work indicates.[9] It may also reflect institutional differences - not only the structural differences noted above, but also greater bargaining intensity or militancy on the part of European unionists which developed in response to heightened expectations of their members in the light of their more rapid economic progress in the recent past, in response to pressures for and against wage egalitarianism, and in response to the combined influence of high rates of inflation and steep tax progressivity.

Although European assessments of economic effects of collective bargaining have been more adverse in some respects than American views, they were not associated with so dismissive an attitude towards the institutions. Partly out of deference to the greater numerical and political strength of the unions in Europe, partly out of greater reluctance to experience higher levels of unemployment, incomes policies were pursued more insistently in Europe than in the United States in an effort to induce restraint in the exercise of union bargaining power. In Europe these policies have been designed more to restrain real wages in the interest of increasing, maintaining, or restoring international competitiveness, profitability, and ultimately employment than in the interest of restraining domestic inflation. Moreover, in-

---

[9]Daniel J.B. Mitchell, "International Convergence with U.S. Wage Levels," in Barbara D. Dennis, ed., **Proceedings of the Thirty-Sixth Annual Meeting,** December 28-30, 1983, Industrial Relations Research Association (Madison, Wis.: IRRA, 1984).

comes policies in Europe were often made part of "social contract" packages which may have offered pecuniary compensation to workers (in exchange for restraint on negotiated wages and labor costs) in the form of wage indexation, price controls, tax reductions, expanded social benefits, or favored treatment for low-paid workers. They sometimes offered nonpecuniary compensation to workers or their unions through varying forms of worker participation in management or capital-sharing schemes or even to various measures of institutional protection of more centralized union institutions. Moreover, when it became impossible to avoid recourse to deflation, incomes policies were sometimes designed to complement deflationary measures in the hope of increasing their efficiency in holding down costs and thus minimizing unemployment.

In recent years compensation money has been running out and social welfare budgets have been pared, while unemployment (as noted above) has risen to levels approaching - and in some cases exceeding - those prevailing in the United States and which Europeans had previously regarded as politically unacceptable. The persistence of these conditions, along with major loss of blue-collar employment in traditional manufacturing jurisdictions, might support the view that what is generally perceived abroad as a decline in American unionism portends a similar decline in other countries - that economic convergence portends institutional convergence. Indeed, we shall point to certain structural and organizational developments in postwar European industrial relations which recall earlier developments in the United States and which some might regard as evidence of an ongoing process of institutional convergence in the postwar period. Before doing so, however, we should consider the influence of some historic forces which contributed to a divergent development of trade unionism and collective bargaining in Europe and in the United States, for these influences have survived into the postwar era.

American Exceptionalism and Institutional Difference

Three pronounced characteristics of American labor relations have contributed to this divergence. The most obvious and most commonly remarked one has been the relative weakness of radical politics and unionism, which has, of course, been evidenced by the absence in this country of major Socialist (Labor) or Communist parties of the types with which union movements in other countries have been closely associated. Another characteristic was identified by Slichter, Healy, and Livernash as the prevalence in the United States of "strongly individualistic and highly competitive employers who have been aggressively hostile to unions and who have been willing to go to great extremes in order to destroy them."[10] And the third characteristic was noted by Slichter as "the fact that the bargaining power of most unions is greater than their organizing power."[11] At first blush this third proposition might seem odd: we tend to regard bargaining

---

[10]S.H. Slichter, J.J. Healy, and E.R. Livernash, **The Impact of Collective Bargaining on Management** (Washington, D.C.: The Brookings Institution, 1960), p. 34.

[11]S.H. Slichter, "The Changing Character of American Industrial Relations," **American Economic Review Supplement** (March 1939), pp. 121-137; reprinted in J.T. Dunlop, ed., **Potentials of the American Economy** (Cambridge, Mass.: Harvard University Press, 1961), p. 221.

power and organizing power as moving in the same direction - the greater the latter, the greater the former, with the degree of organization ultimately achieved imposing an upper limit on bargaining power. However, while evidence of union bargaining power in organized firms, as manifested in a sizable difference between union and nonunion wages, may furnish an incentive to nonunion workers to form and join unions in their own firms (as remarked above), it also furnishes both incentive and opportunity for their employers to resist organization. Indeed, causation may sometimes run in the opposite direction: incomplete organization may make for greater bargaining power in the organized sector of an industry if unionized firms hesitate to take a strike for fear of losing market share to competitors - at home or abroad - who are not in the same bargaining jurisdiction. Taken together, the second and third attributes suggest that the power of employers to keep unions out may exceed their power to resist specific demands once unions are established. Thus the second and third attributes can be squared with each other readily enough.

It was more difficult to reconcile the last two attributes with the first, at least for the early exponents of pure and simple trade unionism. Gompers' economic case against the radicals boiled down to the assertion that capitalism would generate a positive rather than a negative trend of economic growth and that as the employer's ability to pay was continually replenished, collective bargaining would pay off ("more and more") for the workers. At the same time, if workers are convinced that collective bargaining can pay off for them, it ought to pay off for the employers as well by offering the workers an alternative to socialism, anarchism, even trust-busting. If the employers had seen things that way, they would not have been so aggressively hostile to businesslike A.F. of L. unions whose loudly proclaimed commitment to the "sanctity of contracts" contrasted pointedly with the IWW's loudly proclaimed commitment to "no contracts."

But the attitude of employers, in Europe as well as in the United States, ultimately depended on their assessment of the credibility, first, of the radical threat and, second, of the bargaining alternatives. Abroad the threat was most dramatically expressed by a series of general strikes in the first decade of this century - in Sweden (1902 and 1909), Belgium (1902 and, earlier, 1893), Holland (1903), Italy (1904), France (1909) - and during and after the first World War - Italy (1914), Norway (1916), France (1920), Denmark (1920), Britain (1926). These strikes were called for a variety of objectives, political as well as economic. They were led by Socialist-affiliated union federations, but in Italy and France, the labor movements contained strong syndicalist elements whose influence was reflected in a strong aversion to "permanent" or "continuous association" and collective bargaining as well as to parliamentary political activity; they were high rollers who gambled on instant revolution generated via the "row in the piazza" and general strike. But this was a gamble which the employers in those countries could afford to take. Moreover, collective bargaining was not a promising option for them, although if they had felt more obliged to proffer it to the weakly institutionalized unions they might have strengthened the position of the more prosaic and conventional groups within those unions.[12] These historic attitudes persisted. Val Lorwin wrote: "In most French private industry, genuine collective relations have scarcely been tried." And Daniel Horowitz observed that "The Italian trade union movement during much of its history has not been able to focus upon those problems - the marketplace problems - which have been the overwhelming concern of the trade union movement of countries like the United States, Great Britain, or the Scandinavian Countries."[13]

In Germany, the Netherlands, and Scandinavia, the Gompersian conditions were much more closely approximated than they were in southern Europe - or in the United States. The Socialist parties to the north were able to present a more coherent, persistent, and, especially at the end of World War I, serious challenge, while the unions were better gaited, ideologically and organizationally, to collective bar-

---

[12]Ashenfelter and Johnson found it"...puzzling why so much of the work force remains unorganized" if differentials between union and non-union wages were as large as previous econometric studies had found them to be; they ultimately concluded that the net effect of unions on these relative wages was not significantly different from zero. What their analysis ignored was that a combination of union bargaining strength and organizing weakness could continue to be a combination of relatively rising union wages and relatively declining degrees of organization. Cf. O. Ashenfelter and G.E. Johnson, "Unionism, Relative Wages, and Labor Quality in U.S. Manufacturing Industries," **International Economic Review** (October 1972), pp. 488-508.

[13]V.R. Lorwin, **The French Labor Movement** (Cambridge, Mass.: Harvard University Press, 1954), p. 190; Daniel L. Horowitz, **The Italian Labor Movement** (Cambridge, Mass.: Harvard University Press, 1963), p. 1.

gaining. Thus in the Netherlands the failure of the general strike of 1903 marked the end of serious syndicalist influence within the unions. Revolutionary ferment at the end of World War I generated organized employer resistance. But this was soon followed by Parliament's acquiescence in demands by moderate Socialist, Catholic, and Protestant unionists for extensive social legislation, the establishment of a multipartite High Council of Labor and ultimately the passage of legislation (1927) which regularized the legal status of collective agreements.[14] The influence of war time and its revolutionary aftermath was especially marked in Germany where, under the Stinnes-Legien Agreement of 1918, employers agreed to recognize and bargain with the unions, which in turn (to quote Gerald Feld-

___

[14]J.P. Windmuller, **Labor Relatons in the Netherlands** (Ithaca: Cornell University Press, 1969), pp. 9, 28, 30, 52-53, 232-233. It might also be noted that, following the lead of Germany in the 1870s, the period prior to World War I witnessed the rise and spread of modern social legislation, and that in Germany at least the original impetus was provided by "a governmental campaign to destroy the growing social democratic movement." (P. Flora and A.J. Heidenheimer, "The Historical Core and Changing Boundaries of the Welfare State," in **The Development of Welfare States in Europe and America** (New Brunswick, N.J. and London: Transaction Books, 1981), p. 17. Other factors of course played a role in subsequent development of social welfare; and concerning the period following World War II Harold Wilensky found a tendency by left-wing regimes to hold down public spending on welfare programs where they were without serious challenge for power by conservative Christian Democratic parties. ("Leftism, Catholicism and Democratic Corporatism," in **ibid.**, pp. 345-382. See also **The Welfare State and Equality** (Berkeley: University of California Press, 1975).

man), "accepted the continued existence of private property and employer organizations - a significant matter since Germany was undergoing a revolution ostensibly under Socialist leadership...."[15] In Sweden a political strike in 1902 by the recently formed Swedish Federation of Labor (LO) in support of the franchise - which was a critical issue for unions and their Social Democratic allies in other countries as well - furnished the occasion for the formation of a strongly centralized Employers' Confederation (SAF), which later in the decade led some highly successful lockouts against economic strikes by the unions. In the latter, however, recognition was not an issue; it was granted in the metal trades in 1905, and T.L. Johnston wrote that SAF was designed to be "armed and ready to fight against the policy and tactics of the unions, **not** the unions as such."[16] Walter Galenson discerned a prevailing spirit of "almost class consciousness" among employers in Norway and Denmark, although they formed strongly centralized bargaining institutions, not in response to extraparliamentary political activity on the part of the unions, but in order to bargain with them on a more advantageous basis.[17]

---

[15]G.D. Feldman, "German Business Between War and Revolution: The Origins of the Stinnes-Legien Agreement," in G.A. Ritter, ed., **Entstehung und Wandel der modernen Gesellschaft** (Berlin: de Gruyter, 1970), p. 313.

[16]T.L. Johnston, **Collective Bargaining in Sweden** (Cambridge, Mass.: Harvard University Press, 1962), pp. 17, 32, 69-70.

[17]W. Galenson, **Labor in Norway** (Cambridge, Mass.: Harvard University Press, 1949), p. 80; **The Danish System of Labor Relations** (Cambridge, Mass.: Harvard University Press, 1952), p. 71.

Near-class consciousness was conducive to the production of a public good in the form of strong employer associations, especially in industries composed of large numbers of small-scale producers where it was in everyone's interest for everyone else to offer united resistance to national (or regional) unions. The Scandinavian associations acquired and exercised strong, explicit authority over their affiliates, reserving the right to order and approve stoppages, to fine disobedient members, and to conclude collective agreements. In these countries, employers' associations accumulated strike insurance funds and conducted lockouts. German associations even circulated blacklists of strikers and furnished strike-breakers, and they required their members to sever business relations with unaffiliated firms that did not respect lockouts.[18] In addition to protecting the individual employer from whipsaw action, multiemployer bargaining restricted collective bargaining largely to the determination of pay and working time at industrywide levels, which resulted in control over the production function at plant level being left to the discretion of local management. This meant that the unions were essentially excluded, for bargaining purposes, from the plants. In 1905, the Swedish employers enshrined the principle of management prerogatives in a provision (Article 23) which was inserted in all the collective agreements within the purview of SAF and which stated that "the employer is entitled to direct and distribute the work of his enterprise, to engage and dismiss workers at his own discretion, and to em-

---

[18]P. Taft, "Germany," in W. Galenson, ed., **Comparative Labor Movements** (New York: Prentice-Hall, Inc., 1952), p. 269.

ploy organized or unorganized workers as he sees fit." The last provision was of no practical importance; but SAF, threatening a general lockout, successfully defended Article 23 in a series of strikes in 1906. After World War I the establishment of works councils became an active issue, especially in Germany where left-wing Socialists and Communists saw in such councils the potential for worker control; but they were viewed by the unions as potential competitors - particularly in Holland and Germany where plural and parallel unions existed - and by management as a threat to their traditional prerogatives. In the end they were confined to subordinate and nonadversary roles.[19]

While protection against whipsawing reduced the cost of resistance to employers by protecting their market shares during a stoppage, another function of industrywide bargaining - to ensure uniform settlements - tended to reduce their potential gains from taking a strike. This feature was popular among small-scale employers, for whom such an arrangement to "take wages (and therefore prices) out of competition" was a welcome throwback to the precapitalist past.[20] Under the Weimar Republic the Minister of Labor was empowered to "extend" the terms of collective agreements to nonsignatory employers,[21] which

---

[19]Taft, **op. cit.**, pp. 278-284; Windmuller, **op. cit.**, pp. 399-407; A. Sturmthal, **Workers Councils** (Cambridge, Mass.: Harvard University Press, 1969), pp. 15-16, 159-162.

[20]Glenson, **op. cit.**

[21]Taft, **op. cit.**, p. 284.

foreshadowed the introduction of similar provisions in other countries in the 1930s and 1940s.

Large-scale firms had less to gain directly from entering into centralized arrangements with unions. Some of Holland's giants bargained directly; but elsewhere large-scale firms fell in with (Norway) or even helped to initiate (Germany) the pattern of association bargaining. They were motivated by class interest as well as more narrowly individualistic interests. The German industrialists were reacting to political instability and "the failing power of the state and government" in 1918.[22] In the deflationary environment of the early 1920s employers launched what scholars in virtually every country called "employer counteroffensives" to reduce real and sometimes nominal wages, which touched off major stoppages of work, while unions lost membership under the impact of high levels of unemployment. Nevertheless, recognition as such was not in question. Moreover, by the end of the decade organizational losses in these countries had been largely recouped. The great vicissitudes of depression, social reaction, and war in the next two decades swept away institutional structures or drastically altered their behavior; but when Germany and the countries of northern and central Europe emerged from the Second World War, they either revived or established bargaining arrangements which bore the strong imprint of custom and past practice.

---

[22]Quoted in Feldman, **op. cit.**, p. 327.

Experience in Britain resembled experience on the continent in some important respects. Unionists were exposed to syndicalist and socialist influences, participated actively in politics and ultimately helped to form a new major party which sent union representatives to Parliament and which professed socialist aims. Union militancy increased markedly in the generation preceding the First World War and again in the postwar decade. Employers combined to offer resistance, and, even when effective, resistance was followed by multi-employer bargaining. But in even more important respects the British experience was distinctive. To begin with, the political motivation of British unionists tended to be pragmatic and reformist rather than ideological. The dominant socialism preached by political leaders and some union leaders was homespun doctrine which "owed more to Mill than to Marx... and was strongly disinclined to accept the class-struggle as the instrument of change."[23] Although nationalization of some prominent industries, notably coal, was effectively pushed, the appeal of British socialism was primarily egalitarian and humanitarian, and it concentrated effectively on statutory protection of unions in their bargaining and political activities and on a comprehensive program of social legislation. In the second place, while British unions engaged determinedly and repeatedly in industrywide stoppages and in sympathy strikes which revealed strong feelings of class, this activity was essentially directed to concrete bargaining objectives - retaining practices which technological change had

---

[23]G.D.H. Cole, A **Short History of the British Working-Class Movement, 1789-1947** (London: George Allen & Unwin, 1948 ed.), p. 287.

rendered inefficient or resisting pay cuts after World War I.[24]

In the third place, British employers were neither as organization-minded nor as motivated by class consciousness as their employees. They did not exploit the potential advantages of industrywide bargaining very thoroughly. Instead of facilitating retention by management of control over work practices, standards of output, and pay systems at the workplace, industrywide bargaining in Britain paved the way for a "movement" of highly autonomous, militant, and sometimes radical shop stewards, who bargained aggressively in such areas after the Amalgamated Society of Engineers had conceded the employers' right "to admit no interference with the management of their business" following an effective lockout in 1897-98.[25] The shop stewards flourished during the First World War and again during the economic revival in the second half of the 1930s when their influence was revealed in a large number of unofficial strikes and in the emergence of wage drift. In the Second World War, as in the first, the stewards played a prominent role; and so this unique heritage was carried forward into the present era.

---

[24]Referring to the General Strike of 1926, Renshaw notes: "Unlike the Government, who denounced the strike as a political threat to constitutional government, the TUC insisted it was purely sympathetic industrialization spread over the whole country. Cf. P. Renshaw, **The General Strike** (London: Eyre Methuen, 1975), p. 154.

[25]Quoted in H. Phelps Brown, **The Origins of Trade Union Power** (Oxford: Clarendon Press, 1983), p. 135.

Although British unionists had established well-institutionalized "continuous associations," British employers were marked by what Phelps Brown has referred to as "a reluctance to combine"[26] in the period preceding the First World War. Subsequently they resigned themselves to more continuous association with one another, but they did not endow their organizations with either the powers or the purses enjoyed by employer associations on the continent. They were fond of ascribing their aversion to ceding authority to centralized institutions to individualism and competitiveness. Yet on the whole they seem to have appreciated the price-maintaining properties of wage bargaining through associations more than they did its adversarial advantages. (Phelps Brown wrote that the Victorian employers "believed in competition...[but] they disliked price-cutting."[27] That spirit was itself conducive to employer recognition of unions, but to weak bargaining thereafter. Recognition was not the product of class action by large-scale employers in response to their perception of a threat to the social order.[28] Such a threat was in the final analysis not regarded as very strong. Even the big sympathy strikes, which threatened the public health and safety, were,

---

[26]Ibid., p. 45-46, 109-110, 141, 143.

[27] Ibid., p. 205.

[28]In 1928, after the tension and tumult surrounding the General Strike of 1926, Sir Alfred Mond originated an appeal to the TUC and the two central employers' organizations to set up a National Industrial Council, but the large-scale firms did not support the proposal (ibid., p. 125).

as noted above, called in support of nonpolitical objectives. Moreover, the government of the day rested on a sufficiently stable social order to cope with public emergency disputes.

Thus, with respect to the first of our two Gompersian conditions for employer acceptance of collective bargaining, British experience contrasts somewhat with the experience of the non-Latin continental countries in which employers did react in part to political strikes or to political threats from the radical left. And British experience resembles experience in France and Italy in which there was more political motivation behind industrial action, but employers generally did not seriously attempt to buy political stability with collective bargaining. With respect to the second Gompersian condition, British experience diverged from the French and Italian in that the British union movement certainly wanted and could deliver collective bargaining. In that respect British unions were like those of the other countries on the continent, but in recognizing and bargaining with them through associations, British employers appeared to be intent on minimizing neither political risks nor settlement costs. If they were attempting to minimize anything, it was possibly costs (psychic as well as pecuniary) of stoppage (as distinct from the combined costs of stoppage and settlement).

American employers faced a combination of background conditions which were more similar to the British combination than to the conditions found either in Italy and France or in the other continental countries. Certainly Gompers' second condition obtained: what he had to offer was a union movement which was more single-mindedly committed to securing and exploiting the method of collective bargaining than any movement abroad. But, partly for that reason, the first condition - a serious and sustained challenge from the left - failed to obtain; and so by implication Gompersian doctrine had more to offer to employers abroad than in its country of origin. Gompers did have something else to offer to American big business, however, which was unique to their circumstances - opposition to an antitrust reaction which sprang from populist roots and an agrarian tradition of deep suspicion of large-scale organizations. But there were no takers here either. (Ironically, the unions were tarred at least as thoroughly as big business with the antitrust brush; even more ironically, the reinvigoration of the union movement owed much to the recrudescence of antibusiness sentiment during what was widely perceived as a failure of the business system in the Great Depression of the 1930s. Regulation, rather than trust-busting, was the chosen instrument of the reformers on that occasion, however; and big unions could be championed as a "countervailing power" to big businesses in the spirit of the second-best.)

We have seen that it was relevant for large-scale employers in some other countries to consider buying off radicalism with collective bargaining - and to minimize the cost of the latter by entering into centralized bargaining arrangements. There was a spate of industrywide bargaining in the United States in the late 1890s which coincided with a trustification movement and which, as in Britain, was partly valued by the participating employers for whatever help it could provide in taking wages out of competition.[29] But in more concentrated industries, large-scale employers did not need collective bargaining for that purpose; and such collaboration in the labor markets as they found it advantageous to engage in was mainly for purposes of avoiding recognition - e.g., by circulating blacklists - rather than negotiation. The task of repelling boarders was lightened by judge-made law: at a time when Parliament was granting British unions blanket immunity from actions at tort and prosecutions for conspiracy, American judges were still going farther than British judges ever had done in issuing injunctions against labor unions and were subsequently to deny unions exemption from antitrust legislation. During World War I, changes in both the political and economic climate were conducive to the growth of unionism as well as an upsurge of radicalism in the United States and in Europe; but American employers were not disposed to forestall the latter by accepting the former. Instead, when large-scale enterprises did become interested in buying off radicalism after the end of the war, they sought to buy off unionism as well by offering high wages, an array of other benefits - including morale-oriented personnel management policies - to their own employees directly, and to minimize the associated costs by exploiting the human investment potentialities offered by reduced turnover and increased tenure of employment.[30]

---

[29]L. Ulman, **The Rise of the National Trade Union** (Cambridge, Mass.: Harvard University Press, 1955), pp. 519-535.

[30]S.H. Slichter, "The Current Labor Policies of American Industries," **Quarterly Journal of Economics** (May 1929), pp. 393-435.

At the same time, employers resumed their old practices of direct opposition to unionism through a widespread open-shop drive which capitalized on the "red scare" of the early postwar period by calling itself the American Plan. And, as Jacoby's work emphasizes, once the threat of industrial unrest had subsided and union growth had been reversed in the 1920s, many firms that had adopted personnel management reforms abandoned them and returned authority to production-oriented foremen and their "drive system."[31]

So, while heightened employer resistance in Britain and Europe was confined to the terms of settlement in the 1920s, in the United States it was often aimed at disestablishing unions and returning to prewar patterns of labor relations which contrasted markedly with European prewar patterns. As a result the great explosion of organization in the United States had to wait for a catastrophic event, the Great Depression, which churned up widespread industrial unrest, a convulsion within the union movement, and ultimately the enactment of a revolutionary new public policy - all of which allowed for the extension of industrial unionism into the manufacturing sectors of the economy. The unrest of the 1930s, however, found an outlet in New Deal reform politics rather than in European-style left-wing politics; and the new CIO unions, notwithstanding some strong radical influences within their ranks, promptly exhibited some of the most prominent characteristics of the older busi-

---

[31] S.M. Jacoby, "Industrial Labor Mobility in Historical Perspective," **Industrial Relations** (Spring 1983), pp. 272-274.

nesslike model - the primacy of more narrowly oriented collective bargaining over political activity and the dominance of the national unions over the central federation (whose offspring many of them were).[32] Hence even in the 1930s there was not a real incentive for employers to wean workers away from radicalism by forming associations and offering collective bargaining in its place; some would say that President Roosevelt had attended to those chores. Nor was the desire to lead the quiet life by setting a floor under wages through multiemployer bargaining strong enough to extend recognition, although after the invalidation of the NRA and its codes of fair competition in 1935, a substitute device for avoiding the widespread wage and price cutting which had occurred earlier in the depression might have been found in industrywide bargaining. (U.S. Steel's mysterious recognition of the Steel Workers' Organizing Committee, which occurred in the absence either of a strike or an election - neither of which the union believed it could win at the time - may have been so motivated. If so, however, the other firms in the industry refused to follow their price leader; they successfully staved off recogni-

---

[32]Even Communist-led unions in the United States, like the UE and the ILWU, developed highly efficient bargaining habits. This distinguished them from the Communist union movements in France and Italy, which tended to subordinate, if not avoid, bargaining - partly because of ideological aversion, but also because of their aversion to any consequent weakening of the authority of their central federations with which they were linked to their respective Communist parties.

tion in the Little Steel Strike of 1937.)[33]

It may be that the competitiveness which, according to Slichter, Healy, and Livernash, fueled the resistance of American employers to union recognition also deterred many of them from bargaining together after recognition had been forced on them, although multiple-employer bargaining has been prevalent in the most atomistically competitive industries.

Single-employer bargaining with national unions has been more prevalent in the United States than in Europe; and it was conducive to a widening of the scope of bargaining to include issues originating at the plant level - such as employee discipline, internal wage structures, incentive pay systems, job descriptions, work assignment, and production standards - which in Europe had remained subject either to the employer's discretion or, in the case of Britain, to bargaining with shop stewards who were not under the effective control of the national union. The American development was in part the product of wartime wage controls and a no-strike pledge by the top union leadership: the adoption of multistage grievance procedures (with arbitration) afforded the membership an alternative outlet to wildcat strikes and, together with the exten-

---

[33] L. Ulman, "Influences of the Economic Environment on the Structure of the Steel Workers' Union," **Proceedings of the Fourteenth Annual Meeting of the Industrial Relations Research Association,** 1962, pp. 1-11. For a more sober and balanced account of this episode, see Irving Bernstein, **A History of the American Worker, 1933-1941: Turbulent Years** (Boston: Houghton Mifflin, 1970), pp. 466-473.

sion of the dues-checkoff and union security provisions, could reinforce the presence and authority of the national union at the workplace. The scope of bargaining was further extended to include a wide range of nonwage benefits, which elsewhere have been left more to the welfare state to provide, but provision of which in this country has testified to the spirit of business unionism among the membership who have insisted that their unions attend to their differentiated interests in the domains of security and equity as well as pay.

In its own turn the wider range and complexity of issues on the bargaining table was conducive to a lengthening of the duration of collective agreements, from one to two and ultimately, in most cases, three years. This has contrasted with the one-year agreement that has been typical in Europe (but not always in Germany and Sweden) and, as noted above, has been credited with allowing greater flexibility of real wages in response to monetary expansion in the 1970s. It should also be noted, however, that the American long-term agreement was originally proposed by large-scale employers in the late 1940s and was designed in part to accommodate aversion to risk and uncertainty on their part as well as among their organized employees. The latter were to be protected against inflation, partly by cost-of-living escalator clauses and partly by scheduled interim wage increases. The latter permitted real wages to rise although, it was contemplated, in line with productivity. Management could gain from greater certainty in the movement of future labor costs and, to that extent, output prices, and also from less frequent exposure to strikes. (Wildcat strikes within the contract period were presumptively barred by no-strike clauses, which were generally regarded (by the courts as well as the parties) as a quid pro quo for management's acceptance of the grievance procedure with arbitration and hence of the encroachment on managerial prerogatives and autonomy - which had been better defended on the European continent.) Indeed, econometric studies, although seeking to explain why strikes occur, have isolated some negative trends in strike activity, at least through the 1960s.[34] Evidence of a decline in the frequency of strikes would be consistent with the theory of Hicks - who really sought to explain why strikes occurred only rarely, by attributing them to poor bargaining information or practice - because all this institutional elaboration of collective bargaining, especially in large-scale industry, had been taken to bespeak a progressive "maturing" of industrial relations in the United States and increased sophistication of the parties.

But Hicks' theory also concluded that industrial peace is bought by the employer, with payment of "Danegeld," rather than by the unions (through the exercise of discretion in the exploitation of their potential bargaining power). Although competitive equilibrium theory in the postwar period has belittled the

---

[34]O. Ashenfelter and G. Johnson, "Bargaining Theory, Trade Unions, and Industrial Strike Activity," **American Economic Review** (March 1969), pp. 35-49; B. E. Kaufman, "Bargaining Theory, Inflation, and Cyclical Strike Activity in Manufacturing," **Industrial and Labor Relations Review** (April 1981), pp. 333-355 (at 347-48); and "The Determinants of Strikes in the United States," in **ibid.** (July 1982), pp. 473-490.

possible economic impact of unions (and of any other monopolistic endeavors in the private sector), studies have generally attributed major portions of observed union-nonunion wage differences to the operation of collective bargaining (after controlling as best they could for other influences). Through the 1960s, however, wages in the more heavily organized industries rose less rapidly than nonunion wages. Since this was a period when strike activity was down, the leaders of the national unions, maneuvering between minimally acceptable levels of compensation, etc., to the membership and maximum negotiable levels, may have bargained with some discretion in the interest of holding down strike costs and in response to the wage-price guidelines of the Kennedy and Johnson administrations. But in the 1970s, union wages outran nonunion wages. The role played by the operation and by the extension of escalator clauses under long-term agreements in the developments of the 1970s has been analyzed separately by Flanagan, Jacoby and Pearl, and Mitchell.[35] Since the marked increase in COLA coverage in the first half of the decade occurred at a time when the incidence of strikes increased sharply, the former might be reasonably interpreted as reflecting an increase in bargaining pressure exerted by the unions in response to inflationary threats to minimally acceptable levels of compensation.

---

[35] R.J. Flanagan, "Wage Concessions and Long-Term Union Wage Flexibility" (mimeo., 1984; forthcoming in **Brookings Papers on Economic Activity**); S.M. Jacoby and M.Y. Pearl, "Wage Dispersion and Labor Market Contracting" (mimeo, 1984); D.J.B. Mitchell, "Labor Relations Over the Past Five Years: Implications for the Future" (chapter 12, below).

Then, in the early 1980s, when the economy was subjected to severely contractionist policies and particular industries were also subjected to intensified competitive pressures (from deregulation in telecommunications and transport and international competition in manufacturing), long-term contracts were reopened, nominal wages were frozen or actually reduced for 2-1/2 million workers covered by major agreements, and union wages lagged behind nonunion wages for the first time in a decade. As Flanagan points out, this virtually unprecedented wage flexibility was accompanied by a sharp decline in strike activity. The association of lagging union wages and reduced strike activity recalls the 1960s; but in the later period unions tended more to refrain deliberately from resisting wage cuts or freezes in the interest of preserving employment than simply to avoid strike costs and losses. In some of the most celebrated instances of "concession bargaining," extreme illiquidity left the firms in no condition to weather shutdowns; in such cases unions refrained from exploiting their perversely enhanced bargaining power. But that suggested that concession bargaining would not indefinitely outlast the crises that provoked it. Indeed, in some cases national unions refused to accommodate distressed employers - and their local unions - when they believed that accommodation could jeopardize industrywide wage standards which they sought to protect against downward competitive pressures - as they had done in the pre-Wagner Act era. Even the concession bargaining which did occur did not typically disturb the postwar structural innovation - the long-term agreement with a cost-of-living escalator clause - although the terms of compensation in the latter were reduced in various cases. And in many instances unions sought to obtain concessions from employers in the form of increased job security - e.g., advance notification of shut-downs, limited guarantees of continued plant operation, commitments to invest in modernization of facilities - in exchange for their wage concessions.

In short, American unions have been able to exercise considerable bargaining power within the framework of their long-duration agreements; nor have the latter, notwithstanding their enforceable no-strike clauses, prevented strike activity from being greater (relative to the size of the work force) than in most of the other industrial democracies in the postwar period.[36] Management paid "Danegeld" for whatever insurance they obtained against strikes and wage-price instability; by the same token, the unions did not pay for their insurance against inflation with lower wages. In this respect, management could be regarded as more averse to risk than the unions. (This is in contrast to early versions of implicit contract theory which sought to explain the existence of wage rigidity together with involuntary unemployment in unorganized, competitive labor markets by assigning greater risk aversion to employers than to workers. But a more recent version concludes that unemployment is produced when entrepreneurs are more risk-averse than workers.)[37]

---

[36]Cf. Flanagan, Soskice, and Ulman, **op. cit.**, pp. 9 (Table 1-2) and 225 (Table 5-3).

[37]C. Azariadis and J. Stiglitz, "Implicit Contracts and Fixed-Price Equilibria," **Quarterly Journal of Economics**, Vol. 98, 1983 Supplement, pp. 1-21.

Nor was the historic aversion of employers – or of the general public – to unionism ended by the passage of the Wagner Act of 1935. Within a few years after the passage of that landmark measure, state legislation was enacted which departed from the federal model and foreshadowed Taft-Hartley by softening restrictions on employers and specifying unfair labor practices by employees. The long decline in the proportion of NLRB elections won by unions actually began shortly after the end of the Second World War, although the proportion of workers organized rose through the 1950s. Nonunion employers returned to the carrot-and-stick approach of the 1920s, although in a somewhat more sequential manner. In the prosperous 1960s, it was often feasible to attempt to buy off unionization (with its feared restraints on managerial discretion and plant productivity), but subsequently, as profit margins declined, nonunion employers found preemptive wage raising less economical and relied more heavily on methods of direct opposition. Their stick was considerably lighter than the pre-Norris-La Guardia and Wagner models, but thanks to Taft-Hartley it was heavier than it had been in the 1930s and 1940s. Moreover, they became increasingly aware that under the latter legislation a variety of Fabian tactics before and after representation elections could be sanctioned. They were also made aware that the penalties for violating the National Labor Relations Act are light; it had depended originally for its enforcement on a presumptive respect for the law – a presumption which has since been weakened. Increased effectiveness of direct resistance to organizational attempts helped to turn the terms of trade with preemptive wage increases in favor of the former. So did the bargaining power of the unions which, by increasing union wages relative to nonunion wages, tended to raise the cost of preemptive wage increases relative to the costs of direct resistance.

The ability of unions to raise relative wages was due to their organizing weakness as well as their bargaining strength; they were unable to raise "entry-preventive prices" along with their negotiated wages and, of course, in the case of imports the probability that a potential "entrant" would be deterred by the prospect of American unionization was zero. Moreover, as we have already mentioned, the organizing weakness of unions could actually increase their bargaining power as the growth of nonunion competition increased the immediate threat of loss of market share in the event of a shutdown taken by unionized employers to resist union demands. Union bargaining power and organizing weakness could thus be mutually reinforcing, as has been the case in such industries as construction, trucking, meat packing, basic steel, autos, tires, and, earlier, textiles and full-fashioned hosiery. In some of these industries, large-scale firms could open nonunion plants (especially in the South) or invest in capacity abroad; such employers might rather run than fight.

Evidence of a more long-term nature, however, consisting of positive rather than negative relationships between the extent of organization and the effect of collective bargaining on wages, suggests that the processes decribed above can be self-limiting. A brake could be applied through the exercise of self-restraint by unions in the interest of increasing the competitiveness of their employers. The effectiveness of this mechanism depends heavily on the willingness and the authority of the national union, which must be concerned with the demand and cost conditions prevailing throughout the unionized sector of the industry as a whole. But when it might be willing to take the long and broad view, its ability to do so might be circumscribed by the typical reluctance of local unionists to forego bargaining gains when their employers are making profits on a companywide basis. And in some industries in which local unionists were willing to make concessions to keep illiquid employers in business, national unions were opposed on the grounds that to do so would compromise "national" wage standards - which in the previous century the national union had primarily been established to protect. In the early 1980s two century-old credos were revived in at least two of the older national unions (the Machinists and the Mine Workers) in justifying opposition to the granting of concessions: (a) wage cuts in one firm or sector would simply be matched by wage cuts in others (including nonunion firms); and (b) the only way to solve the problem caused by the inequality of bargaining power and organizing power was to "organize the unorganized" and that could best be done by demonstrating bargaining aggressiveness in the unionized sectors. (This latter, of course, could not address the problem of imports.)

The alternative approach is to reduce the bargaining power of the unions. A tilt, or reversal of bargaining power in unionized sectors of industries - or in domestic sectors of international industries - can occur when cost differences become sufficiently large to make losses of market share resulting from bargaining concessions to unions exceed losses of market share incurred during shutdowns. Increased cost disadvantages could also combine with larger pools of nonunion labor, especially at higher levels of unemployment, to make recourse to "replacements" a preferable strategy of employer resistance to siege warfare, despite the predictable increase in the levels of violence on the picket line provoked by the use of strikebreakers.

History will doubtless record that in the 1980s the bargaining power of American employers was increased by legislated deregulation of domestic transport and telecommunications and by currency appreciation as well as by the cumulative effect of relative increases in the costs of unionized enterprises. These developments nurtured a "hard" managerial line - a greater disinclination to take as given not only various arrangements which had originally been negotiated to serve as frameworks for subsequent negotiations over substantive issues, but also, in some cases, the bargaining relationship itself. This hard line was reflected in the weakening of several formal industrywide structures, the rupture of some long-standing "pattern" relationships, and also a tendency, as noted above, for large-scale firms to institute "double-breasted" operations by opening nonunion facilities.

Whether increased employer bargaining power proves to be associated with stabilization rather than further deterioration of the extent of unionism will depend on whether the unions find it easier to discount the outcome of struggles in which their bargaining potential has been reduced than deliberately to reduce their bargaining intensity.[38] The historic record of procyclical strike activity suggests that the unions would refrain more often from striking as the odds against their winning strikes are increased; if that proves to be the case, the decline in union membership might approach some socioeconomic asymptote which would be determined by such factors as the size of the blue-collar work force, the magnitude of the government sector, and the going level of populist distrust of large-scale enterprise (whose perceived decline in international competitiveness has entailed a loss of public esteem). Hence the United States would be neither the only nor the first industrialized democracy to dispense with a union movement- But the present situation of the American unions does call to mind the title which Perlman and Taft affixed to the penultimate chapter in Commons' **History:** "Struggling Against Decline."

Institutional Convergence and Its Limits

In most of Europe employer activity continued to be focused primarily on terms and

---

[38] E.P. Lazear, "A Competitive Theory of Monopoly Unionism," **American Economic Review** (September 1983, pp. 631-643, models an equilibrium union-nonunion wage differential resulting from the ability of the union to raise the union wage without incurring bargaining resistance from unionized employers, but subject to the constraint that in so doing it is also increasing the extent of nonunion operation and is varying the level of the nonunion wage. This model does not allow preemptive wage-setting by nonunion employers and (ultimately for that reason) requires that workers displaced from the union sector will be frictionlessly reemployed in the same industry under nonunion conditions.

conditions of employment during the postwar period, although in the 1950s Italian employers engaged in their equivalent of the American open shop drive of the 1920s, and in both Italy and France the prewar tradition of determining wages and working conditions in the virtual absence of collective bargaining was maintained into the late 1960s. In other countries the greater prevalence of association bargaining, as well as provision in some countries for governmental extension of the terms of settlement to nonmember firms, made for the virtual absence of such manifestations of the American hard line as recourse to strike breakers and the substitution of nonunion for union operations - although multinational firms in Europe, as in the United States, could substitute foreign for domestic operations. To the extent that these tactics could find historic precedent in the United States but not in Europe in the interwar period, their recent revival in the former country might be regarded as a continuation of the historic expectionalism of American industrial relations, in the light of which the divergent movements in union membership is understandable. The same interpretation might find support in the persistence of the traditional strength of left wing politics in Europe, which served as a source of direct and indirect support of unionism and collective bargaining and which contrasted with the rapid re-emergence of a traditional political climate in the United States that (at its most favorable) generated no comparable support to unions in this country. But before succumbing to the temptation to project divergent membership trends, as well as any other indicators of institutional robustness into the future, one should note that certain postwar developments have tended to make European bargaining institutions and even their political environment resemble their American counterparts a bit more closely than might have been predicted on the basis of prewar custom and practice.

These developments, which were referred to in the first section, had the effect of weakening both industrywide or more centralized bargaining structures and managerial control over working conditions at the workplace. Industrywide bargaining could facilitate employer resistance and protect wage and price levels from being undercut when labor markets were slack (although not when unemployment was extremely high); under the relatively low levels of unemployment in the postwar period, especially between the mid-1950s and the mid-1960s, competitive and bargaining pressures tended to raise rather than lower wages relative to centrally negotiated rates, contributing to wage drift and also to a weakening of the ability of employer associations to maintain a united front of resistance to the national unions. On the other hand, the great postwar expansion of international trade, together with low rates of inflation in the United States in the first half of the 1960s which held down world prices of manufactures, furnished a strong incentive to hold down costs and raise productivity in other countries as they found themselves in balance-of-payments difficulties. To accomplish the former task, many European countries turned to policies of direct wage restraint; and in the second half of the 1960s they had recourse to deflation as well. Productivity was raised as a result both of the growth of large-scale, capital-intensive enterprises at the expense of smaller, low-cost firms[39] and of attempts within firms (especially the larger ones) to improve capacity utilization by increasing production standards and by "rationalizing" their working practices and internal wage structures to provide more efficient incentives as well as adequate supplies of labor, especially in various skilled categories. The larger firms had less use for national employer associations than smaller employers. National associations could not protect them against loss of market shares to foreign competitors during strikes or as the result of settlements which were uniform only within national jurisdictions. On the other hand, they often allowed the wages in their plants to rise more rapidly than centrally negotiated rates in order to attract or motivate labor or to make peace with disaffected or aggressive groups of local unionists. This tended to weaken the associations in countries in which they continued to accommodate the interests of their more numerous, smaller, and higher-cost members.

Meanwhile, these downward pressures on real-effort wages sharply disappointed the (rising) expectations of production workers which, as David Soskice pointed out, erupted in a series of shop floor strikes in 1968-70 that occurred in the absence of either exceptionally low unemployment or exceptionally high prior

---

[39]With the growth of international trade during the 1960s, there was a tendency within industries for increasing concentration within the major countries of the European Economic Community to be associated with decreasing concentration in the area as a whole. Cf. A. Jacquemin and A. Kumps, "Changes in the Size Structure of the Largest European Firms: An Entropy Measure," **Journal of Industrial Economics** (November 1971), pp. 64-66.

rates of inflation.[40] Soskice attributes the local and spontaneous origin of these strikes to the unwillingness of official national unions or confederations to defy official incomes policies or break fixed-term contracts (in Germany and Italy) and/or their inability to respond to grievances in the plants or less skilled workers in industry and in the public sector (whose rising wage egalitarianism constituted an important source of increased worker militancy). As a result, attempts by employers to tighten (or in the case of Britain, to restore) control over work practices and wage determination in the workplace resulted in the abrupt intrusion of adversary unionism into what had been effectively preserved as the exclusive presence of continental management since the prewar period.

Up to this point, these postwar European developments on both the management side and on the union side can recall prewar American experience. The combination of expansion of geographic market areas and increased industrial concentration experienced by Europe in the 1960s had been experienced in the United States in the last quarter of the nineteenth century. In that earlier episode large-scale American firms had been able to resist collective bargaining in any form; and later, after the widespread extension of collective bargaining in the 1930s, the tendency of such firms to go it alone found expression in pattern bar-

───────────────
[40]D. Soskice, "Strike Waves and Wage Explosions, 1968-1970: An Economic Interpretation," in C. Crouch and A. Pizzorno, **The Resurgence of Class Conflict in Western Europe Since 1968** (New York: Holmes & Meier, 1978), Vol. 2, pp. 221-246.

gaining in such industries as autos, aircraft, electrical manufacturing, and nonferrous metals. (In the 1960s and 1970s American and European traditions collided when various U.S.-based multinational firms attempted to resist joining domestic employer associations in European countries, although in some prominent instances they were induced to do so by a combination of union and association pressure.)

The European wildcat strike episodes in 1968-70 can be viewed as a belated European version of the American organizing episode of the 1930s. Of course, they arose out of different historic contexts and could tap quite different wellsprings for the intense ideological support which each received. But both consisted in part of responses at the grass roots to an accelerated pace of work and also to heightened insecurity, although in the American case the deterioration in actual conditions had been far greater, while the later European situations were marked by a decline in conditions relative to heightened expectations as well as to prior experience. Both episodes were distinguished by spontaneous activity by workers in the plants, although in the earlier episode this was (literally) organized and supported by experienced and aggressive leadership furnished by the breakaway unions of the CIO, whereas in the later uprisings most of the European establishments were caught as flat-footed by developments as the leadership of the AFL had been in the early 1930s. (The Italian confederations were notable exceptions.) In both instances, employer-cultivated institutions in the workplace - e.g., company unions in the American basic steel industry and works councils in Europe - went native and played adversarial roles - although this was not the case in Britain where shop stewards had long been operating autonomously and aggressively. In both cases low-paid, nonskilled workers were the chief organizational objects of the exercise. Since such groups had been unionized in most of Europe since the end of the last century, the organization of industrial unions in the U.S. manufacturing sector marked a catch-up with the Europeans. But the American catch-up was really a leap-frogging exercise: the new American unions promptly engaged in adversarial relationships with management at the workplace and at companywide levels, whereas in continental Europe the unions generally had been effectively excluded from such activity until the events of May 1968 in France set off a round of heightened militancy among already unionized workers. Finally, each episode generated a "structural break" with prior wage behavior, raising the rate of money wage increases associated with any given level of employment or capacity utilization. This historical comparision thus illustrates that an increase in militancy, or bargaining intensity, among already organized workers can have (qualitatively) the same economic impact as an increase in the extent of organization or of bargaining coverage (assuming an unchanged degree of bargaining intensity). (Either an increase in organization or of intensity can generate higher rates of wage inflation by raising the equilibrium real wage and the equilibrium rate of unemployment, although monetarist theory has reserved this role for the former since it assumes that unions at any level of organization invariably bargain at maximum intensity. What our historical comparison underscores is the obvious fact that a surge in union organization is simply a surge in militancy among those previously unorganized.)

Our two historical parallels reflect similar responses to similar changes in certain economic determinants of unionism and collective bargaining. Neither parallel has been completed. Industrywide bargaining structures in concentrated European industries have not been abandoned, nor has industrywide bargaining in Europe suffered erosion from defections and nonunion competition as have some of the American systems. Effective union representation of semiskilled production workers in Europe has been increased, but the challenge to employer control at the workplace has not developed into vertical extension of formal collective bargaining from industrywide to plant levels and by a corresponding extension of control by national unions over shop stewards (although Italy has provided a partial exception to this generalization). Naturally, the changes in the economic determinants of employer and union behavior discussed above could not be expected to close the gaps completely, especially in the absence of facilitating changes in the political and ideological influences which have long made for institutional divergence. In addition, the imprints left on American unionism and collective bargaining by extension of market areas, the rise of large-scale enterprise, and later by the Great Depression were strongly reinforced by the adoption of a unique set of legal prescriptions for bargaining behavior (the National Labor Relations Act) and subsequently by the wartime environment which followed the 1930s.

In the latter connection, it might be useful to contrast the policies of wage restraint that were implemented in both areas in the periods immediately following those in which union militancy and bargaining power had sharply increased - in the 1940s in the United States (to which reference was made in the previous section) and in the 1970s in Europe. Incomes policies have relied on one or more of three methods for their implementation: persuasion and exhortation, compulsion (or coercion), and compensation.[41] Under the wartime conditions prevailing in the 1940s in the United States, methods of persuasion could be more effective than in peacetime, and methods of compulsion or coercion were more accessible. Nevertheless, the policies were designed to restrain real as well as nominal incomes at very high levels of employment, and elements of compensation had to be included in order to abate restiveness among local unionists and to secure the authority of the national union officers who actively participated in the formation and administration of the policy.

The compensatory measures included the encouragement of union security clauses (of the maintenance-of-membership variety) and the check-off of union dues by the employer in order to prevent the erosion of union membership (which in fact expanded greatly during the war). They also included encouragement of grievance procedures under collective bargaining to provide a safety value for worker discontent and an alternative to wildcat strikes. This procedure formally involved the national union in the disposition of membership grievances and the administration of the collective agreement; in so doing it provided a vehicle for the enforcement of negotiated seniority rules, which had been widely negotiated at the

---
[41]Flanagan, Soskice, and Ulman, **op. cit.,** pp. 660-664.

insistence of unions in the 1930s and which complemented the newly established federal system of unemployment compensation, as a result of which layoffs became a preferable alternative to "work-spreading." And, while compensation had to be primarily nonpecuniary in nature, the tripartite War Labor Board permitted the negotiation of private pension and "health and welfare" schemes on the grounds that they were less inflationary (on the demand side) than wage increases. This laid the groundwork for making collective bargaining complementary to the social security system in many unionized sectors. In addition, national unions were allowed (within limits) to redress wage "inequities" by negotiating over job classification and incentive systems, which had the effect of institutionalizing wage drift. In such ways did the wartime system of wage control encourage the institutionalization of American collective bargaining and helped the method of collective bargaining to attain parity with, if not Gompersian primacy over, the "method of legislative enactment" in increasing security and equity on the job as well as wage income.

In peacetime deflation is a more feasible policy option than in wartime, so that, if incomes policy fails to reduce the bargaining power exerted by unions sufficiently at a given level of employment, the level of employment itself might be lowered and in that way union bargaining power (further) reduced. In postwar Europe, nevertheless, the political feasibility of demand deflation had been quite low, and it was further reduced in the early 1970s by the apprehension that increased unemployment would touch off another wave of wildcat strikes in countries in which such strikes had occurred.

Unions, on the other hand, felt under pressure from their members to deliver greater wage increases, which compounded the difficulties confronting the authorities. Even where more centralized bargaining structures tended to predispose union leaders to some self-restraint, they could at best be expected to take into account the employment interests of their own members. As a result, real wages could rule at levels which, while sufficient to permit high levels of employment to obtain within the unionized work force, would preclude sufficient opportunities for outsiders, notably young people and other new entrants to the labor force where in fact unemployment was most highly concentrated. When the employment target of the government exceeded levels which were minimally acceptable to the unions, the authorities came under pressure to adopt expansionist and inflationary policies to reduce real wages in order to absorb more of the unemployed. But in order to avoid the adoption of such policies - which could ultimately prove self-defeating while entailing adverse consequences for competitiveness and profitability - the authorities turned to a variety of formal and implicit "social contract" deals with the unions in an effort to buy wage restraint.

European compensatory cuisine in the 1970s, however, offered a different and richer menu than the lean cuisine served up in wartime America. To begin with, there was greater recourse to pecuniary compensation which (in different times and places) included reductions in heavily progressive income tax rates and increases in the amounts and variety of social welfare benefits, sometimes offset by increased employer contributions. The latter contrasted with the earlier American device of negotiated fringe benefits. In the second place, when European social contracts included the rectification of "inequitable" wage structures as a compensatory item, they attacked the problem primarily in a centralized way by biasing wage or price norms in the direction of wage equality rather than permitting unions and employers to bargain out their own "exception" at plant, company, or industry levels.

In the third place, while managerial autonomy and discretion at the workplace continued to be challenged in the 1970s, the challenges did not result in any substantial increase in the scope or institutionalization of collective bargaining as had occurred earlier in the United States. The administrative and judicial roles played by the American grievance procedure had been preempted by older institutions and doctrines in Europe. Labor courts performed the function of interpreting collective agreements while affording the aggrieved employee direct access to an authority outside the framework of collective bargaining for the redress of grievances against the employer. (This included protections against "unjust dismissal," a protection which has been absent in the common law - at least until recently in all but a few state jurisdictions - and therefore has constituted a unique property of the collective bargaining relationship.)

"Codetermination" offered another alternative to collective bargaining and the grievance procedure. It was first established and became most fully developed through legislation in West Germany, where "labor directors" are elected to supervisory boards by the employees of the enterprise. Some of the labor seats are reserved for outside union representatives, but the great majority are nominated by the works councils. Legally mandated extensions of this system provoked bitter political opposition from the employers who feared that it would become an alternative not only to collective bargaining, but to capitalism as well. In fact, German labor directors have honored their obligation to support the profitability and efficiency of the enterprise, but this only confirms the suspicion of critics like American unionists for whom schemes of "worker participation" or "control" revive memories of the company unions of the 1920s; they prefer the adversarial relationship which was preserved and formalized in the grievance procedure. In Germany codetermination tended to reinforce the autonomy and influence of the works councils, but the councils are legally excluded from the system of collective bargaining, whereas the grievance procedure had been partly designed to reinforce the authority of the national union at the work place.

Finally, some European unions did attempt to secure some institutional protection, partly in exchange for wage restraint, but, as discussed earlier, with only limited success at best. The German unions secured the passage of legislation to raise the number of works directors in larger firms to equality with directors representing the shareholders, but the result fell short of attaining de facto "parity" and, as noted above, provoked a bitter political row. Efforts to restrict certain negotiated gains to union members also failed in Germany as they did in the Netherlands (where they provoked grassroots resistance from nonunion workers). British unions secured the repeal of restrictive labor legislation passed by a Conservative Government in 1971 as the result of a coal strike (1973-74) and the subsequent election of a Labour Government pledged to seek wage restraint. But this was essentially a defensive victory; and it was ultimately nullified by the passage, under another Conservative Government, of acts (1980, 1982) which, among other things, virtually outlaw the closed shop and apparently go further than the American Taft-Hartley Act in proscribing picketing by workers at other than their own places of work. The Swedish Federation of Labor devised a "wage earner" fund whereby the proceeds of a tax on profits would be used to secure shares in company equity which would be transferred to union-controlled funds. It was supposed to generate resources for investment and at the same time to protect the central bargaining machinery by siphoning off some of the profits earned by firms in the export sector to which the restive metalworkers' union had been denied access by the "solidaristic" (egalitarian) wage policy. But the plan provided no tangible compensation for the wage earners (who could neither receive dividends nor sell the new shares), and any nonpecuniary compensation it might provide by way of the prospect of socialized (union) ownership of industry served as a red flag to employer and shareholders, 100,000 of whom vented their discontent in a "march of pinstripes" in the capital. The LO, however, conditioned their cooperation in wage restraint on the adoption of such a plan, and a new Labour Government, anxious to reduce real wages and costs through major currency devaluation, passed legislation, although in a watered-down form. But it prevented neither the dissolution of the 33-year-old centralized bargaining structure, from which the Employers Confederation withdrew in 1983, nor the disaffection of the metalworkers.

In both the United States in the 1940s and in Europe in the 1970s, wage restraint was accompanied by nonwage gains which resulted in higher labor costs to employers. In the American episode these cost increases were chargeable to collective bargaining. In Europe they were not: they showed up in increased social security or payroll taxes or in the form of unproductive or excess employees as the result of employee recourse to the labor court system or, it should be noted, as the result of legislation requiring advance notification or (as in France) official authorization of mass layoffs. The difference is significant in that the elaboration of collective bargaining in the United States furnished the employer with an additional and potentially powerful disincentive to operate in a "union-free environment," which is lacking when a larger portion of nonwage costs are determined outside the domain of bargaining and must be borne by union and nonunion employers alike. The bargaining process helped unions to raise those costs, since their political bargaining power was a function of their bargaining power over wages, but employer resistance against such cost increases - and against the various anticapitalist alternatives discussed above - could most effectively be concentrated in the political arena. But that calls for united activity through employer associations, which in turn could strengthen association bargaining on the wage front, making breakaway activity less attractive - (and nonunion operation less visible) as an alternative.

This tendency reinforces - and is reinforced by - prewar traditions of employer participation in association bargaining, for political as well as economic reasons, while it runs counter to the weakening of industrywide structures under the pressure of intensified international competition and tight domestic labor markets. The latter has given way to much higher levels of unemployment which obviously reduced the temptation of more prosperous and aggressive firms to grant wage increases in excess of those negotiated by industrywide associations. In the United States severe recession and high levels of unemployment - but also deregulation in certain sectors - has weakened industrywide bargaining in some prominent instances by inducing and enabling firms to undercut association settlements or standards. In Germany, on the other hand, employers have continued to offer strong united resistance against union demands. Nor has the continued cohesiveness of employers' associations there and elsewhere been due to a major reduction in union bargaining intensity; recall that the unions have been assigned a generous share in the blame for the rise in European wages relative to wages in the United States in the late 1970s and early 1980s. The appearance for the first time in a quarter-century of high levels of unemployment within union jurisdictions as well as in the nonunion periphery of the labor force does not appear to have reduced union bargaining intensity or resulted in bargaining concessions on the scale experienced in the United States. (In part the difference has been one of appearance rather than substance, due to the prevalence of long-term agreements in the United States which were dramatically broken into.) In Europe the principal result seems to have been a switch in union priorities in the direction of job protection without much disposition to give way on the wage front - e.g., the resistance of the Italian unions to reductions in wage indexation and the militant reaction of the Swedish metal workers to recent increases in the profits gained by their employers in the wake of currency depreciation. The big German metal workers' union has taken the lead in a wider European push for a shorter work week at correspondingly higher hourly rates of pay. Union militancy has been countered by employer militancy, but the latter has been contained within its centralized structure and has been confined to the issue at hand. "I would never say that we wanted weak unions," said an official of the central employers' federation; "We have an interest in their remaining strong and stable."[42] (The German employers of 1984 bear a remarkable resemblance to the German employers of 1918.) On the continent, at least, the old tradition of employer support of trade unionism in the interest of social and political stability - the case which Gompers had tried to make in the United States - has thus far survived in an increasingly uncongenial economic environment.

Summary and Conclusion

Postwar trends in membership place the organizational decline of American unions (in the private sector of the economy) in international perspective and call into question the continued viability of a distinctive system of collective bargaining found in the United States. They also invite speculation about the future of unionism and industrial relations in European countries which in recent times experienced certain events and conditions similar to those that had previously been experienced

---

[42]Ibid., pp. 681-685.

in the United States, where they had strongly influenced the development of industrial relations. Three of these were considered in this paper.

The first consisted of the extension of competitive market areas and an associated increase in the economic importance of large-scale, multiplant enterprises. In nineteenth-century America, both conditions were conducive to the strengthening of national unions; and the widening of competitive areas was conducive to the spread of industrywide bargaining in more competitive industries, but not in most highly concentrated industries where large-scale firms were generally able to resist recognition of unions until the 1930s. In postwar Europe, the growth of international trade and of multinational enterprise tended to weaken the effectiveness of bargaining in national associations.

The second event consisted of the organizing activity in the United States in the 1930s which extended collective bargaining not only horizontally, i.e., into industrial sectors and occupational categories where it had been largely absent (or excluded after the First World War), but also vertically, or down to the plant level where it was soon involved in such productivity-related areas as job security, production standards, and the handling of employee grievances. The waves of wildcat strikes in Europe at the end of the 1960s and the beginning of the 1970s presented an analog to the American events of the 1930s. Although the European episodes mainly involved increased militancy among union members, they did entail both the extension of effective representation to low-paid, less skilled groups and the introduction of adversarial relations in the plants.

Finally, higher levels of unemployment and slack in the labor markets prevailed in the United States than in Europe in the postwar period up to the 1980s. During the 1970s and early 1980s the disparity between the bargaining power of American unions and their organizing power was especially marked: unemployment was not sufficiently high to prevent union wages from significantly outpacing nonunion wages, but labor market slackness combined with lower profitability to make nonunion operation a feasible as well as an attractive option for many employers. In Europe tight labor markets in the 1960s contributed to the weakening of industrywide bargaining and employer associations, but subsequent higher levels of unemployment removed this source of weakness without facilitating significant employer defections and recourse to strikebreakers and nonunion operation.

Thus employer resistance to unionism abroad has been largely confined within the bounds of collective bargaining. It need not be assumed, however, that unorganized American employers are a breed apart from unionized employers either at home or abroad. It might be reasonably assumed that employers anywhere would prefer nonunion operation to collective bargaining, but it might also be assumed that they would prefer the latter to either sufficiently costly employee unrest or a noncapitalist economic order. In many European countries, the last class of alternatives was sufficiently strong to make collective bargaining the preferable alternative for employers, especially in those industrial sectors in which employers were sufficiently large in size and few in numbers to take class interests into account in formulating policy in the arena of industrial relations. The outcomes have differed widely from time to time and country to country, but leftist alternatives have by no means atrophied - **viz.**, the wildcat strikes and some of the more ambitious manifestations of worker control - and so they have continued to act as a counterpoise to intensified economic pressures.

William Ouchi

4

Some Informal Remarks on the M-Form Society

When I was sitting down to write the last chapter of **Theory Z** some three and a half years ago, I intended to make it a grand statement on what I thought the role of government should be in restoring the competitive edge to American business. I said to myself, "Just suppose that every manager and every company in America were to do everything exactly right, then would all of our problems go away on the economic front?" And I concluded sadly that they would not. They would not because there remains a very serious problem of coordination between business and government.

Every company operates with a large number of common endowments. Some of them are physical, such as plentiful energy, land, and clean air. Others are social endowments, such as universal literacy, well established higher education with a research and development base, and honest and stable government. But there is one further endowment which we do not possess, but which other countries do. That endowment is the capacity for collaboration between business and government.

Professor Jay Barney and I have spent the last three years with a team of sixteen scholars at UCLA trying to learn something about business-government relations. As we looked more deeply into the problem, I reached the conclusion that it is entirely possible that your children and mine will never be able to look forward to the day when they will enjoy two cars, a boat, and a three-bedroom house in the suburbs. This is because a good deal of the prosperity that we have enjoyed for the past several decades has come about for reasons largely of industrial monopoly.

Before World War II, only 5 percent of the total GNP of the United States depended on trade. In 1950 it was still only 5 percent, and in 1960 it was still only 5 percent, but today it is 14 percent of our GNP. This is higher than most European nations and approaches the 17 percent of Japan. At the end of World War II, anyone who wanted to buy a ship, airplane, or oscilloscope had to buy it in North America. Much of the industrial plant of Germany, France, the United Kingdom, and Japan had been destroyed. For nearly forty years now, we have enjoyed an unprecedented period of industrial monopoly. While those countries were rebuilding, we supplied their needs.

Each of us can think of a time when there has been a monopoly, perhaps because a company had a better product or because it had government protection. Whenever there is a monopoly the stage is set for superstitious learning. In the case of a company, it means that when there is a monopoly the management can stay home and watch reruns of "Let's Make a Deal" and yet sales and earnings continue to rise each year. But typically the management won't stay home; instead they'll come to work. They'll work hard, but no matter what they do, sales and earnings will rise. In consequence they will learn, and learn deeply, that they know how to manage that business. But that learning is in every way superstitious. It is just as superstitious as the learning by a primitive tribe that knows that if they perform a ceremony each evening the sun will return twelve hours hence. Probably one member of that tribe, an intuitive scientist, said, "I bet this is a bunch of hooey. I bet if we cut out this ceremony the sun would be back anyhow." And probably one of his colleagues said, "I bet you're right, but why take a chance?" Superstitious belief is difficult to change.

It occurs to me that a good deal of what we believe today about the underlying nature of our economy and how it should run is superstitious belief. We have, on the one hand, an economic superstition which declares that the way to maintain the economic vitality of our economy is to cause each company to act entirely on its own in every way. In any industry, companies "A" and "B" should be made to stand in opposite corners, with government in another corner. No combination of the three should be permitted to come together because what results will not be good. On the other hand, there is a superstition which argues that political-economic gridlock is the inevitable price of democracy.

This political-economical superstition has been expressed most recently and forcefully by Mancur Olson, a distinguished political economist at the University of Maryland.[1] Olson ob-

---
[1] Mancur Olson, **The Rise and Decline of Nations** (New Haven: Yale University Press, 1982).

serves that in any country that has a long period of peace, those who are like-minded will find one another and form a special interest group. In time, these special interest groups will come to oppose one another. They will grow like weeds and ultimately will choke off the capacity of the nation to arrive at a national consensus, and therefore choke off its capacity to maintain economic vitality. He observes that in every Western nation, such as in the United States, there has been a period of prosperity after the nation either lost a war or suffered a revolution. Those two catastrophic events are so completely upsetting that they will disorganize the existing interest group politics and make it possible to form a new national consensus. That will produce many years of economic growth until the weeds grow and once again choke off further growth.

What does this mean in the terms of an industry? It means that an industry that is young needs a certain form of regulation on the one hand, and of support on the other. But when that industry matures, it needs a very different form of regulation, and of support, if it is to maintain its competitive vitality. It means that we cannot sustain competition unless we can change the rules of the game to meet the conditions at hand.

Baseball remains the great American game. It remains competitively vital, in part because the rules are changed from time to time. When the pitchers got too big and strong, the mound was lowered. When the pitchers became too specialized, they introduced the "designated hitter." Basketball retains its competitive vitality because when the players got too big, goal-tending was outlawed, and when the game became too defensive, they put in the shot-clock.

If we can't change the rules, we can't maintain the vitality of any competition. What that means is that, as a nation, we must be able to focus our most scarce resource, which is not air, water, or land, but political will. If we can focus our political will, then we can bring about the changes in the rules that are necessary to allow each sector of our economy to retain and regain its vitality. But to focus in that way, we must engage in social choice. The implication is that we're not going to answer everyone's problems at once, but rather that we're going to focus our energies on solving one set of problems at a time. Then next year we will focus on the next set of problems.

In a democracy, we cannot engage in social choice unless those not chosen will support the designated choice. But who will support a choice that leaves him or her with an empty bag? No one, unless they know with certainty that there will be serial equity. Each party must be certain that over a series of events, decisions, and years, that their sacrificial support today, or their selfishness today, will be remembered and repaid in kind tomorrow. How can we know that there will be serial equity? Only by constructing units of social memory: the institutions which have the stability to remember and to repay both those who have been flexible and those who have been unreasonably rigid. What does it mean to think about putting in place a structure like this? Whenever we think about the problems of managing our economy, we turn by tradition to political scientists or to macroeconomists, but never to the scholars of business. Today, some of our largest companies exceed in size and complexity some of the smaller national economies. You can't push the analogy too far because even the largest company is much simpler than the smallest nation or state. But we have learned some important lessons about how to manage and organize a large, complex enterprise. These may be important lessons for managing our nation.

The research of the last seven or eight years has produced some tremendously important innovations in the microeconomics and the sociology of large organizations. One of the most consistent findings is that there are only three forms of corporate structure that are possible in the large enterprise.[2] The simplest and most familiar of these is the U-Form or unified organization, more commonly known, perhaps, as a functional organization. It is called unified because the operating units have to stand as a group. None of them can exist or survive on its own. Furthermore, it is impossible to assess the performance of any one department in a clear manner. As a result, when there is a dispute between functional departments, the only person in the organization who has the right set of incentives and information to make the tradeoffs between them is the chief executive. One consequence is that as a U-Form company grows, the number of decisions that must be made by the CEO becomes overwhelmingly large. Then the company bogs down.

---

[2]Oliver E. Williamson, **Markets and Hierarchies: Analysis and Antitrust Implications** (New York: The Free Press, 1975).

are semi-autonomous, that is, each stands alone and makes its own product line, but all of them draw upon some common resources such as corporate laboratories, marketing staff, or some manufacturing plant. One result is that the company is in an intermediate stage between centralized and decentralized. It is decentralized in the sense that each division is asked to operate as though it were a small entrepreneurial business so that the benefits of nimbleness and flexibility can be obtained. But on the other hand, because it is impossible to measure with precision exactly what has been contributed by each unit, it is necessary that all behave together as a team, and that there be some substantial capacity for memory about the subtleties of who has been flexible or rigid in the past.

When an M-Form company works well, it is because the middle managers work as a team. To work as a team does not mean that they all share the same goals, nor does it mean that they love one another and walk arm-in-arm toward the future. It means, simply, that they trust one another sufficiently to be willing to confront one another directly and argue toe-to-toe when they have a dispute, for example, over the design of the new information system. If they will work together as a team, confront one another, and fight out their differences, then they can make a joint recommendation to the executive office and the company works well. But if the middle managers will not do that, but instead each attempt an end run and go directly to the chief executive and say, "Please do it my way," the result will be that: (1) the corporate staff will balloon in size in order to study all of the claims and counterclaims, (2) the decision making will become

The second pure form of organization is the H-Form or holding company. In the true H-Form company the operating units have come in by acquisition and are involved in unrelated businesses. That means that there is no transferring of intermediate products or services between them. It means, as a result, that it is possible to measure with some precision the profitability and the return on investment attributable to each operating unit. The major task of the executive office is to conduct an internal capital market. It announces, for example, "We have a capital budget of $50 million this year, gentlemen; submit your bids." The operating units bid for capital by offering promised rates of return: "I'll earn you 28 percent, 29 percent or 34 percent." The task of the financial staff is to cast a cold and skeptical eye on these typically optimistic expectations, boil them down to something more readily believable, and then allocate capital on the basis of expected return. However, in an H-Form company the capacity of the units to coordinate together is very limited, so that the corporate office, representing the organization as a whole, contributes little beyond summing the pieces. The research of the last several years very strongly implies that large companies of U-Form and H-Form are low-profit performers in the long run.[3]

The high performing type in the long run is the M-Form, or multidivisional organization. In the true M-Form company the operating units

---

[3]See, for example, Richard P. Rumelt, **Strategy, Structure, and Economic Performance** (Boston: Division of Research, Graduate School of Business Administration, Harvard University, 1974).

113

The M-Form company can do both. That is the
lesson of business that can be applied to the
governance of our nation.

What does the M-Form suggest at the level
of an entire industry, rather than at the level
of a single firm? Consider the structure of
the microelectronics and computer industries in
Japan. The computer industry was born in the
United States in 1944 with the design of Mark
I, a joint venture between IBM and Harvard University under a contract from the federal government. In 1946 the first commercial prototype machine, ENIAC, was built by the Univac
Corporation.

The computer industry in Japan was born
roughly twelve years later, the first computer
being produced by a joint venture between NTT
and the University of Tokyo. That first computer in Japan was followed by both individual
company research and by a series of joint research and development projects with acronyms
such as FONTAC, DIPS, and PIPS. In 1964 the
Japanese computer industry was just starting to
get off the ground when IBM introduced the System 360. The 360 was so vastly superior to any
business machine on the market that it and its
successors drove GE and Xerox out of the computer business and threatened to destroy the
Japanese computer industry as it was being
born.

The Japanese responded with a strong form
of protectionism which no one would argue was
fair to IBM. In addition to protectionism,
they began a new joint R&D project in 1965, the
Super Computer. This was to be a copy of the
IBM 360, but the Super Computer came to fruition just as IBM introduced the next genera-

116

more and more centralized in the chief executive, and (3) soon the middle management will start to complain that the company is top-heavy, the staff intrusive, and decisions too slow, without realizing that they themselves have created the problem. Another way to say this is that the essence of the M-Form organization, when it succeeds, is that it achieves a balance between competition on the one hand and teamwork on the other. That is precisely the problem that we face in our government.

The Japanese Diet is a bicameral legislature. It has 763 members and meets in a one-year session. In a typical one-year session, the Diet entertains 150 proposed new bills. Of those, on the average, 100 are proposed by the ministries and 80 percent of those pass into law. Of the remaining fifty, which are proposed by the Diet members and which are of the "pork-barrel" variety, on the average 18 percent pass into law. Overall, 60 percent of the proposed bills pass into law.

The U.S. Congress is also bicameral, has 535 members, and meets in a two-year session. There are 22,000 bills proposed in the typical two-year session. Of those, on the average, 2.5 percent pass into law.

It is relatively simple to construct a situation in which there is only competition between individuals and no teamwork. It is also relatively simple to construct a situation in which one emphasizes only teamwork without individual competition; but neither of those works very well. It is extremely difficult, whether in an economy or a company, to have simultaneously an emphasis on a great deal of competition and on a great deal of teamwork.

ject that would require the bringing together of companies producing apparel, textiles, fibers, sewing machines, robots, machine tools, lasers, computers, and software, along with several unions. There isn't any way for us to gather all of those people in and get them to agree on how to do this. If you can find a way, let us know."

That is precisely the problem which faced the Japanese computer makers in 1975. What did they do? They turned, first of all, to JEIDA, the trade association which represents the computer makers, and asked JEIDA to formulate a plan. JEIDA member companies agreed on a plan which involved a joint VLSI research association. Then, on behalf of its members, JEIDA went to the next higher level trade association, the EIAJ, which represents the makers of not only computers, but of consumer electronics, power generators, and the full range of electrical goods. They said to the members of the EIAJ, "Would those of you not in the computer industry temporarily set aside some of your own pet projects so that we, as a group, can get behind the VLSI joint R&D idea? In other words, would you stand aside so that the traffic may flow through the intersection, rather than everybody trying to jam into the intersection at once saying, 'me, me, me', thus producing political-economic gridlock." And the members said yes.

Then the EIAJ, on the part of its members, went to the Keidanren and asked for their support. Here we need some explanation about the Keidanren, because there is nothing like it in the United States. The Keidanren is a private organization initiated by business. It is organized a little bit like the United Nations.

The "security council" equivalent consists of 812 of the largest companies of Japan, typically not more than three per industry. There is a small staff of perhaps fifty professionals, and there are 110 general trade associations which hold membership. Each of those associations has as its members specialized trade associations, and they and their members represent one million medium-sized and small companies.

The Keidanren is not a unit of central planning, but instead resembles a great big "boxing ring." When there is a dispute between the chemical companies and the mining companies, between the life insurance companies and the securities companies, or between the banks and the thrifts, they can step into this "ring," put up their dukes, and have it out. When there is a dispute between big business and small business they can step into this "ring" and they can "duke around." If and when they reach a consensus, they can go with one voice to speak to their government and lobby as a group.

The seven companies approached MITI through two separate avenues. The first avenue was through the MITI staff, which, unlike the U.S. Department of Commerce, invites participation from business. The MITI staff is organized in the simplest matrix one can imagine. There are several industry bureaus, each of which is subdivided into industry specialties, so that if you are in the shoe business, there will be two or three staff members who do nothing but maintain contact with and know everybody in the shoe business. Then there are several issue bureaus which cut across industries, but all you need is your contact man in the shoe section and he can instantaneously, through this matrix, put you in contact with everyone who will be important in whatever it is you have in mind. With a big issue like VLSI, however, you go, in addition, to the MITI discussion councils.

MITI maintains thirty-eight industry discussion councils, of which the most important is the Industrial Structure Council. The one which deals with the computer industry is the Aircraft-Machinery Council. The several proposals currently before the U.S. Congress have called for the formation of a National Economic Planning Board whose membership would be one-third labor leaders, one-third business leaders, and one-third government officials. Compare that and think about its implications for the structure of the Industrial Structure Council. The Industrial Structure Council has eighty-two members of whom **none** is a government official. It is a private voice - a boxing ring into which come twenty-eight representatives of trade associations, twenty people representing their own manufacturing companies, eleven university professors, four leaders of major labor federations, three leaders of the largest consumer groups, two senior members of the press, and fourteen others representing groups such as the Council of Mayors and the Council of Governors. Now imagine such a diverse group achieving a consensus; it then needs no power beyond the power of free speech to attract the attention of the appropriate government officials.

The computer companies were able to activate a network that was already in place instead of having a chaotic scramble in which everyone is standing up and shouting at the same time. There was a more reasoned dialogue and communication among all of the parties who had an interest in this problem. In addition, these institutions possess a stability and permanence which comprise a social memory. As a result, everyone has an incentive when entering into this discussion to behave in a reasonable way.

Agreement was reached that there could be a four-year project from 1976 through 1979 and that the technology goal would be to move an order of magnitude from the then state-of-the-art 16K RAM, to the 1,000K device, and from the 100 gate to the 1,000 gate logic device. Here, we might think, were all of these Japanese competitors linking arms with one another and marching off down the road happily together. We can't possibly imagine IBM, DEC, Honeywell, NCR, and Hewlett-Packard contemplating such a thing.

Upon closer inspection, however, what we see is not seven companies happily expressing their allegiance to country and to emperor. What we see, instead, is something much more familiar. We see seven companies, each of which at the outset intended to send to the project their least experienced young scientists, each hoping to contribute as little as possible and get back as much as possible. What we see is the normal amount of pettiness, of jealousy and elbowing for position. What we see is perfectly normal self-interested human behavior, but working within a system that has a memory.

One of the first disputes was over the composition of the project. Of the seven possibilities, one company, NTT, didn't want to join. NTT had the most advanced microelectronics research and felt they had little to gain and perhaps a lot to lose. Because the other six companies were all big suppliers to NTT, they couldn't put pressure on them and NTT never did join. Oki, on the other hand, wanted very much to be in the project, but the other companies didn't want Oki in. So they got together within JEIDA and drafted an agreement stating that "any company could join the project" as long as it possessed this specific set of technology, which they knew Oki did not possess, and Oki was cut out.

The five remaining companies then said to the government, "Now we're ready; we have the consensus; send us the money." And the government said, "Not so fast. Where's the joint lab going to be?" The companies said, "What joint lab? You're going to send us the money. We're going to do the research in our own labs and we're going to meet once a month and exchange papers." And the government said, "You must really think we're dumb. The public is not going to stand for large outlays of public funds for your companies. There has got to be a joint physical laboratory with human bodies in it that gives at least the appearance of true teamwork." The companies had been intending to focus their research on the 64K RAM, but when they heard this they realized that if there were a joint lab in which they worked on next year's products, they might lose some proprietary "know-how." So they changed their target to the 1,000K RAM, which was so distant technologically that there was little know-how to lose, and all agreed that there would be a joint lab.

But where was the lab to be? The three-company CDL group insisted that it had to be their location. The NTIS group insisted that it had to be their location. They argued for several months, but there was no hope of compromise. Finally, in desperation they turned to the head of JEIDA and said, "You choose and we'll abide." After a little study and a lot of fancy footwork, a location was picked. Everyone moved in.

When they moved into the laboratory, everyone knew that their plan would be to send their least experienced and youngest scientist in order to contribute as little as possible, and to get back as much as they could. The laboratory chief scientist was a highly respected man from the government electrotechnical lab (ETL), Dr. Tarui. Tarui did two things. First, he started out with the fact that there were only three research projects, but there were five companies plus ETL. He specified six separate research projects so that each of the participating groups would have a project director. Then he announced that he would personally interview each of the scientists sent to the joint lab. He did not imply that he had the right to choose or to refuse anyone, but the simple knowledge of certain discovery within this system of memory was sufficient to deter such behavior, and everyone sent their best.

The lab opened, but the walls between units were thick, so thick that most of the scientists didn't come to the lab in the first months. Many were afraid that their friends back at their own corporate labs would think them of questionable loyalty. Mr. Nebashi, the lab director, responded to this problem. He insisted that the executive and operations committees, which consisted of top executives from the five participating companies, must have monthly meetings at the lab. As they came each month, they began to see that the other scientists were at least as good as theirs and that they had a good deal to learn. They started to pass down the word, "Perhaps we should really work together. Perhaps we should open up." Meanwhile, each night Nebashi began to practice what he called "whiskey operations." This involved gathering up a couple of armloads of scientists each night, taking them out and drinking with them. After a couple of months of this, the walls came down, and people went to work.

At the end of four years, the joint lab had filed 1,000 patent applications, from which they expect ultimately to achieve 500 patents. They had achieved the technology for the 256K RAM and the 1,000 gate logic device. At the end of the project, in 1979, the lab closed and the scientists went home. Dr. Tarui took a position at the Tokoyo University of Science and Agriculture. Nebashi took a job at IBM/Japan.

In the interest of candor and of balance, note that Oki, which was not a part of the project, was the first company to test the commercially viable 256K RAM. But consider the implications of this example. In 1975, many observers were predicting that Fujitsu would fail. Fujitsu was the main Japanese computer maker. In 1975 many in Silicon Valley were saying that the so-called Japanese threat in semiconductors would never come to pass. By 1982, Fujitsu had replaced IBM as the major vendor of computers in Japan. The Japanese makers as a whole had taken over their home market.

During this period, it appears that IBM and other U.S. computer makers suffered from unfair treatment and protectionism. In addition, throughout this period, the U.S. government had IBM under the threat of a Department of Justice anti-trust suit. So on the one hand, IBM was working against its government and against seven Japanese companies who were working together and **with** their government. Yet IBM held its own reasonably well. On the other hand, it is undeniable that what we see here is a new way to think about managing an economy and it is a view which violates some of our most deeply held underlying beliefs about what works and about what should be. If we find this example to be troubling, worrisome, and fearsome in some respects, perhaps that is because it works.

What do we do in the United States when we're faced with a problem like this? Consider an example. In 1978 the United States was, we thought, in the grip of the OPEC cartel. The public was clamoring for energy independence and the U.S. Congress had to act. There was the sun shining away, twelve hours a day. In 1978 the American Physical Society published a report on photovoltaic solar energy, in which they contended that it was impossible that photovoltaic solar energy could account for more than 1 percent of the total electricity needs of the United States in fewer than fifty years. What was needed, they said, was a steady stream of financial support for basic R&D, $20 to $30 million a year for the next twenty years.[4] In that same year the U.S. Con-

---

[4]Original sources for this and other specific facts may be found in William G. Ouchi, **The M-Form Society: How American Teamwork Can Recapture the Competitive Edge** (Reading, Mass.: Addison-Wesley, 1984).

gress allocated $1.5 billion for photovoltaic solar energy research in the United States over a ten year period.

Have you ever asked yourself how we distribute R&D money in the United States? Do we do it the way the Japanese do? Is there a dialogue, a discussion, a debate with the government? How do you distribute $1.5 billion of R&D money in America? The way they did it was to make an arrangement with four labs that at least knew something about photovoltaics, the MIT Lincoln Lab, Sandia, Solar Energy Research Institute, and JPL. These they assigned to review the applications. The scientists at those four shops knew a lot about photovoltaics, but they had no political power and no reason in the world to deny a company a project, since that company might be a future supporter of theirs. The result was that in the first two years of the project, they granted 402 research contracts to 250 different organizations. There was no provision for any form of conversation between them, and no attempt at coordination. Many experts would say that in the year 1978 there were not 250 individual scientists in the United States capable of photovoltaic solar research.

The whole project was such a disappointment, despite several individual successes, that it was cancelled by the Congress in the third year of its operation, except for $32 million a year of basic R&D funding. The real tragedy of this example is what we learned from it. The scientific establishment learned once again that you can't depend on government funding. The Congress learned once again that business will always over-promise and under-deliver. The public learned once again that you can't trust any of them.

But the story isn't always a disappointing one: consider another example. The Soviets have more ships, more airplanes, more men under arms, and more tanks than we do, and probably always will. Our military edge is a technology edge, primarily an electronics edge. That edge used to be twelve to fifteen years; now many people would say it's down to two to three years. The problem is that in 1960 the Department of Defense purchased 60 percent of all of the output of the U.S. semiconductor industry and so they got exactly what they wanted. But today the nondefense uses of semiconductors are so much more vast, that the DOD now buys only 4 percent of the industry's output and has to take what it can get off the shelf. What it can get off the shelf is not radiation hardened and doesn't have the tremendously high speed that is needed for weapons guidance, control, and detection. The semiconductor devices must be radiation hardened and capable of executing 12 billion additions or subtractions per second and be on a chip the size of your thumbnail. The problem is that the semiconductor firms that have the technology don't understand weapon systems and don't want to learn how to navigate Pentagon bureaucracies. The computer companies that understand the software don't have the semiconductor technology, and the defense contractors that understand the Pentagon don't have the computer or the semiconductor technology.

The solution is that for the first time in the history of our republic there are six company teams comprising the very high speed integrated circuit (VHSIC) project. Each team combines the knowledge of the semiconductor hardware, computer software, and defense systems knowledge. Working across the three military branches, everyone is a team (IBM has the only one-company team). Although the project is only half completed, the early reviews suggest that it is succeeding.

But let's return now to thinking more generally about the model of business/government relationship and what it means. What we see in Japan is approximately an M-Form structure. First, in the business community the principal group is the Keidanren which I have mentioned already. Then there is the Keizai Doyukai, which consists of a thousand individuals rather than corporate members who conduct studies and issue position papers on more general topics such as an aging population, cost of health care, or the need for green space. Next is the Chamber of Commerce with 478 chapters across Japan which represents small and medium businesses primarily. Finally, there is the Nikkeiren, a federation of 30,000 companies which exists for the purpose of carrying out a dialogue with the major labor unions. There is conversation between them other than that which occurs across the bargaining table. Because this structure is in place, the "boxing rings" are available, and the system has a memory, there can be a conversation rather than a chaotic yelling of everyone at once.

Some might think that the Japanese don't care about small business. There are many ways to define small business. One standard definition is any business with fewer than twenty employees if it is in manufacturing or fewer than five if it is in service. By that definition, 20 percent of the U.S. labor force works for a small business, as compared with 50 percent in Japan.

What the Japanese have done for small business is impressive. Japan has forty-seven prefectures, each roughly akin to a state in the United States. In each prefecture there is a federation of the many different kinds of organizations which are intended to help small business. In the larger cities there are chambers of commerce, an average of ten in each prefecture. In the small towns which do not have a chamber, there is a Society of Commerce of Industry, an average of eighty-two in each prefecture.

The local government bureaus coordinate with the national small business organizations such as the People's Finance Corporation, which makes loans to small business. There is also a Small Business Corporation, owned by the government, to make small business loans. Then there are three MITI councils, which are exclusively devoted to the interests of small business, as well as a whole bureau within MITI that does nothing but focus on small business. All of these resources are brought to the local level through the coordination of the prefectural federations.

What structure do we have in place in the United States? We have the basic units necessary for an M-Form organization. We have the National Federation of Independent Businesses with 600,000 small business members, the Business Roundtable, which represents 196 of the biggest companies in America, the National Association of Manufacturers with 50,000 manufacturing members, the Chamber of Commerce with medium and small business members, and the American Society of Association Executives. Within one industry, the electronics industry, we have several specialized associations, such as the EIA, AEA, SIA, SAMA, and CBEMA. But they won't work through those more general associations, and often the member companies won't work through their own specialized association. Everybody wants to go directly to government because they know that there is no social memory in place. If they get into a "boxing ring" or a group process they will be asked to wait, and they know that if they wait, they won't be remembered. If we don't have the units of social memory, then we condemn ourselves to the kind of political-economic gridlock that Mancur Olson foresaw.

If the Department of Commerce isn't presently very useful, that's because the business community doesn't care and doesn't put pressure on it to get organized and properly staffed. If the trade associations in America aren't useful, it's because their members don't care. Last year I spoke at a meeting at one of the major U.S. trade associations. It was a typical association meeting: the time was winter and the place was Florida. I spoke one morning and they played golf in the afternoon. They had another speaker the next morning and then they played tennis. They had a speaker the third morning and then they went fishing. Now, I love fishing, golf, and tennis, and I'm not trying to be goodie-two-shoes about this, but I said to these fellows, "Look, when you're out on the golf course this afternoon waiting to tee-up, let me ask you to think about something. Last month I was in Tokyo where I met your counterpart association which has the 200 companies that are your direct competitors. While you're out on the golf course this afternoon, they're back there in Tokyo having meetings from 9:00 a.m. until 10:00 p.m., Monday through Friday, for three months straight.

They are sorting out their product standardization policies, just as you're trying to do, so that a customer can buy an oscilloscope from one vendor and an instrument from another vendor and plug them together. They're trying to sort out their recommendations to the government on product safety standards instead of arguing before a federal board for twelve months about what the safety standard should be and holding up everybody in new product introduction. They're trying to "duke out" their differences on what they really want by way of export assistance, legislative reform, and so on and so forth, so they can go to the government with one voice. You tell me who's going to be in better shape five years from now.

In 1969, the maximum tax on capital gains was raised from 20 percent to 49 percent. In 1970, there was one-fiftieth as much venture capital available for small businesses as there had been the year before. It just dried up. One of the people who was hurt by that was a fellow named Ed Zschau, who was running a little fifty person company in Silicon Valley. Ed Zschau was suffering because of the difficulty in raising capital. In 1976, Jimmy Carter was elected president. As you remember, he campaigned against the three martini lunch. His tax bill was going to raise taxes on business and one of his key targets was to raise the capital gains tax even more. Ed Zschau was a member of a group of small businessmen who are members of the American Electronics Association and who met for their annual two day meeting in Washington, D.C. One of the people who spoke to them at their breakfast was Representative Al Ullman of Oregon, who was then chairman of the House Ways and Means Committee. Ullman said to these high-tech small businessmen,

"I've got good news for you. I'm going to sponsor a provision in the 1978 tax bill to do away with the double taxation on corporate dividends." His audience sat there on their hands and looked glum. Ullman couldn't believe it. He thought they'd stand up and cheer. They said to him, "Let us give you some help, Congressman Ullman. None of us pays corporate taxes. All of our companies are start-up companies. Any profits we make go back into buying equipment on which we get depreciation. So we never pay taxes to begin with. If you reduce taxes on corporate income or dividends, that's going to make investments in the large, stable, mature companies more attractive and make it even harder for us to get capital. What we need is a cut in the capital gains rate." Ullman said to them, "Look, if you guys really feel this way, you must remember that democracy only works when there is an involved citizen." That night, the AEA had a dinner at which Ullman was present again. The president of the AEA said, "I'm proud to announce that the AEA has formed a task force on the cost of capital and it is headed by Ed Zschau."

It was the first time Ed Zschau had heard of it. Ed Zschau, however, was fast on his feet. He started a drive in Washington to cut the capital gains tax and his position was: "We think it should be zero, but we'll take a rollback to 20 percent." The Chamber of Commerce wouldn't help. The members of the Roundtable and the members of the NFIB couldn't agree, so neither took a position. It was Ed Zschau, with volunteers from Silicon Valley who ran their own businesses, who were trying to get the cut in capital gains. They didn't know that a couple of concerned citizens couldn't have an impact among all the pros in Washington. They went before the Congressional hearings and told their stories. They did their research and spoke to anybody who would listen. To make a long story short, in 1978 Jimmy Carter, who wanted to raise business taxes, signed a bill that cut the capital gains tax from 49 percent to 28 percent.

In 1981 the AEA, headed by Ed Zschau, went back again and got the tax cut from 28 percent to 20 percent. They were joined by the Massachusetts High Technology Council, the Semiconductor Industry Association, the Scientific Apparatus Makers Association, the Electronics Industry Association, and others.

In 1982 Ed Zschau entered the Congress as the elected representative of Silicon Valley. Twelve months later the New York Times dubbed him the star of the freshman class in the House of Representatives.

I don't believe that the idea of national central planning is any wiser than that of corporate central planning. No one can see into the future. In a large company, the people who are best equipped to see into the future are the 23-year-old "rookies" who are working close to the customers and the technology. But they don't have the wisdom to make major policy judgments. The best "strategic plan" is to have a good conversation between the rookies, who know what they're doing, and the top executives, who may not know what they're doing, but who have wisdom. As long as there is conversation between them, the organization will make its way to the future.

The best national economic policy is an involved citizenry. Durkheim predicted that, in a mass urban nation like ours, if the only form of political participation most people have is the vote, then the democracy will wither because voting is a too impersonal and too distant form of democracy. There must instead be a host of intermediate organizations which knit people and interest groups together.

Another way to put the problem of industrial policy, in my view, is to observe that we don't have enough special interest groups in America. I don't belong to a special interest group because there isn't one that fits enough of my interests closely enough to get me to join. There are twelve pizza parlors within ten minutes of my house, so I can get any kind of pizza that I could possibly want. There aren't that many civic or interest groups in my neighborhood. Why? Because none of these special interest groups talks to each other, and as a result none of them has much influence. If none of them has much influence, who will want to start up yet another special interest group that's also going to have no influence? Nobody. If we can knit them together, then they will all have influence on one another. Then there will be a tremendous flowering of new kinds of special interest groups, or intermediary institutions. This network can knit our society together. Right now the only people who have reliable influence in Washington are the eighty-five or so companies that can afford to maintain large permanent staffs. If you can't afford a forty to sixty person staff in Washington, you aren't a player. That means that the other 99 percent of us are locked out of a part of the political process. What we need to do is to lower the cost of political participation by building the institutions that can make it easy for people to participate.

I visited the headquarters of Tohmatsu, Awoki and Company, the largest CPA firm in Japan and a division of Touche, Ross International. I sat down with five of their senior partners who said to me, "You must understand that in Japan nobody cares about reported company earnings. Therefore, the fundamental job of the CPA is different in Japan than it is in the United States. In the United States, the stockholders of a large, public company know so little about the business that they must rely on the accountants' definition of earnings. Therefore, the chief function of the CPA in the United States is to come up with a completely understandable and standardized definition of earnings. But in Japan, the owners of the company are so well informed and so close to the company, that they already know how it's doing this year and how it is going to do next year as well. There's very little that the CPA can add to their understanding. His task, instead, is to help them build the information system that keeps them informed every day."

Our research team studied the financing of the 814 publicly listed electronic and aerospace companies in the United States and in Japan. We found that the weighted average cost of capital, of equity and of debt, is far higher for the American company than it is for the Japanese company. It translates into a major competitive disadvantage. Why is that? The reason in essence is that there cannot be an effective relationship between the owner of a company and the manager of the company at arm's length, but that is what we have in the United States. Another way to say it is that in the United States the typical company, say a big chemical company, will have 300,000 shareholders. If you have 300,000 shareholders, what is the likelihood that they are going to know what's going on in the company? Suppose you're the management and you say, "I want to communicate to my shareholders some of our five year plans for capital investment and automation. Let's send them a fifty page report." What are they going to do with that fifty page report? They're going to throw it in the rubbish can. If you only own 1/300,000th of a company, you have no incentive to spend more than two minutes discovering what's going on, let alone attempting to influence the management. It's easier to sell your shares and buy something else. That is what produces the short-run pressures on American management.

But you might say "Wait a minute; that chemical company is probably financed 30 percent through debt. Certainly the bank, even though it isn't allowed to own shares, must be governing the company." Not so. In the United States, our bankruptcy law does not allow the bank to try to influence the management of a company to which it makes the loan. If the bank can't influence the management, and the owners can't influence the management, that means that nobody "owns" American business. No one can exercise the rights of an owner over these companies. Now, I ask, how can you have a free enterprise system, based on private property, if there are not effective property owners?

Akio Morita, the chairman of Sony, remarked several months ago, "Our lead bank is the Mitsui Bank. They own some of our shares. They represent the other banks that own some of our shares. Their chief function is to keep an eye on me, the chairman of the company, and to look out for the rights of all of the other owners of Sony, as well as the customers, employees, suppliers, and everybody who has an interest in the corporation. If they conclude that I'm not doing my job right, they can kick me out. In most American companies that's not possible."

The only remedy we have is the unfriendly takeover, but things have to get extremely bad before that remedy comes into play. The situation in the United States is one in which even the big stockholders, such as the bank trust departments, pension funds, and insurance companies, which among them own more than one-third of all the equities of American business, are fiduciary trustees. They are not able to exercise any governance over the company whose shares they own. As a result, there is nobody who oversees the operations and behaves like an owner of many of the largest U.S. firms. Our large businesses are so large today that it is typically not possible for a single family or a few individuals to own them. There needs instead to be some institutional form of ownership, and the most logical institution is the bank. We prohibit banks from doing that by law.

Why do we prohibit banks from owning the equity shares of nonbank businesses? The restriction is rested in the National Banking Act of 1864. It was the end of the Civil War and the U.S. Treasury had been depleted. In addition, it was very important to symbolically reunite the nation. The big banks of the day were issuing their own bank notes as their private currency. In order to solve both problems, the Senate passed a bill which put a tax on all private bank currencies and allowed banks to obtain the new U.S. bank notes primarily by buying securities of the U.S. Treasury.

In 1865 a federal court held that because the law had not given banks the explicit right to own nonbank securities, they were thereby forbidden to do so, because they would be competing against the Treasury Department for scarce capital. That need has long since passed, but the law is still on the books. It seems to me that it's another example of a change that we need to make and that needs to be carefully examined.

These examples, I hope, have been stimulating, but many will feel that this simply lies too far beyond the American experience; that there's something about it that's too collective, too homogeneous, not individualistic enough.

Let me tell you a little bit about Minneapolis. Minneapolis is a city of 500,000. The Twin Cities have about a million people. They haven't had an easy time of it economically in Minnesota. Seventy percent of the state of Minnesota is covered with trees. Their first industry was timbering. They clear-cut the forests, used their assets, and they had nothing. Then they found the Mesabi range, the richest deposit of iron ore in the world, thirty miles long by one mile wide. It supplied 65 percent of all the iron ore used in the United States until about the turn of the century. Once again the money flowed east and afterward all they had was a big hole in the ground. The other major industry was grain. By the year 1900 there were 500 flour mills operating in Minnesota. Today Minnesota is a center of electronics, financial services, and retail industry. Four out of the five major computer mainframe makers in the United States have either their corporate headquarters or a major plant in Minneapolis.

How did they accomplish what every other American city would like to accomplish? Minneapolis is anomalous in yet another way. In 1965 one of the major companies moved its corporate headquarters out of the center city to the suburbs. Everybody feared it was the beginning of the end: the loss of tax base, white flight, and urban decay. Today Minneapolis has a thriving downtown. It has the $400 million Nicollet Mall and a pedestrian skyway system which connects the forty blocks of the center of the city. The skyway keeps pedestrians away from the cold, above the traffic, and they've stayed downtown to live, work, be entertained.

Minneapolis-St. Paul is thriving. How did they do it? Minneapolis is anomalous in still another way. The average U.S. company donates .6 percent of pretax earnings to charity each year. The estimates are that there are approximately 100 companies in the United States that donate 5 percent or more of pretax earnings to civic groups each year. Sixty percent of those companies are in Minneapolis.

How do we explain that behavior in this day of self-seeking, profit-minded, individual firms? When we look closely at Minneapolis what we see is a structure of social memory that very closely resembles what we find in Japan. In Minneapolis the Citizens League consists of 3,000 ordinary citizens like you and me, each of whom pays $20 a year to join. Anybody may join a study group for the purposes of writing a position paper on the need for downtown parking, green space, pedestrian circulation, or better elementary school education.

The Chamber of Commerce runs the Five Percent Club and brings together the small and medium businesses to fight out their differences with one another and then go to the other groups. The Downtown Council consists of the small shopkeepers and the big bankers, everybody who cares about the future of downtown. Their president one year was the head of a local coffee shop, the year before that the head of the largest bank, and another year it was the head of the Lutheran Brotherhood.

The Minnesota Association of Commerce and Industry, MACI, brings together the farmers, manufacturers, and service companies so that they can "duke it out" when they have a difference. The Minnesota Project on Corporate Responsibility brings together 200 companies so that they can be educated several times a year on what it means to be a good corporate citizen and on how to make it happen.

The Minnesota Business Partnership consists of the forty-two chief executive officers of the biggest companies in Minneapolis including the heads of General Mills, Pillsbury, 3M, and Honeywell. What do these forty-two do when they get together? Do they scheme, do they plot? Do they figure out how to grind the common man down? Not at all. They go out on field trips like so many school children. They get together in groups of three, four, and five and call on the mayor, governor, legislative leader of the opposition, and heads of the major labor unions: the kinds of people whom each of them individually would be reluctant to see, and who are never going to come see them.

They establish a dialogue between business and government. Because each of these organizations is linked to the other, there are not only a host of "boxing rings," they also have become the social memory in Minneapolis.

It seems to me that we have before us a national agenda. In outline it really isn't very complex. We need to build the units of social memory which will enable us to engage in the process of social choice. Through social choice we can focus our scarce resources, and it is that focus that will allow us to achieve prosperity. The basic building blocks are in place. In the business community we have the American Business Conference, the Conference Board, National Association of Manufacturers, Chamber of Commerce, National Federation of Independent Businesses, and the Roundtable. Most of them are new organizations, formed to meet a new need. They ought to be linked to one another. If they will confront one another when they have differences and "duke it out," nose-to-nose, we'd be going a long way in the right direction.

Business is only a part of the solution. There needs to be as well a means through which we can connect the other semi-autonomous units of an M-Form society to one another. We need to have, in addition to the business organizations, a similar network within the labor community. There must also be an organization that causes the farmers to fight out their differences with one another. The municipalities and the states, because we are one nation undivided, have to have a way to interact within this network. The consumer and civic groups must be involved.

Last spring I had a parking lot conversation with a friend. It was one of those fifteen minute discussions at the end of an evening, an extended good-bye. I was talking to a fellow named John Doyle, who is the vice president for R&D at the Hewlett-Packard Company. He oversees the stream of inventions that is his company's lifeblood. It was the kind of discussion that is best held in the semi-darkness of the parking lot of a Chinese restaurant, where the dim light conceals your commonness and permits you for a moment to discuss matters of state, to pretend you're Hobbes, Locke, or Adam Smith. Five years ago John was reading books on management, on productivity, and on creativity at work, but more recently he has been reading books on economic history. Most of the books explain in painful detail why our current economic malaise is both inevitable and irreversible, why we should gracefully accept our fate of poverty as the British have learned to accept theirs. But John has the mind of a scientist. He is a skeptic. He is skeptical that anything is impossible, that anything is inevitable, that anything widely believed is true. He said as he headed for his car, "You know that the really important inventions have all been impossible. It was only after they appeared that the scholars rushed around to construct new theories to explain their existence."

It seems to me that it is that spirit of pragmatic and optimistic skepticism with which we should approach our perhaps superstitious beliefs about what it is that makes our economy tick and our nation survive. We owe it to ourselves to search for a better way.

Caren Siehl

5

Corporate Culture: Managing The Magnetic Force

The success of an organizational leader within the organization is contingent upon the development of shared meaning through a coherent system of beliefs and guiding values. As the eminent organizational researcher Philip Selznick (1957) clearly argued:

> The formation of an institution is marked by the making of value commitments, that is, choices which fix the assumptions of policy makers as to the nature of the enterprise, its distinctive aims, methods and roles. The institutional leader is primarily an expert in the promotion and protection of values. Leadership fails when it concentrates on sheer survival. Institutional survival, properly understood, is a matter of maintaining values and distinctive identity.

While chairman of the board of IBM, Thomas J. Watson, Jr. (1963) posited a similar argument when he said:

> The basic philosophy, spirit, and drive of an organization have far

more to do with its relative achievements than do technological or economic resources, organizational structure, innovation, and timing. All these things weigh heavily on success, but they are transcended by how the people in the organization believe in its basic precepts and how faithfully they carry them out.

What Is Culture?

Some researchers and practitioners suggest that organizations should be conceptualized as cultures. They favor the view that culture is something an organization is, rather than something an organization has. Those who have argued that culture is a socially constructed system of shared beliefs and values would find it inconsistent to think of systematically developing or attempting to control the phenomenon. As stated by Karl Weick (1983) in **Fortune** magazine in responding to a recent article on managing corporate culture: "Organizations don't have cultures, they are cultures, and this is why culture is so difficult to change."

However, other managers and researchers, particularly those searching for predictable means of organizational control and improved methods of organizational management, hold the belief that culture can, to some degree, be managed. This view of organizational culture stems from the belief that organizations produce cultures. As the introductory paragraph indicates, one of the critical tasks of management involves the construction and maintenance of a system of shared values. Such values are one component of the phenomenon defined as organizational culture by those who suggest that organizations produce cultures and that culture can be managed.

Although definitions of culture are available, their primary shared attribute is vagueness. An amalgamation of some of the more interesting definitions would result in the following: corporate culture can be thought of as a magnet which holds a company together through a sharing of patterns of meaning. The culture focuses on the values, beliefs, and expectations that employees come to share.

It is important to reduce the vagueness of such definitions if culture is to be developed and managed by organizational leaders. A more concrete and complete definition of organizational culture would suggest that a culture consists of three major components: content, forms, and perceptions of company practices.

The first component, the content of an organizational culture, consists of the core values of the organization. The content of a culture can be divided into two parts: espoused values and inferred values. It is important to distinguish between espoused values and inferred values because, as will be discussed below, these may differ.

Espoused values are those values in which employees say they believe. They are the values which employees espouse to be important. Espoused values are communicated directly. For example, top management might espouse values through a statement of corporate objectives or management philosophy. Such values define the basic philosophy or mission of the company. Sometimes the espoused values of top management concern technical issues such as the one which Ken Olson, the founder and president of Digital Equipment Corporation expresses as: "Our job is to make a good product. Growth is not our primary goal. After making good products, growth is a natural occurrence." Or, espoused values can be financial in nature as is reflected in an underlying value of Data General: "We're in this business to make money. It just so happens that the computer business is the best way to do that. But if we could make more money selling rye bread, we should consider doing that." Often the espoused values are humanistic and emphasize the importance of the people and customers of the company. Espoused values of this type are embodied in the slogans of Dana Corporation's "productivity through people" and IBM's "IBM means service" and "respect for the individual." DuPont's "better things for better living through chemistry" and GE's "progress is our most important product" are other examples of espoused values which may help to shape the way people interact and process information about the organization.

Espoused values are what employees say. Inferred values reflect what employees do. Inferred values are those values which are inferred from employee behavior and from the second and third components of culture, cultural forms and perceptions of company practices.

Cultural forms, the second component of culture, are often indirect, implicit, and subtle means of value expression. Such forms include jargon or a special language, organizational stories, rituals and ceremonies, and humor. Most people tend to consider cultural forms to be unimportant and unrelated to company performance and therefore not worth examining. According to this point of view, jargon makes accurate communication difficult, organizational stories are often misleading glorifications of the past, and rituals, like retirement dinners, are a waste of time.

Contrary to this point of view, cultural forms are well worth examining in detail. They can be the key to understanding employees' reactions to the espoused values of top management. For this reason, each of the cultural forms just mentioned is discussed in some detail below.

A special language or jargon is one of the most common cultural forms. Jargon is a vocabulary that is comprehensible only to enculturated employees. Jargon is composed of words or phrases expressing both cultural values and technical issues. For example, at one well-known computer firm, an employee casually assumed that the following sentence could be understood: "The heuristics scheduler in the TOPS-20 makes it a superior multi-user time-sharing system when compared to the VMS, RSX, or IAS."

Humor is another cultural form. Frequently, jokes specific to an organizational context make fun of cultural outsiders, specifically employees who fail to conform to company norms or are members of competing firms. When employees laugh at such jokes, they are demonstrating the distinction between cultural insiders and outsiders. To people who are not employees of the company, the jokes usually do not seem funny. Jokes, like jargon, create a boundary between cultural initiates and those who are not initiated.

Values can also be inferred from another cultural form, organizational stories. An organizational story is defined as a coherent event or short sequence of events based on organizational history; about the company or its representatives; and known or shared by a group within the company. Such stories have heroes, frequently the founder or top executives of the firm. Organizational stories recount an event ostensibly drawn accurately from the corporation's history. An organizational story has two basic parts, the story text itself and an underlying moral or message. Values can be inferred from each of these two parts. For example, the following story is frequently told in a large, high-technology corporation:

> Susan Sanders, a secretary of a sales unit in Northern California, had been working for the company for about two years. She was well-respected by everyone - her manager, the sales people, and other secretaries. She was extremely skillful and her performance had been rated as excellent. Due to her efforts, Susan's manager did not need to direct his attention to proofreading or correction tasks. Susan also had a pleasant personality. In fact, she was one of those people who was generally cheerful, even on bad days. During her second year with the company, Susan's husband, who worked for another company, was promoted to a new job in Arizona. Although he would be losing a valued employee, Susan's manager approved her request for a transfer to a branch office in Arizona. This office was not hiring at the time but gladly accepted her transfer, knowing that her skills would be helpful in some capacity in the future.

The moral of this story was expressed as: "We believe that people are clearly our most important asset and we take pride in treating our employees well."

Inferred values are also transmitted through rituals and ceremonies. Rituals are behavior patterns which are formalized or stylized and which are repeated in that form. Employees at many corporations, for example, infer the value of the importance of individual employees and their families from the ritual of the annual company picnic or retirement dinners. Not coincidentally, these rituals usually include activities like dancing, drinking, or informal chatter about families. These rituals act as status equalization activities, which temporarily ease, and sometimes even reverse the usual status differentials between high and low level employees.

Finally, physical arrangements can be used as an important cultural form. The design of the workplace, employee dress, executive "perks" such as reserved parking places, access to the corporate jet and the executive dining room can all act as symbols which communicate values. Values can be inferred from the shared interpretation of the meaning of such symbols. For example, Renn Zaphiropoulos, chief executive officer of Versatec, Inc, an electronics equipment manufacturer, personally helped to design his company's main building. He communicated values of open, rapid, and direct communications through an open space office arrangement and by banning locks on the few offices that had doors. In addition, in keeping with the value of being customer oriented, Zaphiropoulos ruled out reserved parking spaces for himself and other executives and located customer and visitor parking as close to the building as possible.

Values can also be inferred from the third component of culture, employee perceptions of company practices, that is, the everyday activities of the managers of the company. The most enduring and effective practices for transmitting values lie in a firm's human resource system. Specifically, such practices include selection procedures, training programs, performance appraisals, compensation, and promotion procedures. Management may espouse a set of values which are incongruent with employee perceptions of the values being expressed and reinforced by management practices. This would result in espoused values and inferred values being in conflict. On the other hand, management's espoused values may, in fact, be reinforced by the values expressed through company practices.

For example, recruitment, or selection of new employees, can be the initial step in reinforcing espoused values. The selection process can sort out cultural deviants before they enter the organization. Both the prospective employee and the corporation are faced with a matching task during the job interview process. Research has indicated that a "realistic preview" of both the attractive and less attractive features of a job can reduce disillusionment and can help the individual to achieve a better match with an organization. The realistic job preview can be extended to a realistic culture preview by making as explicit as possible in the interviewing process what the culture of the organization is like.

Training can also be an important management practice. Part of the training process can involve the learning of a distinctive cultural perspective in order that future events can be interpreted within a framework shared by organizational members. At US Homes, for example, different groups of managers meet on three successive evenings every two weeks to discuss a book chosen by the president to reinforce specific values, or to elicit discussion along certain lines. Other companies insist that formal training sessions be led by key line managers who are usually best able to exemplify and articulate the espoused values of top management.

The evaluation system, beginning with performance appraisal and compensation policies, and culminating in promotion decisions, can also be used in an attempt to reinforce cultural practices. Employees who understand and support the espoused values can be part of the "fast track" and receive promotion opportunities. At DEC, for example, where one of the espoused values of top management is a high level of customer service, sales employees are encouraged to meet both reasonable and unreasonable demands of users. Performance is measured by customer satisfaction and salespeople are promoted accordingly. This, in turn, influences other employees' perceptions of what it takes to get ahead in the company. Values can be inferred from such perceptions.

Although values can be easily expressed through human resource systems, other practices can also be used to communicate cultural priorities. The list is endless, but it includes how time is allocated on meeting agendas, whether a subordinate takes all problems up through channels, how long an employee must wait to get an appointment with his or her boss, or even whether an appointment is necessary at all. Employees can read the value-laden signals implicit in practices such as these.

In summary, organizational culture is a multidimensional phenomenon. The first component of culture, the content, consists of shared values, both espoused and inferred. Espoused values are those values in which employees say they believe. Inferred values are those values which are inferred from the second and third components of culture, cultural forms and employee perceptions of company practices. Cultural forms include jargon, humor, organizational stories, rituals, and ceremonies. Management practices are centered in the human resource management system and include selection, training, compensation, and promotional practices.

Why is Culture Important?

The development of a pervasive corporate culture is important because cultures serve four, perhaps five, useful functions. First, cultures can offer a shared interpretation of organizational events, so that employees know how they are expected to behave. Second, in addition to these cognitive functions, pervasive cultures have emotional impact, lending an aura of excitement, if not inspiration to employees' work lives. For example, cultures can generate commitment to a set of corporate values or management philosophy, so that employees feel they are working for more than a paycheck. Culture gives employees something they can believe in, as well as a reason for investing extra time, effort, and creativity in their work.

Having a distinctive cultural reputation helps firms to compete successfully in hiring and retaining skilled employees and in producing top quality goods and services. Organizational cultures also generate commitment by giving members a sense of community. Values shared among employees provide for the integration of individuals into the work setting, a kind of individual-to-organization linking. Such a sharing of values can bind members to the organization. Third, culture creates and maintains boundaries. In- versus out-groups arise which help to define who is and is not appropriately behaving within the organizational context. Fourth, cultures also serve as organizational control mechanisms, formally labeling some patterns of behavior as prohibited and encouraging others. Finally, the presence of a strong humanistic culture has been tied, by implication if not firm empirical evidence, to increased productivity and profitability.

Managing Corporate Culture

The power of culture as a means of generating commitment and as a means of implicit control has been demonstrated. The ultimate end product of research into this means of control would be statements of contingent relationships that have applicability for those trying to effectively manage organizations. There is a need to better understand whether culture can be managed. It would seem that rather than striving for an unequivocal yes or no in response to the question of managing culture, a more fruitful approach would be to explore under what conditions it would be more likely that culture could be managed. In other words, the question of managing culture should be changed from "Can culture be managed?" to "If so, when and what components of culture can be managed?" In the pages that follow I will suggest a set of conditions which might be conducive to managing culture, and discuss how and what components of culture might be managed under those conditions. Lastly, I will outline several potential problem areas which may impinge upon the management of culture.

Times of Transition and/or Crisis

Companies face times of transition and/or crisis throughout their existence. Because of the interdependency between a company and the environment and the almost inherent uncertainty of parts of the environment, it is inevitable that change in the form of a transition or crisis will occur. Such transitions include the firm's move from one stage in the organizational life cycle to the next; changes in the top management team; government deregulation; and product obsolescence. Times of transition create a condition under which culture could be managed. There are several reasons why the potential for managing culture exists during these times. Employees may themselves feel a need to change from a culture based on one type of values, such as entrepreneurial values during the initial stage of an organization's life, to one based on very different values, such as long-term growth and stability during later stages in the life cycle. Employees may be looking for a new direction and may be open to attempts to move the culture accordingly. In addition, transitions are often accompanied by the resignation or replacement of some members of upper management of the company. This change could breed the opportunity for other changes, such as those accomplished by managing the culture. Particularly, if employees have been dissatisfied with the past, transitions create an opportunity to manage the culture in ways which would appear to be leading to a brighter future. Finally, transitions give rise to a condition analogous to the unfreezing stage necessary for socialization. During this time a void exists which can be filled by managing culture in order that refreezing can occur with the values cast in a new, predetermined image. However, it could be argued that, the foregoing reasons notwithstanding, a time of transition or crisis would be unlikely to create a condition under which culture could be managed. It is precisely during a time of transition or crisis that employees would cling to the stability of the past in order to maintain some degree of certainty in the midst of change.

How Might Culture Be Managed?

For the reasons outlined above, a transition and/or crisis creates a condition under which culture might be managed. It is necessary to understand what components of culture might be managed under this condition, what means could be used in managing these components, and what players may be involved in the management. Referring to the definition suggested above, culture consists of several different components including espoused and inferred values and the means of expressing and reinforcing those shared values. Managers, for example, may share the same set of espoused values but may express those values to their subordinates using different means, including different behavioral styles. In attempting to manage culture during a time of transition, it is possible to change only the means of expressing the espoused values, while the values themselves remain the same; or it is possible to change both the espoused values and their expression, hence changing inferred values as well. The examples below will illustrate:

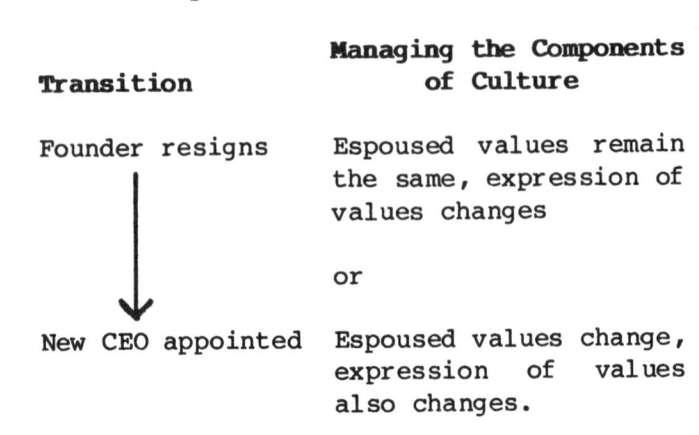

Transition	Managing the Components of Culture
Founder resigns ↓	Espoused values remain the same, expression of values changes
or	
New CEO appointed	Espoused values change, expression of values also changes.

If the company has not been successful prior to the transition or crisis occurring and/or employees are unhappy and dissatisfied with the current shared values, then one would expect the management of culture to involve replacing both the shared values and the means and ways of expressing the values. If, on the other hand, the company has been generally successful, the employees not dissatisfied, and the transition has occurred without loss of respect for management, the management task becomes more complex. One may attempt to change both the values and the expression of values in order to refocus the company and find that employees are loathe to change their shared values because of past success. If, in fact, the values can make the transition, it may be more appropriate to leave the values untouched and to manage the ways the values are expressed. This would seem to be the strategy employed by the top managers of two of the most admired U.S. companies (**Fortune** magazine survey, 1983). John A. Young, the president of Hewlett-Packard, reports:

> We have had a set of corporate objectives that have been in place, guiding the practices of our company for years and years. Dave Packard and Bill Hewlett (founders of the company) didn't even write them down until we had been in business for twenty years....They are a kind of glue - the basic philosophy, the basic sense of direction, sort of a value set - that draws everyone together.

Warren H. Phillips, CEO of Dow Jones, concurs while discussing quality, a long-standing corporate goal:

> We set high standards of performance in terms of quality. Financial excellence follows that. That sounds kind of cornball, but we find that it works. The companies on your list have gotten there due to a long period of pursuing quality.

In addition to considering what aspects of culture may be managed, it is important to suggest what means may be used. As described above, research has shown that values are expressed using a number of different forms including special language, rituals, stories, and organizational practices. These could all be potentially used to manage culture during a time of transition. It has been found that the most effective ways to manage culture are through verbal, one-to-one communication and role modeling. Role modeling provides employees with an opportunity to observe a specific instance of behavior from which they can begin to develop new mini-theories concerning situations in which this behavior would be appropriate. Role modeling and one-to-one communication can provide relevant, current information in a timely fashion. This would seem to be particularly important during a time of transition.

Finally, the question of who might be involved in managing culture during times of transition should be raised. The set of potential managers would include the CEO, middle managers, and members of work groups or subcultures. It would seem that if any of these players had an explicit interest in managing the culture, the time of transition would give them an opportunity to do so and their attempts would have an effect. The CEO, because of his/her position and the resulting focus on the position, normally has the most influence. However, if strong subcultures exist, such influence may be mitigated, if not obscured, by the values shared within the subculture. In addition, the influence of a new CEO may be overshadowed by the influence of more immediate personnel who are explicitly attempting to manage the culture.

Trouble Spots in the Management of Culture

There are four predictable trouble spots in the process of managing corporate culture: the absence of a clear and internally coherent set of espoused values; over-reliance on direct methods of communicating values; a dysfunctional conflict between the espoused values of top management and the values being inferred from the actual practices of the firm; and the existence of pockets of ignorance and resistance. The four potential problem areas will be briefly discussed below.

First, one of the most important and difficult tasks of top management is to decide what values should be shared, what objectives are worth striving for, and specifically what values should be espoused. Companies need a clear and internally coherent set of values. Without a clear set of values, employees can work at cross purposes. Without internal coherence, a set of espoused values can increase the confusion of employees.

Second, once top management has selected a clear and coherent set of values, the next step is to communicate these values to employees in a memorable and convincing fashion. Many managers prefer direct methods of communication; if they have something to say, they say it. This results in lists of corporate objectives or statements of a philosophy of management. Such direct methods of communicating values are often reacted to with skepticism and may be dismissed by employees as corporate propaganda. Managers who rely heavily on direct methods of communicating their espoused values run the risk of being ignored or disbelieved. Indirect methods of conveying values, such as the use of cultural forms and management practices, can be more effective in having employees remember and believe in what is being communicated.

Third, discrepancies between espoused values and the values being expressed through cultural forms and practices can be dysfunctional.

When management espouses values which are not translated consistently into management practices, employees can be put into a double bind. They cannot trust what management says and they do not know whether to translate espoused values into action. In cases such as this, the discrepancy can easily be dysfunctional for employees at all levels in the firm, causing a kind of cultural schizophrenia.

Finally, employee reactions to management's espoused values and the values being expressed and reinforced through cultural forms and company practices may lead to pockets of ignorance or pockets of resistance. If employees are unaware of the values of top management, a pocket of ignorance will arise. If, however, employees are aware of the values but do not agree with them, a pocket of resistance may be created. Within this pocket of resistance, subcultures may develop which focus on values which conflict with the values of management. The first step in dealing with these problems is to determine where in the organization pockets of resistance and ignorance are located. The next step is to determine the source of the problem and deal with it accordingly.

Conclusion

Corporate culture has been hailed as an important means of making an organization work effectively. As suggested, one of the critical tasks of the manager and leader is the creation and maintenance of a system of shared values, one of the key components of a culture. This paper has attempted to increase the understanding of culture in order that managers may more effectively manage it. All organizations have cultures. The decisions faced by managers are: (1) whether to become part of the culture creation and maintenance process; and (2) if so, to decide which means are most appropriate given the cultural context. Hopefully, the ideas presented in this paper will aid managers in making these critical decisions.

SELECTED BIBLIOGRAPHY

Organizational culture research has its roots in Philip Selznick's **Leadership and Administration** (Row, Peterson, 1957) and Burton Clark's **The Distinctive College: Antioch, Reed, and Swarthmore** (Aldine, 1970). Four books, oriented toward the professional manager, are largely responsible for the recent renaissance of interest in this topic. William Ouchi's **Theory Z: How American Business Can Meet the Japanese Challenge** (Addison-Wesley, 1981) and Richard Pascale and Anthony Athos's **The Art of Japanese Management** (Simon & Schuster, Inc., 1981) drew heavily on Japanese models of corporate culture. Thomas Peters and Robert Waterman studied the cultures of unusually profitable American companies in **In Search of Excellence** (Harper & Row, 1982), as did Terrence Deal and Allan Kennedy in **Corporate Cultures** (Addison-Wesley, 1982).

Some have taken a critical view of the work that aroused this interest in culture. Edgar Schein disputed the reliance on Japanese models in "Does Japanese Management Style Have a Message for American Managers?" **(Sloan Management Review,** Fall 1981). The claim that cultures express an institution's distinctive competence or unique accomplishment was questioned by Joanne Martin, Martha Feldman, Mary Jo Hatch, and Sim Sitkin in "The Uniqueness Paradox in Organizational Stories" **(Administrative Science Quarterly,** September 1983).

Others have taken a closer look at particular cultural phenomena. Organizational stories, legends, and myths have been studied by Alan Wilkins and Joanne Martin; for example, see "Stories and Scripts in Organizational Settings," in Albert Hastorf and Alice Isen (eds.), **Cognitive Social Psychology** (Elsevier-North Holland, 1982). For an excellent sampling of papers about a wide range of cultural phenomena, including organizational stories, rituals, humor, and jargon, see the collection edited by Louis Pondy, Peter Frost, Gareth Morgan, and Thomas Dandridge, **Organizational Symbolism** (JAI Press, 1983).

Another approach has been to study the functions served by different types of cultures. For example, John Van Maanen and Stephen Barley have studied occupations in "Occupational Communities: Culture and Control in Organizations," in Barry Staw and Larry Cummings (eds.), **Research in Organizational Behavior,** Vol. 6 (JAI Press, 1984). Caren Siehl and Joanne Martin have studied the enculturation process for new employees, producing a quantitative, easily administered measure of culture in "Symbolic Management: Can Culture Be Transmitted?", a chapter in the **Annual Leadership Series,** Vol. 7 (Southern Illinois University Press, 1984). Although the recent academic research is scattered in a variety of scholarly journals, books integrating this literature are being written by a number of people, including Edgar Schein, Meryl Louis, and Joanne Martin.

Eric G. Flamholtz, Yvonne Randle and Maria Lombardi Bullen

6

Human Resource Accounting: An Overview

Introduction

During the late 1960s, managers, behavioral scientists, financial analysts, and accountants became increasingly interested in the idea of accounting for people as organizational resources. Initially, the notion was to "put people on the balance sheet," because it was recognized that people are valuable resources and corporate financial reports are deficient if they do not reflect the status of human assets.[1] More recently, there has been a growing trend towards developing methods of accounting for human resources as managerial tools rather than for purposes of financial reporting. Some business organizations have already begun to develop systems of accounting for their human resources.[2]

---

[1] James C. Hekimian and Curtis H. Jones, "Put People on Your Balance Sheet," **Harvard Business Review,** Vol. 45 (January-February 1967), pp. 105-113.

[2] See Eric G. Flamholtz, **Human Resource Accounting** (San Francisco: Jossey-Bass Publishers, Inc., 1985).

This introduction to human resource accounting as a managerial tool deals with the basic questions about human resource accounting which are of concern to management:

- What is human resource accounting?
- What is its history?
- What is its role in managing people?
- How can we account for human resources (i.e., how can we measure investments in people, their replacement cost, and their value to organizations)?
- What are the different types of human resource accounting systems and for what kind of organization is each system most appropriate?

Concept of Human Resource Accounting

Human resource accounting (HRA) has been defined by the American Accounting Association's Committee on Human Resource Accounting as "the process of identifying and measuring data about human resources and communicating this information to interested parties."[3]

In a literal sense, "human resource accounting" means accounting for people as an organizational resource. It involves measuring the costs incurred by business firms and other organizations to recruit, select, hire, train,

---

[3]American Accounting Association, **Report of the Committee on Human Resource Accounting,** The Accounting Review Supplement to Vol. 48 (1973).

and develop human assets. It involves measuring what it would cost to replace an organization's human resources. It also involves measuring the economic value of people to organizations. Thus, human resource accounting means measuring the investment made by organizations in people, the cost of replacing those people, and the value of people to the enterprise.

The term "human resource accounting" should not only be viewed literally, for it also has a figurative or symbolic meaning as well. It is not only a system of measuring the cost and value of people to organizations; it is also a way of thinking about the management of people. It suggests the need to think of people as valuable organizational resources, resources whose value may be appreciated or depleted as a result of the ways in which they are managed.

History of Human Resource Accounting

The field of human resource accounting has been developing since the 1960s and is an outgrowth of the convergence of several independent but closely related streams of thought, as well as the fundamental change of the United States postindustrial economy into a service economy. These developments have fostered a growing awareness that human capital or human assets are the distinctive feature of today's economy and a major part of today's organizational assets.

Growing Recognition of the Importance of Human Assets

It is increasingly recognized today that the United States is experiencing a fundamental restructuring of its economy.[4] Specifically, the economy is in the process of a qualitative transformation from an industrial economy to a service-based economy, just as there was the prior transformation from an agricultural economy to an industrial economy. This transformation, which began at about the end of World War II, has led to changes in the composition of the labor force not only in the sectors in which people are employed, but in the nature of the types and levels of skills demanded.

At present, we are rapidly becoming a knowledge-based economy, and the services provided are increasingly what may be described as high-technology services - the product of considerable amounts of training and experience. Thus, the economy is increasingly comprised of white-collar, technical, and professional personnel. The distinctive feature of the emerging economy is that there is a growing emphasis on human capital (the knowledge, skills, and experience of people) rather than on physical capital. A related attribute is that the development of human capital is costly and requires significant investments both by individuals and the organizations in which they are employed.

Impetus for Development of Human Resource Accounting

Under agricultural and industrial economic structures where the extent of human capital

---

[4]For a discussion of the nature of this transformation see Alvin Toffler, **The Third Wave** (New York: Bantam Books, Inc., 1980) and James Cook, "The Molting of America," **Forbes** (November 22, 1982), pp. 161-167.

was significantly less than it is today, the theories and methods of accounting did not treat either people or investments in people as assets (with the exception of slaves who were viewed as property). However, with the increasing importance of human capital at the level of the economy as a whole, as well as at the level of the individual firm, a great deal of research has been designed to develop concepts and methods of accounting for people as assets. This field, described in more detail below, has come to be known as human resource accounting.

HRA is, at least in part, a recognition that people comprise human capital or human assets. Thus, the economic theory of human capital is based upon the concept that the skills, experience, and knowledge which people possess are a form of capital. Theodore Schultz, whose work on the economic theory of human capital received the Nobel Prize, has stated: "Laborers have become capitalists not from a diffusion of the ownership of corporation stock as folklore would have it, but from the acquisition of knowledge and skills that have economic value."[5] In his review of the history of the development of the economic theory of human capital, B.F. Kiker indicated that the early economists who recognized the concept of human capital included Adam Smith, Petty, Say, Senior, List, Von Thunon, Roscher, Walras, and

---

[5]Theodore Schultz, "Investment in Human Capital," **The American Economic Review,** Vol. 51, No.1 (March 1961), p. 3.

Fischer.[6] The two methods used by economists to measure the amounts of human capital were based upon cost-of-production and capitalized-earnings procedures.

Human resource accounting has also developed from a parallel tradition in personnel management known as the "Human Resources School," which is based upon the premise that people are valuable organizational resources and therefore ought to be managed as such. Personnel theorists such as George Odiorne and organizational psychologists such as Rensis Likert have treated people as valuable organizational resources in their work.[7] For example, in **The Human Organization: Its Management and Value,** organizational theorist Likert states that "every aspect of a firm's activities is determined by the competence, motivation and general effectiveness of its human organization."[8]

There is also support among some of the early accounting theorists for treating people as assets and accounting for their value, even

---

[6]B.F. Kiker, "The Historical Roots of the Concept of Human Capital," **Journal of Political Economy** (October 1968), pp. 481-499.

[7]George S. Odiorne, **Personnel Policy: Issues and Practices** (Columbus Ohio: Charles E. Merrill Books, Inc., 1963); Rensis Likert, **New Patterns of Management** (New York: McGraw Hill Book Co., 1961).

[8]Rensis Likert, **The Human Organization: Its Management and Value** (New York: McGraw Hill Book Co., 1967).

before the nature of our economic structure changed and human capital increased in importance. For example, D. R. Scott pointed out that "a trained force of technical operatives is always a valuable asset."[9] Similarly, W. A. Paton has stated that "in a business enterprise a well-organized and loyal personnel may be a much more important asset than a stock of merchandise."[10]

In addition to academic theorists, practicing managers have for some time recognized the importance of human assets. For example, the 1966 annual report of Uniroyal stated: "Our primary resource is people. [We are] essentially a collection of skills - the varied expertise of our 68,000 employees....Uniroyal has plants and has capital, but most of all, it has people."[11]

Taken together, these various streams of thought have led to the conclusion that organizations possess a valuable asset in the people who are in its employ, and that the people themselves are a form of capital, human capital. During the 1960s this recognition led to both academic research and business development of concepts and methods of measuring the cost and value of people as organizational assets; and to the present-day field of human resource accounting.

---

[9]D.R. Scott, **Theory of Accounts,** Vol. I (New York: Henry Holt Co., 1925), p. 258.

[10]William A. Paton, **Accounting Theory** (Chicago: Accounting Studies Press, 1962), pp. 486-487.

[11]Uniroyal, Inc., **75th Annual Report - 1966,** 1967, p. 10.

Brief Survey of Research in Human Resource Accounting

One of the earliest approaches to measuring and accounting for the value of human resources was developed by R. H. Hermanson, an academic accountant, as part of his Ph.D. dissertation, and later published as a monograph in 1964.[12] Hermanson's principal concern was that conventional financial statements fail to reflect adequately the financial position of a firm because they do not include human assets. Hermanson developed "the unpurchased goodwill method" to measure the value of human assets possessed by a firm and acquired through the normal course of operations by recruiting and training, but which have not been purchased by an acquisition of one firm by another.

In 1966, a group of researchers consisting of R. L. Brummet, E. G. Flamholtz, and W. C. Pyle began research on human resource accounting at the University of Michigan.[13] This research was designed to develop concepts, models, and techniques of measuring and accounting for the cost and value of human assets as well as developing possible applications for such measurements. Their work led to a variety of theoretical concepts and models as well as

---

[12] Roger H. Hermanson, **Accounting for Human Assets**, Occasional Paper No. 14, (East Lansing: Bureau of Business and Economic Research, Graduate School of Business Administration, Michigan State University, 1964).

[13] R.L. Brummet, E.G. Flamholtz, and W.C. Pyle, "Human Resource Measurement: A Challenge for Accountants," **The Accounting Review** (April 1968), pp. 217-224.

applications of these approaches in actual organizations.

Under the direction of William C. Pyle, the R. G. Barry Corporation, headquartered in Columbus, Ohio, made the first reported attempt to develop a system of accounting for a firm's investment in people.[14] This system was intended for managerial rather than financial reporting purposes.

The first experimentation in an actual organization with the measurement of the value of human resources was done by Eric G. Flamholtz.[15] Flamholtz developed a theoretical model for the measurement of an individual's value to an organization, termed the stochastic rewards valuation model. This model, which has since undergone refinements, was recently applied to the valuation of registered retail representatives at a securities brokerage firm.[16] The model is described below, in the section on Human Resource Accounting Measurement.

Since the early studies by Hermanson, Brummet, Flamholtz, and Pyle, there has been a considerable body of theoretical and empirical

---

[14] W.C. Pyle, "Accounting for Your People," **Innovation,** No. 10 (1970), pp. 46-54.

[15] Eric G. Flamholtz, "The Theory and Measurement of an Individual's Value to an Organization" (Unpublished Ph.D. Diss., University of Michigan, 1969).

[16] See Flamholtz,"A Model for Human Resource Valuation: A Stochastic Process with Service Rewards," **The Accounting Review** (April 1971), pp. 253-267; and Flamholtz, **Human Resource Accounting.**

research in both the United States and abroad to develop concepts, models, and methods of accounting for people as organizational assets, and the field as a whole has come to be known as human resource accounting.[17]

In 1983, Flamholtz completed a project for the U. S. Office of Naval Research involving the application of human resource accounting methods.[18] He is currently directing a second research project on the application of Human resource accounting to naval personnel management issues for the U.S. Office of Naval Research. He has completed a similar research project for a major U.S. financial institution.[19] In addition, he has conducted an evaluation of basic research programs and future research opportunities for the application of human resource accounting and human capital Theory to U.S. national productivity problems for the National Science Foundation.[20]

---

[17]For a description of the field's status as of 1979, see Eric G. Flamholtz, "Human Resource Accounting: State of The Art and Future Prospects," **Annual Accounting Review,** Vol. 1 (1979), pp. 211-261.

[18]Eric G. Flamholtz, **Personnel Turnover Cost and Management in Naval Operations** (U.S. Office of Naval Research, May 1983).

[19]Eric G. Flamholtz and Richard A. Kaumeyer, Jr., "Human Resource Replacement Cost Information and Personnel Decisions: A Field Study," **Human Resource Planning,** Vol. 3, No. 3 (1980), pp. 11-138.

[20]Eric G. Flamholtz, "An Evaluation of Basic Research Progress and Future Research Opportunities with Respect to the Applications of Human Resource Accounting and Human Capital Theory to National Productivity Problems," (Unpublished report prepared for the National Science Foundation under contract no. OM, Order No. 77-SP-0858, requisition no. 1614).

Human Resource Accounting's Managerial Role

A major purpose of human resource accounting is to serve as a system of providing measurements of the cost and value of people to an organization. From a managerial perspective, human resource accounting is intended to help decision makers base decisions on a cost-value calculus, that is, on an assessment of the costs and value involved in a decision.

Measurement of the cost and value of human resources is needed (1) to facilitate planning and decision making by personnel management staff, and (2) to enable top management to evaluate the effectiveness with which human resources have been developed, conserved, and utilized by lower levels of management (especially in large decentralized companies). More specifically, management needs measurements of the cost and value of human resources to make decisions in all phases of the human resource management process: acquisition, development, allocation, conservation, utilization, evaluation, and rewards.

Acquisition of Human Resources

The acquisition of human resources involves recruiting, selecting, and hiring people to meet the organization's present and anticipated personnel needs. The first step in human resource acquisition is to forecast personnel requirements; when they have been forecast, management must translate its personnel needs into a "personnel acquisition budget." This is essentially a process of cost estimation.

Human resource accounting can be useful in budgeting personnel acquisition. It can provide measurements of the standard costs of recruiting, selecting, and hiring people, which can be used to prepare proposed personnel acquisition budgets.

Personnel selection is another process in which human resource accounting can play a role. In making selection decisions, managers need measurements of the economic value of alternative job candidates. A personnel manager, for example, faced with a choice among several attractive candidates for a job, would, ideally, like to choose the person possessing the greatest future value to the organization. However, measurements of the expected value of people are not presently available, except in terms of nonmonetary surrogates such as scores on tests of "managerial potential." Thus, if monetary measurements of the expected value of people were available, personnel managers could use decision rules for employee selection designed to optimize the expected value of an organization's human resources.

Acquisition and Development Policy

By providing estimates of the current costs to acquire and develop people for various positions, human resource accounting can help management assess the tradeoffs between the costs of recruitment from outside as opposed to development from within. Thus it provides the economic information management needs to assist in formulating personnel acquisition and development policy.

Allocation of Human Resources

The allocation of human resources is the process of assigning people to various organizational roles and tasks. There are several, sometimes conflicting, objectives involved in allocation decisions. First, the task to be performed should be completed in the most efficient way. This may mean that management will allocate the "most qualified" person to a particular job. In addition, however, an organization's human resources must be developed, and management may wish to provide people with the opportunity to develop their skills through on-the-job learning. This suggests that the "most qualified" (experienced) person may not be assigned to a task. Third, management wants to allocate people to jobs which satisfy their needs. Thus, ideally, management allocates people to jobs in a way that will optimize these three variables: job productivity, human resource development, and individual satisfaction.

Human resource accounting can help quantify the variables involved in the allocation decision and express them in the common denominator of monetary units. This will help management understand the tradeoffs involved in allocation decisions, and permit selection of the optimal course of action. For example, linear programming might be used to determine the optimal solution to the personnel allocation problem.

Conservation of Human Resources

Conservation of human resources is the process of maintaining the capabilities of people as individuals and the effectiveness of the human system developed by an organization. Failure to measure the extent to which human resources are being conserved in a division, plant, or department can be costly to an organization. In the short run, for example, a divisional manager can put pressure on people to temporarily increase their productivity or reduce costs, with the effects upon employee motivation, attitudes, and labor relations going unmeasured. As a result, highly trained and skilled employees may become dissatisfied and leave an organization. The cost of replacing them may be substantial.

An organization must account for its human assets in order to prevent their depletion. Managers must be held accountable for conservation of human resources allocated to them. Currently, such conservation is measured in terms of turnover rates. Measures of turnover, however, are inadequate indicators of human resource conservation for two reasons. First, they are historical, and therefore are unavailable to management until after turnover has occurred. Thus, they cannot be used as an early-warning signal to suggest the need for special efforts at conservation. Second, turnover rates do not fully represent the economic impact of turnover, which is more realistically demonstrated by monetary measure.

Human resource accounting can assist management in conserving its human organization by providing an early-warning system. It can measure and report certain (social-psychological) indicators of the condition of the human organization, and management can anticipate trends in these variables prior to the actual occurrence of turnover or decreased productivity. Corrective actions can thus be taken before the fact rather than after the fact.

Utilization of Human Resources

Human resource utilization is the process of using human services to achieve organizational objectives. Human resource accounting can help managers effectively and efficiently utilize human resources by providing a paradigm, or conceptual framework, for human resource utilization.

At present, the management of human resources in organizations is less effective than it might be because it lacks a unifying framework to guide it. Managers have neither a valid criterion to guide decisions affecting people nor a methodology for assessing the anticipated or actual consequences of such decisions. Clearly, the criteria of productivity and satisfaction which frequently underly strategies of human resource management have not been entirely helpful in coping with problems of managing people. Similarly, since it is exceedingly difficult to measure productivity and satisfaction, or to assess the tradeoffs a manager should rationally be willing to make to increase one by decreasing the other, it is not frequently possible to predict the economic consequences of alternative actions with respect to people.

The notion of "human resource value" provides one possible solution to these problems. It can serve as the **raison d'etre** of human resource management; it can simultaneously provide the goal and the criterion for the management of human resources. More specifically, the aim of human resource management can be viewed as the need to contribute to the value of the organization as a whole by optimizing the value of its human assets; the effectiveness criterion can be the measured change in the value of the organization's human resources.

If the aim of human resource management is seen as the optimization of human resource value, then task design, selection, role assignment, development, performance appraisal, and compensation are not merely a set of service functions to be performed; rather, they are a set of available strategies that can be adopted to change the value of human assets, and, in turn, the value of the organization as a whole.

What does this mean for a manager? It means that the manager will have a theoretical framework to guide his/her thoughts, actions, and decisions in regard to people. The framework or paradigm posits that the ultimate guide to decision making involving people is the extent to which human resource value is optimized. It also means that the manager will receive measurements of the extent to which his/her ultimate objective is being achieved, that is, the degree to which the value of people to the organization is being optimized.

Evaluation and Reward of Human Resources

Human resource evaluation is the process of assessing the value of people to an organization. It involves measuring the productivity (performance) and promotability of people.

At present, human resources are typically evaluated by nonmonetary methods. These methods, however, cannot be used in most of the human resource acquisition, development, allocation, and conservation problems and decisions cited above; monetary methods of human resource evaluation are needed instead.

Human resource accounting can be useful in the human resource evaluation process by developing valid and reliable methods of measuring the value of people to an organization. These methods will include both monetary and nonmonetary measurements. They will permit human resource management decisions to be made on a cost-value basis.

Human resource valuation will also have an impact on the administration of human resource reward systems. These systems are intended to motivate and reinforce the optimal performance of people in achieving organization objectives. "Rewards" include compensation and promotion, as well as symbolic "rewards" such as performance appraisals. Human resource valuation will permit organizational rewards to be administered in relation to a person's value to an organization. It will enable management, for example, ultimately to base compensation decisions on the value of people to a firm.

Human resource accounting can also be used to evaluate the efficiency of the personnel management function per se. It can help establish standard costs of acquiring and developing people, and these standards can be compared with the actual costs the personnel department incurs in performing its acquisition and development functions. The variances (deviations) from standard may be analyzed to identify possible inefficiencies in the manpower acquisition and development process.

Measurement of Human Resource Cost and Value

The discussion above suggested how human resource accounting might be useful in managing people. This section briefly identifies and describes the concepts and methods which have been developed to actually account for the cost and value of human resources.[21]

---

[21] A thorough discussion of these methods is beyond the scope of this paper. See Flamholtz, **Human Resource Accounting,** especially chapters 2, 3, 5, 6, and 7.

Measuring Human Resource Costs

Three different concepts have been proposed for the measurement of human resource costs: original cost, replacement cost, and opportunity cost. "Original cost" is the actual, historical outlay incurred as an investment in resources. "Replacement cost" is the sacrifice (cost) that would have to be incurred today to replace an organization's resources. "Opportunity cost" is the maximum amount that resources could earn in an alternative use.

Original Cost of Human Resources. The original cost of human resources refers to the sacrifice that was actually incurred to acquire and develop people. This is analogous to the concept of original cost for other assets. For example, the original cost of plant and equipment is the cost incurred to acquire these resources.

The original cost of human resources typically includes cost of recruitment, selection, hiring, placement, orientation, and on-the-job training (Figure 1). Some of these items are direct costs while others are indirect costs. For example, costs of hiring and placement are direct costs, while portions of the cost of a supervisor's time during training is an indirect cost.

Replacement Cost of Human Resources. The replacement cost of human resources refers to the sacrifice that would have to be incurred today to replace human resources presently employed. For example, if an individual were to leave an organization, costs would have to be incurred to recruit, select, and train a replacement.

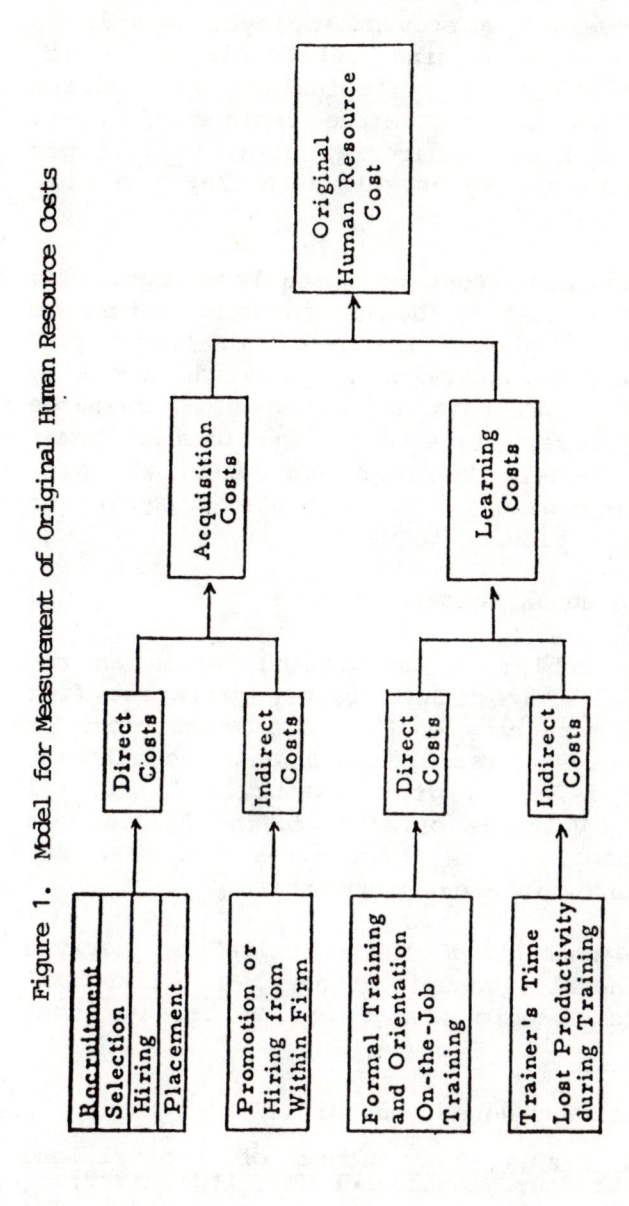

Figure 1. Model for Measurement of Original Human Resource Costs

```
                                          ┌──────────────┐
                                          │   Original   │
                                          │Human Resource│
                                          │    Cost      │
                                          └──────▲───────┘
                                                 │
                         ┌───────────────────────┴───────────────────────┐
                  ┌──────┴──────┐                                 ┌──────┴──────┐
                  │ Acquisition │                                 │  Learning   │
                  │    Costs    │                                 │   Costs     │
                  └──────▲──────┘                                 └──────▲──────┘
                         │                                               │
                  ┌──────┴──────┐                                 ┌──────┴──────┐
           ┌──────┴─┐        ┌──┴─────┐                    ┌──────┴─┐        ┌──┴─────┐
           │ Direct │        │Indirect│                    │ Direct │        │Indirect│
           │ Costs  │        │ Costs  │                    │ Costs  │        │ Costs  │
           └────▲───┘        └───▲────┘                    └────▲───┘        └───▲────┘
                │                │                              │                │
    ┌───────────┴──┐   ┌─────────┴────┐        ┌────────────────┴─┐   ┌──────────┴─────┐
    │ Recruitment  │   │ Promotion or │        │ Formal Training  │   │ Trainer's Time │
    │ Selection    │   │ Hiring from  │        │ and Orientation  │   │ Lost Productivity│
    │ Hiring       │   │ Within Firm  │        │ On-the-Job       │   │ during Training│
    │ Placement    │   │              │        │ Training         │   │                │
    └──────────────┘   └──────────────┘        └──────────────────┘   └────────────────┘
```

Source: Eric Flamholtz, **Human Resource Accounting** (Los Angeles, California: Management System Consulting Corporation, 1983), p. 37.

The replacement cost of human resources typically includes the costs attributable to the turnover of a present employee as well as the costs of acquiring and developing a replacement (Figure 2). It includes both direct and indirect costs. Since replacement costs are intended for managerial uses, they should include opportunity as well as outlay cost components.

Opportunity Cost of Human Resources. The opportunity cost of human resources refers to the value of human resources in their most favorable alternative use. Although nominally a cost concept, this notion of human resource cost is closely related to the idea of human resource value. Hekimian and Jones, who proposed the concept, have suggested a system of competitive bidding to measure it.[22]

Measuring Human Resource Value

The problems of accounting for human resource value are significantly different from those of measuring costs. The measurement of cost involves tracing costs and accumulating them. It is, to a great extent, a historical process. Value is oriented to the future, not to the past. Thus it requires forecasts and is, in turn, inherently uncertain.

The concept of "human value" is derived from general economic theory.[23] Like all resources, people possess value because they

---

[22] Hekimian and Jones, **op. cit.**

[23] Irving Fisher, **The Nature of Capital and Income** (London: Macmillan & Co., Ltd., 1927).

Figure 2

Model for Measurement of Human Resource Replacement Costs

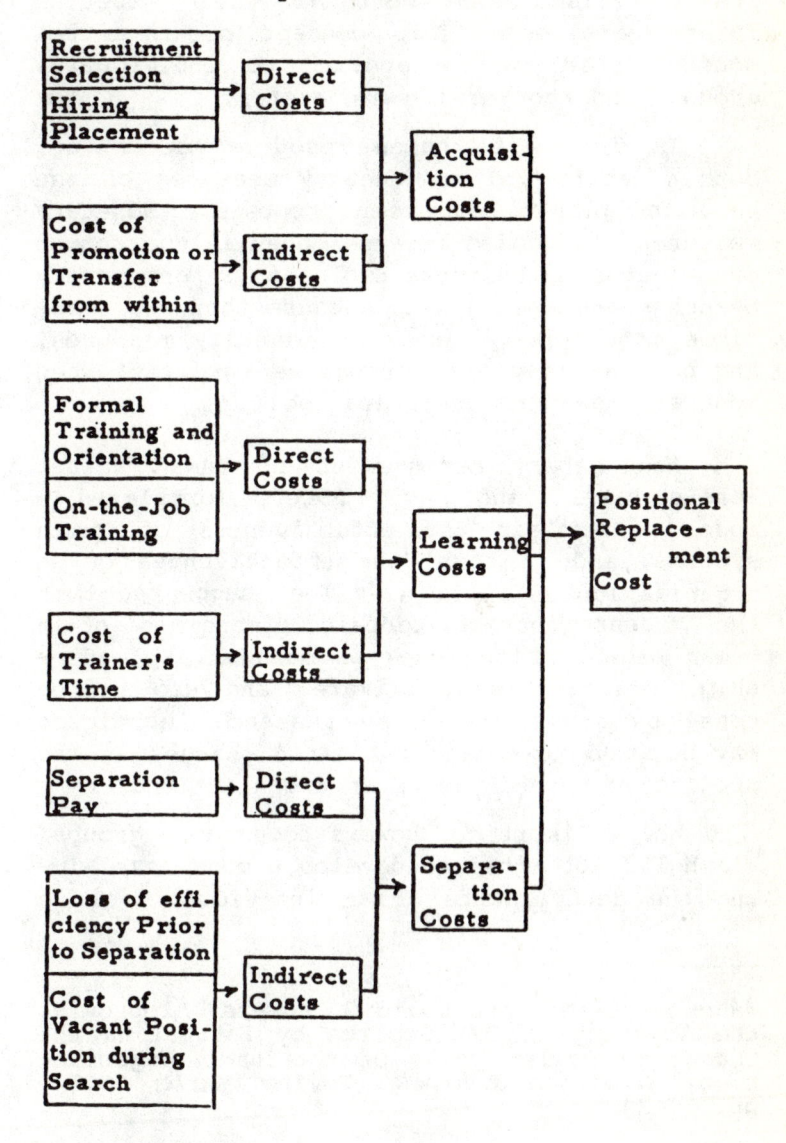

Source: Eric Flamholtz, **Human Resource Accounting** (Los Angeles, California: Management System Consulting Corporation, 1983), p. 37.

are capable of rendering future services. Thus, the value of human resources, like the value of other resources, may be defined as the present (discounted) worth of their expected future services. This concept of human resource value can be applied to individuals, groups, and the total human system.

In developing human resource accounting, both monetary and nonmonetary measures of the value of people have been proposed. Monetary measures are needed because money is the common denominator of business decisions. Nonmonetary measures are needed both because they are sometimes more appropriate than monetary measures, and because they are surrogates (proxies) when monetary measures are unavailable.

Nonmonetary Measurement of Human Value. Rensis Likert and David Bowers formulated a model to explain the effectiveness of human systems, and in turn, the effectiveness of an organization as a whole.[24] They suggested that the measurement of certain dimensions of a human organization (such as managerial leadership, organizational climate, and group process) by means of survey research techniques may be used to obtain estimated changes in the productive capability of an organization.

While Likert and Bowers focused on groups, Flamholtz attempted to develop a model explaining the determinants of an individual's value

---

[24]Rensis Likert and David G. Bowers, "Improving the Accuracy of P/L Reports by Estimating the Change in Dollar Value of the Human Organization," **Michigan Business Review** (March 1973), pp. 15-24.

to an organization.[25] The model, shown in Figure 3, identified the economic, social, and psychological factors which determine a person's value to a firm. It is based on the premise that a person's value is a product of the attributes he/she brings to an organization (such as traits, skills, and motivation) and the characteristics of the organization itself (such as its structure, reward system, management style, and role descriptions).

Monetary Measurement of Human Value.
Several methods for measuring the monetary value of human resources have been proposed. Some are intended to measure value directly, while others are intended as surrogate or proxy measures.

Brummet, Flamholtz, and Pyle suggested a direct approach to measuring a group's value.[26] Their method involved forecasting a firm's future earnings, discounting them to determine the firm's present value, and then allocating a portion to human resources based upon their relative contribution.

Focusing on the problem of measuring an individual's value to an organization, Flamholtz conceptualized the individual valuation problem as a stochastic process with rewards

---

[25]Eric G. Flamholtz, "Assessing the Validity of a Theory of Human Resource Value: A Field Study," **Empirical Research in Accounting: Selected Studies,** 1972, Supplement to Vol. 10 of the **Journal of Accounting Research,** p. 257.

[26]R. Lee Brummet, Eric G. Flamholtz, and William C. Pyle, "Human Resource Management - A Challenge for Accountants," **The Accounting Review,** (April 1968), pp. 217-224.

Figure 3. Revised Model of the Determinants of an Individual's Value to a Formal Organization

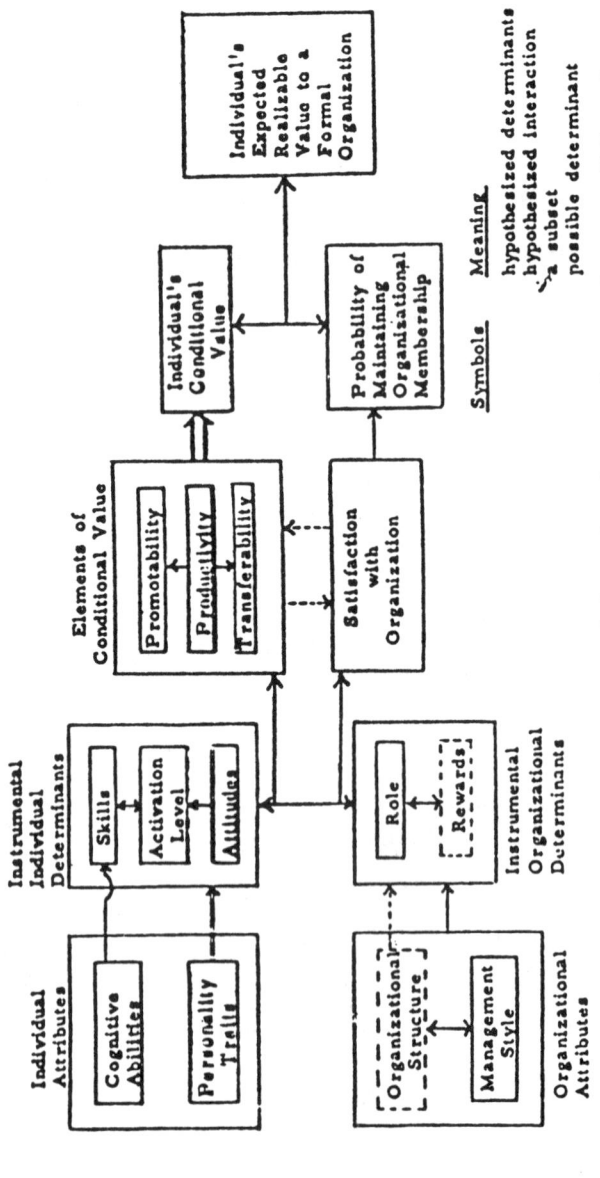

Source: Eric Flamholtz, "Assessing the Validity of a Theory of Human Resource Value: A Field Study," **Empirical Research in Accounting: Selected Studies, 1972,** Supplement to Vol. 10 of the *Journal of Accounting Research*, p. 257.

and presented a "stochastic rewards" model for the monetary valuation of individuals.[27] The model, shown schematically in Figure 4, is based on the notion that a person is not valuable to an organization in the abstract but in relation to the roles (service states) he/she is expected to occupy. Thus, a person is engaged in a process of movement among organizational service states through time. If the individual occupies a service state for a specified time period, the organization derives a given amount of services. Since the states that people will occupy in the future cannot be known with certainty, we must measure the mathematical expectation of a person's services. Thus, to measure an individual's value to an organization, we must (1) estimate the time period during which the person is expected to render services to an organization; (2) identify the service states that the person may occupy; (3) measure the value derived by the organization if the individual occupies the state for a specified time period; and (4) estimate the probability that a person will occupy each state at specified future times. The result is a direct measure of the person's expected value to an organization.

Hermanson proposed two possible techniques for developing surrogate measures of the monetary value of "human resources": the unpurchased goodwill method, and the adjusted present value method.[28] The former involves fore-

---

[27]Eric G. Flamholtz, "A Model for Human Resource Valuation, pp. 253-267; and Flamholtz, **Human Resource Accounting**, pp. 167-173.

[28]Roger H. Hermanson, **Accounting for Human Assets**.

Figure 4

A Three-Dimensional Representation of the
Mobility Experiment as a Stochastic Process
With Service Rewards

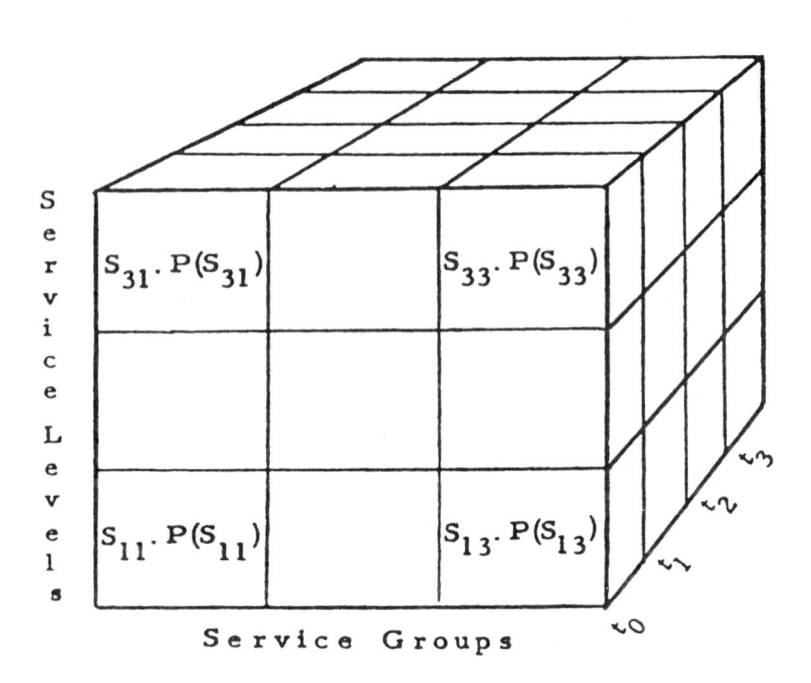

$S_{31} \cdot P(S_{31})$ $S_{33} \cdot P(S_{33})$

$S_{11} \cdot P(S_{11})$ $S_{13} \cdot P(S_{13})$

Service Levels

Service Groups

casting future earnings and allocating any excess above normal expected earnings for an industry to human resources. The approach is based on the premise that human resources are responsible for differences in earnings among firms. The latter method is more accurately labeled the "adjusted discounted future wages method." It involves using the present value of the stream of future wage payments to people, adjusted by a performance efficiency factor, as a proxy measure of human resource value.

Lev and Schwartz also proposed using discounted future compensation as a surrogate measure of human resource value, suggesting that their method could be aggregated to value groups and the total human organization.[29]

A Continuum of Human Resource Accounting Systems

Different organizations require different degrees of human resource accounting capability. One firm may require only the most rudimentary system, while only the most advanced capability may be satisfactory for another company. Similarly, the human resource accounting capability appropriate for a firm at one stage may be quite inadequate at a later stage.

To illustrate the different types of human resource accounting capability, Table 1 presents a continuum of five human resource accounting systems. The table shows various functions of human resource management (human

---
[29]Baruch Lev and Aba Schwartz, "On the Use of the Economic Concept of Human Capital in Financial Statements," **The Accounting Review** (January 1971), pp. 102-112.

Table 1

HUMAN RESOURCE ACCOUNTING SYSTEMS I–V

CAPABILITY PROVIDED BY HUMAN RESOURCE ACCOUNTING SYSTEMS:

Human Resource Management Functions	System I *Prerequisite Personnel System*	System II *Basic HRA System*	System III *Intermediate HRA System*	System IV *Advanced HRA System*	System V *Total HRA System*
I. Human Resource Planning	Manpower skills inventory Replacement tables	Estimated costs of recruiting, training, etc.	Replacement costs	Standard and actual personnel costs Stochastic manpower mobility models Manpower simulations	Stochastic rewards valuation model Human resource value simulations
II. Human Resource Decision-making: A. Budgetary	Personnel Costs included in "General and Administrative" expense	Personnel costs budgeted separately	Budgetary system for recruitment, training, etc. Budget replacement costs	Budget standard and actual costs Original and replacement costs	Human capital budgeting Budget ROI on human capital investment
B. Policy	Traditional selection, training, and placement methods	Value-oriented selection decisions	Recruitment vs. training trade-off analyses	Manpower assignment optimization models	Value-based compensation

	Turnover rates	Turnover cost	Replacement cost	Opportunity cost	Human resource value depletion
III. Human Resources Conservation:					
A. After-the-fact		Attitudinal data	Expected turnover cost (replacement)	Expected opportunity costs Human re-accountability	Expected conditional and realizable value depletion
B. Before-the-fact	N.A.				
IV. Human Resource Evaluation	Performance and potential ratings	Perceived value rankings	Psychometric predictions of potential value Interval scaling of value	Measurements of economic value of groups	Measurement of economic value of individuals
V. Human Resource Management Efficiency Control	N.A.	Comparison of actual costs with historical costs	Comparison of budgeted and actual costs Variance analysis	Comparison of actual costs against standard Variance analysis	Interunit comparison of costs

resource planning, decision making, conservation, etc.) and the human resource accounting capabilities provided by each system level.

Human Resource Accounting System I

An organization with a System I human resource accounting capability possesses most of the personnel systems which are **prerequisite** to the implementation of human resource accounting. System I consists of nominal but very elementary human resource accounting capability; that is, it consists of personnel systems which are aimed at the same functions of more sophisticated human resource accounting systems, but which lack advanced capabilities.

Most well-managed large and medium sized corporations have System I capabilities. Examples are numerous and probably include most, if not all, of the largest U.S. corporations, the so-called "Fortune 500."

Human Resource Accounting System II

In a System II organization, the human resource planning function incorporates estimates of costs of recruitment and training. Personnel costs are budgeted separately and not merely lumped in "General and Administrative" expenses. Personnel policy decisions are based on a cost-value calculus. For example, personnel selection decisions are based on such criteria as a person's expected value to the firm. Decision makers are more aware of the tradeoffs between one person with a high expected conditional value and another with a high expected realizable value. In a System II organization, management not only has data on turnover rates; it also has data on the **cost** of turnover. Thus, turnover is expressed in a more meaningful common denominator. Attitudinal data, such as measures of satisfaction and perceived motivation, are available, and they are used as leading indicators to forecast probable changes in turnover. Under System II, human resource evaluation is based on criteria of perceived value which are obtained by alternation-ranking (totem pole) methods. The efficiency of the human resource management process is assessed, and reports compare actual costs with historical costs of similar activities.

This system is thus based primarily upon accounting for the historical cost of human resources. Several organizations have engaged in experiments to develop this degree of human resource accounting capability, including Honeywell-Bull, Elf Petroleum, AT&T, R.G. Barry Corporation, Touche Ross, and Rank-Xerox.

Human Resource Accounting System III

Under System III, there is intermediate human resource accounting capability. Human resource planning incorporates replacement costs as well as original costs. Budgetary and policy decision making for human resources are subject to more systematic analysis. There is a formal system for budgeting recruitment, training, etc. Personnel needs are planned as a formal part of overall corporate planning, and not just on an ad-hoc basis. Policy decisions involving tradeoffs between human resource variables are subjected to analyses. For example, the choice between recruitment of experienced workers versus hiring and training entry-level personnel is subjected to tradeoff analysis. In System III, the replacement cost of turnover is measured and reported. Managers may be requested to explain controllable turnover. The human resource evaluation process is based on psychometric predications of a person's potential, and value is assessed in nonmonetary terms using interval scaling methods. The efficiency of the overall human resource management process is based on a comparison of budgeted and actual personnel costs, and explanations of variances are required.

In one firm, a United States insurance company, the data derived from a System III capability was used to evaluate the efficiency of personnel planning policies and practices. There was a significant difference between standard personnel replacement costs and anticipated replacement costs. Upon investigation, these differences were traced to inadequate staffing practices.

In another organization, AT&T, an attempt was made to measure the replacement cost of personnel to help control personnel turnover. Flanders reports that AT&T developed a system of "human resource accountability" intended to

> ...increase managerial effectiveness in developing and retaining employees. It accomplishes this by treating employee-replacement costs [hiring, training, benefits, etc.] as if they were capital investment rather than operating expense, and holding managers directly accountable for those segments of the investment that fall within their area of responsibility.[30]

---

[30]Harold Flanders, "The A.T.&T. Company Manpower Laboratory, circa 1971," **Academy of Management Proceedings** (31st Annual Meeting, August 1971) pp. 205-206.

In another firm, a large multinational chemical company, the replacement cost of personnel is measured and used in personnel planning. Similarly, the executive vice-president of a large aerospace corporation once described how his firm had made faculty layoff decisions because of the failure to take into account replacement costs. He stated that the decision would have been reversed if such costs had been recognized.

Human Resource Accounting System IV

An organization with a System IV capability has an advanced human resource accounting system. In such organizations, human resource accounting planning is based on standard personnel costs. Stochastic models are used to forecast personnel mobility and predict future human resource needs. Computers are used to simulate human resource planning, and parameters in the models are varied so that sensitivity analyses can be performed. In the decision-making process, budgets are based on standard costs. Optimization models are used for personnel policy decisions. For example, personnel assignment may be based on optimization methods. Human resource conservation is assessed not only in terms of historical and replacement cost, but also in terms of the opportunity cost of human resources. The organization has an ongoing system of human resource accountability, and one criterion used to evaluate managers is human resource conservation. The firm also has an ongoing turnover control program, and it uses measures of expected opportunity cost turnover as a basis for turnover control decisions. Under System IV, the organization accounts for the value of groups of people but not individuals. The efficiency of the human resource management process is evaluated by comparing actual costs against a standard, and there is a formal system for reporting and explaining variances.

System IV is based upon the use of opportunity costs. At present, there are no firms which have developed such a capability, though a few have developed aspects of the system. For example, an office of Touche Ross & Company has used opportunity costs in accounting for its investment in people. Other firms, including a large multilocation corporation engaged in the manufacture and marketing of a wide variety of electrical products, have developed stochastic manpower mobility models. Such corporations have the present capability of adding opportunity costs to their models to convert them from quantitative to cost-value based models. This would give them the ability to develop a System IV capability.

Human Resource Accounting System V

System V represents total human resource accounting capability. Human resource planning is based on a stochastic rewards valuation model, and simulations of the effects of overall corporate plans on human resource value are performed. In the decision-making process, there is formal human capital budgeting. Return on investment is the criterion employed to assess capital expenditures in human resources just as it is used for other resources. Personnel policy decisions are based fully on a person's expected value to the firm. Human resource conservation is controlled both before and after the fact. **Ex ante,** anticipated human resource depletion is measured in terms of expected conditional and realizable replacement cost. Turnover control programs are initiated when expected depletion is too high.

The System V organization has a human resource accountability subsystem, and managers are charged with the opportunity cost of controllable human value depletion. They are expected to conserve human as well as physical and financial assets entrusted to them. The human resource evaluation process includes the measurement of the economic value of individuals per se, as well as that of aggregates such as departments, plants, or divisions. Finally, the efficiency of the human resource management function is assessed not only by comparison of actual against standard costs, but also by comparison among comparable organizational units. In sum, System V represents maximal human resource accounting capability, measuring the economic value of people to a firm. The system is extremely difficult to develop because it has very stringent data requirements.

At present, a few organizations are developing human resource accounting systems at each stage of the continuum outlined above. More are developing a System II capability than System III capability and more are developing System III capability than System IV. It should be noted that few companies have developed **all** of the elements of a workable human resource accounting system. Rather, most have developed some aspects of a system, while others are experimenting with research projects.

Conclusions

We have presented an introduction to the uses, concepts, and methods of accounting for the cost and value of human resources, and we have defined human resource accounting literally as accounting for people as organizational resources. It was suggested that human resource accounting means not only measurement, but a way of thinking about the management of human resources. We have also examined the role of human resource accounting in the management of human resources, and have identified and briefly described the various concepts and methods of measuring human resource cost value. A taxonomy illustrates stages of different types of human resource accounting systems.

In this chapter we have only touched on the highlights of a relatively new and still developing field. Although we have made some progress on this problem during the past decade, there is a great deal still to be done. Thus, this presentation should be viewed as a report on progress to date in developing human resource accounting rather than as a final report.

J. Curtis Counts

7

The Contemporary Scene in Labor-Management Relations

The contemporary scene in United States labor-management relations is probably best characterized as one of considerable turmoil and upheaval. The transition from a national to a global economy and from an industrial to a service or information economy, and the impact of this transition upon the nature and stability of the work force is importantly affecting traditional labor-management policies and relationships.

Changes in Nature of Work

Changes in the nature of work, the characteristics of workers, and the structure of the work place have rendered invalid the traditional blue collar and white collar descriptions and categories of work. It is estimated that one half of all jobs today did not exist twenty years ago. New products and services are being discovered and new markets are being created with regularity.

Employment growth is not occurring in large institutions and organizations. The 500 largest corporations today employ but 15.6 million workers in a work force of 100 million. This is a zero increase from ten years ago. Employment statistics indicate that during the past ten years about two-thirds of all new jobs occurred in businesses with less than twenty employees.

The economy's shift to high technology and to information and services has polarized jobs into high-level and low-level opportunities. Prior to this shift, workers could enter a firm and move upward from unskilled to semiskilled to skilled jobs. Today's technology is erasing semiskilled jobs and making it very difficult for workers to advance to higher skilled jobs without major retraining.

This polarization of jobs has created the need to acquire knowledge conveniently and economically. The scarcity of skills and the costs incident to the employment of highly skilled employees not only favor the retraining of workers, but are responsible in part for the shift of the educational system out of schools into homes, offices, and learning centers. Importantly, since the prime ingredient in today's products and services is intelligence, it has reemphasized the importance of the worker. It also demands that the process of learning become a lifelong component of the process of work.

The composition of the work force is also reflective of change. The rise in female participation in the work force is staggering. Today 43 percent of the work force is female. This represents about 6 million more women in the work force than there were in 1970. Wider career opportunities and a greater need for two-earner families have contributed significantly to this growth. Today, approximately three of five families include two wage earners.

Women have also made tremendous progress in narrowing the gap in schooling and experience that has hindered female careers. Women now entering the work force have far greater academic credentials than formerly. In 1980, for example, women held approximately half the bachelor's degrees, half the master's degrees, and 30 percent of the doctorates.

Today's work force also includes more older workers than ever before. The trend toward an older work force results from the increase in the median age of the population, from the trend toward the elimination of compulsory retirement, and from relaxed social security earnings restrictions.

Change in Policy Emphasis

The change in the nature of work and the work force has intensified the pressure upon traditional labor-management policies. Job security and the displacement of employees now overshadow compensation as a priority item in labor-management policy considerations. Retraining, pension and severance costs, work sharing, early retirement, shorter work weeks, and legislated benefits are prime subjects of this intensified emphasis.

The pressure for change in traditional labor-management policies that reflect the differing and rapidly changing needs of workers in today's marketplace underscores the requirement for policies that are both realistic and flexible.

Labor Unions

Indeed, this demand for responsive and flexible policies is challenging the viability, purpose, and the future of labor unions. The real and perceived need for unions has declined over the past several years. Although union membership during the 1970s increased from 21.1 million to 22.4 million, the percentage of the organized labor force declined from 24.7 percent in 1970 to 20.9 percent in 1980. Since most of the growth of unions occurred in the public sector, the position of organized labor in the private sector has deteriorated more rapidly than the data would otherwise indicate.

The continuing failure of unions to attract employees into membership stems largely from a failure to adapt to the changing values brought about by the transition from a product to a service economy. Paul Shay, President of Corporations for SRI International, notes that in today's work force there are new values - people who do not want more things and who do not want loyalty to institutions; they are not joining unions and they are not responding to carrots and sticks; they want to be creative and challenged. This failure to adapt to changing values, changes in government regulations and statutes affecting certain key industries such as transportation and communications, and the shift of key labor-management issues from union-management bargaining tables to those in legislative halls, is contributing considerably to the decline of unions.

Today's entrant into the work force, generally speaking, is better educated and more articulate than have been his predecessors. He has not been associated with the struggles of his forefathers to gain equities and work-place dignities that have made unions attractive and powerful. By and large, the entrant is the product of an affluent society, with a set of values and goals not necessarily attuned to wages, hours of work, and working conditions. By the nature of his background and training, he is more inquisitive and more interested in position satisfactions and career opportunities than in the automatic wage progression and job security through length of service offered by union contracts. Further, as a group, the approximately 50 percent of women in the work force are not attracted to unions. Less than one in four females who enter the work force find union programs sufficiently attractive or necessary to command membership.

If the unions are to continue as a factor in the new economy they must broaden their perspective and develop strategies and programs that will attract white collar workers, female and ethnic workers, and employees involved in the new technology. Policies must be developed that appeal to highly educated and skilled employees whose needs differ greatly from those employed in traditional industrial collective bargaining unit occupations.

Union policies and collective bargaining programs must address these differences. Union policies must recognize that high technology employees are more interested in career development and mobilization than in job longevity and security. Worker participation in the organization of work, as well as intellectual fulfillment, educational and training opportunities to protect against obsolesence, scholarships, sabbaticals, and like items could be key ingredients of these programs.

Union-sponsored training programs could fill this need and be a key element to organization both of nonunion workers and those entering the workforce. Union organizations now employ highly qualified attorneys, actuaries, accountants, statisticians, benefit specialists, and other professionals. There appears to be no reason why unions could not employ equally well-qualified high-technology specialists and educators to develop educational and training centers that would attract workers into membership. Moreover, since unions are in the marketplace, such union-sponsored centers could provide the flexibility not found in traditional schools but vitally necessary to keep pace with the changing needs of the marketplace.

Policies that recognize the increasing importance of women in the work place could also enhance labor's organizational strength. Union-sponsored banking and financial services, physical fitness programs, and subsidized day care centers are examples of nontraditional benefits that could provide such appeal.

Regulatory Changes - The Motor Freight Experience

Regulatory changes affecting key pattern-setting industries such as transportation and communications have further accelerated the decline in union membership and power. The motor freight industry, long the source of Teamster strength and leadership, is an outstanding example of the impact of regulatory change upon union organization and influence.

Prior to the passage of the Motor Carrier Reform Act of 1980, it was almost axiomatic that anything transported by truck was carried by a vehicle driven by a Teamster-represented driver. Freight rates were carefully regulated and entry into the trucking industry and the right to move freight between certain points was acquired through grant of authority by the Interstate Commerce Commission, or by purchase from a carrier holding the desired authority or rights. Teamster representation of employees of trucking companies was virtually 100 percent. This combination of limited entry and minimal rate or price competition allowed unreasonable demands to be met without impact on profitability. It led to the National Master Freight Agreement, which became a pattern for union and nonunion companies alike. It also bred unions that became bloated, top heavy, bureaucratized, corrupt, and wasteful.

As noted, prior to deregulation of the industry, operating rights were certified by the Interstate Commerce Commission upon a showing that additional service was or would be required by public convenience and necessity. Carriers were obligated to offer nondiscriminatory service at regulated rates. These requirements provided significant protection from open entry and excessive competition, and in reliance thereon, carriers made substantial investments in such rights. These operating rights, which in some cases represented as much as 50 percent or more of the total book value of a company, became virtually worthless compared with their previous value as a result of the deregulation of the industry. Changes in entry requirements encouraged the growth of private and nonunion carriers, and the ability to adjust rates within broad parameters resulted in price cutting favoring private and nonunion carriers. These changes, plus the loss of assets, seriously jeopardized the ability of many carriers to continue operations and to employ union members.

Reexamination of Policies

Deregulation of the industry opened the door for nonunion operations and seriously eroded the Teamsters' representation monopoly in the motor freight segment of the transportation industry. An attempt to reopen the agreement and to renegotiate certain onerous contractual work restrictions and costly benefits was initiated by management. Although some receptivity to this proposal was exhibited by the union, political pressures by dissidents caused the proposal to be aborted.

Faced with the inability of the Teamsters to organize new entrants into the industry, the continued loss of business and profits through rate cutting, and an inability to increase productivity because allowable hours of work, truck and trailer size and load limits, and speed and travel distances remained statutorily controlled, individual managements began a program of self-help. The elements of the program, which essentially encompassed "double breasted" operations, merger, liquidation, bankruptcy, and concession bargaining are very much a part of the contemporary scene in today's labor-management relationships.

Double Breasted Operations

"Double breasted" is the term applied to an organization that operates as both union and nonunion through two separate, independent organizations. The term and practice, which found their origin in the construction industry, have blossomed and expanded into other industries primarily as a means of getting out from under restrictive work practices, jurisdictional disputes, and subcontracting clauses. The eased entry requirements into the trucking industry made this an attractive method for established firms to meet the rate cutting and other competitive labor cost advantages of the new nonunion carriers entering the trucking industry. Many carriers, rather than establishing a separate independent company, simply liquidated their assets, secured new operating rights, and formed a new company.

Pan American World Airways' recent attempt to establish a holding company, called Pan American Corporation, is a current example of the impact of double breasted operations upon labor-management relationships and policies. This attempt has been vigorously opposed by Pan American unions. The unions, which hold about 10 million shares, or 9.7 percent of Pan American stock as a result of bargained labor contract concessions and productivity increases, are concerned that the holding company will be used to set up a second nonunion airline which would be used to cut Pan American labor costs.

Recent actions by Frontier Holding, Incorporated, in setting up Frontier Horizon, a non-union airline which pays its workers about one-third less than its unionized Frontier Airline Company, and by Transamerica in setting up non-union charter airlines with substantially lower costs than existing airlines, give credence to the concern of the Pan American unions.

Bankruptcy

In addition to "double breasted" operations, increasing resort to the bankruptcy court as a means of voiding union contracts is of major significance to current labor-management relationships.

This accelerated resort to bankruptcy proceedings by troubled companies stems largely from a recent unanimous decision by the Supreme Court in the **Bildisco** case. The decision holds that an employer who filed for reorganization under Chapter 11 of the Bankruptcy Code may obtain a "rejection" of its collective bargaining agreement and may unilaterally alter the terms of that agreement during the time between the filing for bankruptcy and the permission of the bankruptcy court to reject the union contract. Although this route to relief from union contract provisions has been made highly visible by the Supreme Court ruling as well as through bankruptcy filings by major employers such as Continental Airlines, it should not be regarded by employers as a blank check to modify the agreement or to obtain approval of rejection of the labor contract.

Bankruptcy proceedings do not obviate the duty to bargain and to avoid labor strife. Such proceedings do encourage unions to discuss meaningful economic relief when an employer is in financial distress. An employer may reject a union contract only after reasonable efforts to negotiate a contract modification have been made. The bankruptcy court steps in only if the parties are unable to agree, and contract rejection is permitted only upon a showing that the contract is burdensome and that a "careful" balancing of the equities favor its rejection.

The requirement that labor and management make a reasonable effort to negotiate a voluntary modification and that the bankruptcy court balance the equities should provide a healthy incentive to the parties to resolve their differences in a traditional manner and, more importantly, should curtail the ability of bankruptcy courts to permit summary rejection of collective bargaining contracts. Strict adherence to these requirements should serve to protect the rights of the employees.

Despite all the attention bankruptcy proceedings are receiving in today's labor-management scene, it is highly unlikely that bankruptcy proceedings present a practical means of union contract elimination and avoidance, for the following reasons:

1) The vast majority of unionized employers are not in the sort of financial condition for which bankruptcy presents a viable option.

2) The Supreme Court decision does not limit labor's use of the strike weapon against a recalcitrant company. This is true notwithstanding the provisions

of the Bankruptcy Code that prohibits all attempts outside the court to enforce claims against the debtor.

3) A union whose contract has been rejected has a claim against the company for damages as does any other contract creditor.

4) There is still a substantial stigma attached to filing for bankruptcy in terms of a company's credit rating, customer and supplier relationships, and opinions of present and potential investors.

5) Bankruptcy involves a substantial amount of expense and restricts the freedom of management to make major business decisions unilaterally. In essence, the bankruptcy judge becomes the chief executive officer.

In light of all these restrictions, it can hardly be maintained that bankruptcy is a panacea for employers or a thinly disguised union-busting technique.

Collective Bargaining

The larger question is whether bankruptcy proceedings, liquidations, and "double breasted" operations portend a trend away from collective bargaining as we now know it. Does "concession bargaining," in which unions make concessions to employers, and the widespread perception that the power of organized labor is declining, signal a new era in American labor relations? This year's automotive bargaining could provide an answer to these questions.

The 1984 automotive contract will be the first major test of whether United States industry can keep its labor costs under control during an expansionary boom, and whether or not it can supply the initiative and creativeness necessary to provide the flexibility that international competition and the new technology demand.

Fortune magazine terms the negotiations the "labor showdown of the decade." Certainly automotive bargaining results will be a bellwether for other major industries, such as rubber and steel, which will bargain in 1985 and 1986. Owen Bieber, president of the United Auto Workers, in a February 1984 speech to a joint labor-management public conference in Phoenix, Arizona, stated that while the future of collective bargaining is in doubt, the outlook for the automotive industry is good. He noted that record profits exist, technological advances have and are being made, productivity is rising, and more work will be done with fewer workers.

Excerpts from Mr. Bieber's speech underscored these points with respect to the United Auto Workers' automotive bargaining program:

> We'll see auto companies using foreign sourcing. What will we do? We intend to do everything possible to slash the use of overtime. The number of overtime hours worked in auto would have resulted in employment for 95,000 people. It is being used now to avoid recalls, and we intend to face this at the bargaining table.

> The UAW is ready for progress in 1984. We further intend to seek new training and retraining programs.... We will go after this issue in 1984. Workers must not replace and displace with automation. They must be trained and retrained when new equipment is introduced. Management and labor must work together in this area. We at the United Auto Workers must control outsourcing.
>
> We are uncertain about our wage and benefit demands in 1984. We do know that cost of living adjustments are a must. We further believe that workers deserve a share of the profits. Profit sharing must continue.
>
> In the area of health care costs are out of control. The company wants to penalize workers through a co-pay and deductions system. This will not solve the problem since it just transfers the cost to the workers. The UAW will not allow co-pay and deductions at Ford and General Motors.

The position of automotive industry management, as indicated by a General Motors in-house document recently released to the press, is the polar opposite of positions expressed by Mr. Bieber. The General Motors "wish list" includes hefty job cuts, the permanent elimination of both the cost-of-living adjustment clause (COLA) and the guaranteed 3 percent annual wage increase, a two-tier wage structure providing lower pay for newly hired workers, and larger employee contributions toward the soaring costs of health care.

Observers close to the industry anticipate management proposals will seek to increase productivity through union concessions on restrictive work rules and through more flexibility in work assignments and production scheduling. The quid pro quo for changes would be an expansion of profit sharing, employee stock ownership, income guarantee plans, and union-management cooperation and participation in work-place decisions. Company-paid job retraining programs also appear to be high on the list of both union and management. Union efforts to provide job protection by way of retraining will be intensified both at the bargaining table and in Congress.

The key to the success or failure of automotive and other important negotiations in 1984 and succeeding years will be measured by the ability of labor and management to develop nontraditional solutions to bargaining problems. Wage formulas, cost of living improvements, and regular wage increases appear to be a thing of the past. The options unions have today are to sacrifice guaranteed pay and automatic benefits for the job security of those already employed or for a piece of the action. Stock ownership, profit sharing, and some degree of influence on management responsibility such as sitting on company boards of directors and influencing decisions are examples of "pieces of the action."

Traditional labor contract provisions and wage patterns must give way to more flexible and innovative agreements that recognize the new economic realities of global competition, technological displacement, and high operational costs. Bargaining goals should be developed that link wages to profitability and deemphasize automatic wages because of inflation. Awards to individuals should be maximized. Other realistically achievable goals could require workers to invest part of their earnings in the company and to increase contributions to health care, retirement, and other benefit funds in exchange for profit sharing and other forms of income security programs.

There is a fundamental need to develop a system of bargaining that is not crisis oriented and that encourages problem solving during the term of the contract and prior to established bargaining periods. Procedures which provide for the timely resolution of problems that occur during the life of the collective bargaining agreement are sorely needed. Labor-management committees or participation teams can, for example, provide the understanding necessary for a cooperative relationship and increased productivity. The sharing of information can modify attitudes, minimize adversarial relationships, and result in creative and positive policy and practice modifications.

Management

As indicated, today's operating environment is different from the operating environment of the past and will be still different in the future. Today's managers must be prepared to face a participation-minded work force fragmented by race, sex, age, and with different attitudes, motivations, and values.

To cope with this change, management skills must be further developed and the structure, function, role, and style of management must change. The new economy demands practices which emphasize information availability, and human resource potential. Collaborative team-oriented approaches, positive incentives, and material rewards can be positive responses to the demand for new practices.

Most importantly, a management structure that provides for flexibility and that allows for worker participation in changes vital to an organization's future survival and success must be developed. Vitality, vision, and the ability to communicate organization goals are key ingredients of the flexibility required. Hierarchies must become more flexible and lines of communication must be open to and from all levels of the organization. The creation of a work environment in which workers are involved and feel good about it is probably management's greatest challenge.

Public Policy

Industrial competitiveness is crucial to our development and growth. While there is considerable debate involving governmental trading and investment policies, it is clear that the major goal of United States labor-management policies is the creation of a climate that will support the nation's ability to compete in a global economy. Such policies should encourage technological innovation and should provide educational and training support to upgrade and utilize the skills of the work force.

Education has become a market commodity and governmental assistance to retool the educational system to meet the demands of today's labor market is required. Educational requirements must be reexamined on a continuing basis to ensure qualifications relevant to job opportunities. Government has a vital self-interest in providing information and policy support for the flexibility needed by educational institutions to keep pace with change. Government support in the education of America's work force is justified.

The legitimacy of unions must continue to be recognized. Labor-management partnerships and the movement to cooperative relationships must be endorsed as national labor policy. Collaborative processes, mediation, arbitration, and other dispute settlement procedures must be mandated.

Larry J. Kimbell

8

Industrial Policy: A Critical Review of Several Suggestions

Introduction

A variety of critics of the American economy have concluded that the U.S. government should adopt a formal "industrial policy." This phrase means different things to different people, but one thing it always means is that the government should stop preaching laissez faire or free market economics, which it often asserts it does not practice anyway, and start a new phase of economic policy, with government, business, and labor working cooperatively to restore productivity, growth and international competitiveness.

New and formal institutional processes are usually proposed for the cooperative development of industrial policy, with the promise that these new consensus-building processes will lead to more rational choices as to which industries should expand and which should contract. The output, employment, and investment decisions regarding the level of efficiency and location of each of these activities by various industries would obviously be influenced more consciously and explicitly by government policy. But making policy decisions more formally and openly does not necessarily mean more government "intrusion" than under our current ad hoc industrial policy, it is argued, since government policy already influences these decisions in innumerable ways.

Japan is commonly cited with admiration as the best available paradigm for successful industrial policy. Rapid growth in productivity and real wages achieved by hard-working, loyal employees who are secure in their jobs and not afraid of innovation; aggressive international export policies; conscious governmental support for "high tech" winning industries; and government funding to support transitional adjustments for declining industries and regions are hailed as signs of Japan's genius for using industrial policy effectively.

The proponents of industrial policy all share an emphasis on the potential benefits of cooperative decision making, but they differ significantly in their diagnoses of the problems facing the U.S. economy and in the specific solutions they recommend; accordingly, we will proceed by first presenting the main themes of each of the authors and then critically examining the limitations and strengths of their arguments before going on to the next perspective.

Major Contributions to the Industrial Policy Debate

(The following contributors are listed alphabetically by last name of the lead author.)

1. **The De-industrialization of America: Plant Closings, Community Abandonment, and the Dismantling of Basic Industry,** by Barry Bluestone and Bennett Harrison. Basic Books: New York, 1982.

2. **The DRI Report on U.S. Manufacturing Industries,** by Otto Eckstein, Christopher Caton, Roger Brinner, and Peter Duprey. McGraw-Hill Book Company: New York, 1984. This book develops views similar to those I present to critique the Bluestone and Harris thesis, but its authors remain more pessimistic about the difficulties of manufacturing than I am.

3. **Minding America's Business: The Decline and Rise of the American Economy,** by Ira C. Magaziner and Robert B. Reich. Vintage Books: New York, 1983. See also **The Next American Frontier,** by Robert B. Reich. Penguin Books: Middlesex, England, 1983. These are two of the most active proponents of industrial policy and were highly influential with all three leading Democratic presidential primary contenders. Magaziner has also been active in proposing that the state of Rhode Island adopt a "greenhouse compact" which would promote high-tech relocation to that state.

4. **The M-Form Society,** by William Ouchi. Addison-Wesley Publishing Company: Reading, 1984.

5. **The Twenty-Year Century: Essays on Economics and Public Finance**, by Felix G. Rohatyn. Random House: New York, 1983.

6. **The Zero-Sum Society: Distribution and the Possibilities of Change**, by Lester C. Thurow. Penguin Books: Middlesex, England, 1980. Only tangentially related to industrial policy; narrowly conceived by advocate of government intervention to accelerate reallocations while ameliorating their impacts.

Three of the major contributors listed above are selected for detailed discussion and review because they present the purest strands of thinking on three topics in the general debate. These three arguments (outlined below) also span most of the issues raised by others in the literature.

1. **The deindustrialization thesis, as developed by Barry Bluestone and Bennett Harrison.**

The central theme is that basic industry - manufacturing, in particular - is in serious trouble. Investment is inadequate; productivity is chronically weak; job losses will be permanent. The causes of deindustrialization go far beyond (1) the normal, cyclic forces that would depress manufacturing output temporarily, or (2) the high value of the dollar, which would also make foreign goods temporarily more attractive. The critique of Bluestone and Harrison is from a radical-democratic-socialistic perspective and is somewhat more extreme than the critiques by most other industrial policy advocates. Nevertheless, almost all proponents of industrial policy, such as two prominent liberal Democratic advisers, Ira C. Magaziner and Robert B. Reich, also share the view that a serious secular depression is eroding the capacity of America's basic industries. My critique of Bluestone and Harrison will, therefore, be relevant to most other advocates of industrial policy.

2. **The need for new government credit market interventions, a thesis developed by probably its most persuasive advocate, investment banker Felix G. Rohatyn.**

Government leverage is required to restructure loans in distressed industries (and local governments in depressed regions) as well as internationally in the Third World. Private credit markets cannot apply the tough negotiating pressures needed to force labor to accept new realities. With temporary government assistance, many companies and industries can regain financial viability, so the government loans, if carefully targeted by a tripartite board composed of business, labor and government representatives, need not lead to permanent subsidies.

3. **The Japanese-cooperative-paradigm thesis, as developed by William Ouchi.**

Most advocates of industrial policy cite with great admiration the successes of Japan in creating rapid productivity gains, associated rapid increases in real wage gains, industrial tranquility, and enviable export-market penetration throughout the world. These achievements are asserted to be closely related to the active government policies orchestrated by the Ministry of International Trade and Industry (MITI). Ouchi presents one of the most focused and well-informed developments of the Japanese-cooperative-paradigm thesis.

Deindustrialization - The Radical-Democratic-Socialist Critique Developed by Bluestone and Harrison

Barry Bluestone is Professor of Economics and Director of the Social Welfare Research Institute at Boston College. Bennett Harrison is Professor of Political Economy and Planning at the Massachusetts Institute of Technology.

Bluestone and Harrison define "deindustrialization" in the following manner:

> Underlying the high rates of unemployment, the sluggish growth in the domestic economy, and the failure to successfully compete in the international market is the de-industrialization of America. By **de-industrialization** is meant a widespread, systematic disinvestment in the nation's basic productive capacity. (p. 6)

Bluestone and Harrison chronicle a large number of individual plant closings over the past decade: thirteen Chrysler plants, five Ford plants, seven General Motors plants, fourteen U.S. Steel plants, eleven Firestone plants, etc. Since they seem to appreciate the fundamental weakness of anecdotal enumeration - no matter how long the recitation there is risk of being completely unrepresentative - they create a statistic to measure the balance of forces affecting job growth. Their concept is "net job change," the balance of jobs "created" by new plant openings and, for regions, inmigration, less jobs "destroyed" by plants shutting down, and, for regions, outmigration. They conclude that for every 110 jobs created by new plants, there were 100 jobs destroyed by plants shut down. The "frostbelt" was hardest hit: "...in every state of the Northeast, private industry destroyed more jobs through plant closings than it created through new openings." (p. 31)

Sunbelt states, however, were not immune. They summarize the California situation as follows:

> None was more unprepared for such a shock than the state of California. ...From South Gate to Hayward to Sacramento, across the state as a whole, in the single year 1980, at least 150 major plants closed their doors permanently, displacing more than 37,000 workers. The problem has taken on epidemic proportions, affecting industries as varied as automobiles and trucks, rubber, steel, textiles, lumber, food processing, and housewares. (p. 40)

Capital is too mobile, according to their critique. High technology has expanded the range of feasible and effective management, making capital even more mobile than it was before. This means that communities are threatened by sudden and unexpected plant closings, thus forcing local government authorities into granting tax concessions that are collectively useless but result in less social protection. Capital mobility and a weakened social safety net make workers face greater job insecurity, but profits are raised by keeping wages low and unions out.

Their critique of the ills of our economy leads them to recommend:

1. Widen the social safety net instead of reducing it by expanding eligibility and increasing benefits. Higher costs should be paid for by more progressive personal income taxes and higher corporate taxes.

2. Pass plant closing legislation which would (a) mandate advance notice to workers and communities affected; (b) provide income maintenance and retraining benefits to laid-off employees; and (c) make payments to local municipalities to pay for redevelopment purposes.

3. Encourage much greater worker participation through producer cooperatives, capital for worker buyouts of plants threatened to be closed, and support for greater employee stock ownership plans.

The primary answer to this radical critique by Bluestone and Harrison is that their fundamental premise - that America is indeed "deindustrializing" - is simply factually wrong. Once business cycle developments are properly accounted for, the recent performance of the U.S. economy is seen as exceptionally strong, not, as they would have us believe, so weak that the end of capitalism might be at hand.

Recent Expansion Has Been Unusually Strong, Not Unusually Weak

The post-World War II business cycle history of the U.S. economy is compactly described in Tables 1 and 2. The columns are defined by

Table 1. Output, Manhours, Productivity, Wage Compensation and Unit Labor Costs During Postwar Business Cycle Expansions
(Average Annual Percent Change)

	1949-53	1954-57	1958-60	1961-69	1970-73	1975-80	1980-81	1982-84
Output:								
Nonfarm	7.4	4.5	6.4	4.9	6.1	4.8	4.1	9.1
Manuf.	11.5	4.4	9.3	6.2	8.7	5.9	5.2	15.9
Durables	15.8	4.8	10.8	7.1	9.6	6.4	5.8	19.8
Nondurables	5.1	4.0	6.8	5.0	7.3	5.1	4.3	10.6
Manhours:								
Nonfarm	3.9	2.3	2.8	2.2	3.1	3.5	1.5	5.2
Manuf.	7.7	2.2	4.0	2.8	3.8	2.9	0.6	8.4
Durables	12.2	3.1	5.3	3.6	5.3	3.3	0.9	10.8
Nondurables	2.4	0.9	2.4	1.7	1.6	2.2	0.0	4.9
Productivity:								
Nonfarm	3.4	2.1	3.5	2.6	2.9	1.3	2.7	3.6
Manuf.	3.4	2.3	5.0	3.3	4.7	2.9	4.5	7.0
Durables	3.3	1.5	5.3	3.4	4.1	3.0	4.7	8.1
Nondurables	2.7	3.1	4.4	3.2	5.6	2.8	4.3	5.4
Hourly Wage Compensation:								
Nonfarm	7.1	5.0	4.5	5.1	7.1	8.5	9.7	5.0
Manuf.	7.6	5.4	4.4	4.6	6.4	8.8	9.7	5.0
Durables	8.3	5.4	4.8	4.4	6.4	8.8	9.8	4.9
Nondurables	6.2	4.9	3.8	4.6	6.0	8.6	9.2	4.5
Unit Labor Costs:								
Nonfarm	3.6	2.9	0.9	2.4	4.1	7.0	6.8	1.4
Manuf.	4.1	3.1	-0.4	1.2	1.6	5.7	4.9	-1.8
Durables	5.0	3.8	-0.4	1.0	2.2	5.7	4.8	-2.9
Nondurables	3.4	1.8	-0.5	1.3	0.4	5.7	4.7	-0.8
Real Hourly Wage Compensation:								
Nonfarm	3.4	3.6	3.3	2.4	1.9	0.0	-0.5	1.4
Manuf.	4.0	3.9	3.4	1.9	1.3	0.3	-0.4	1.4
Durables	4.6	4.0	3.6	1.7	1.3	0.3	-0.3	1.2
Nondurables	2.5	3.5	2.6	1.9	0.9	0.1	-0.8	1.0

Table 2. Output, Manhours, Productivity, Wage Compensation and Unit Labor Costs During Postwar Business Cycle Contractions
(Average Annual Percent Change)

	1948-49	1953-54	1957-58	1960-61	1969-70	1973-75	1980	1981-82
Output:								
Nonfarm	-4.4	-4.2	-5.4	-2.4	-1.8	-5.9	-11.0	-3.7
Manuf.	-8.3	-9.5	-14.7	-9.5	-7.5	-13.1	-21.1	-8.2
Durables	-14.2	-13.0	-21.1	-14.0	-11.9	-14.0	-24.5	-11.1
Nondurables	0.8	-3.2	-3.9	-2.3	-0.9	-11.6	-15.9	-3.8
Manhours:								
Nonfarm	-4.9	-4.7	-6.0	-2.3	-2.7	-4.0	-7.8	-3.5
Manuf.	-9.7	-10.6	-11.0	-7.3	-9.1	-9.9	-15.0	-9.5
Durables	-15.5	-13.7	-15.0	-10.2	-12.3	-10.1	-19.2	-12.3
Nondurables	-2.9	-6.2	-5.2	-3.2	-4.4	-9.5	-7.6	-5.1
Productivity:								
Nonfarm	0.6	0.5	0.6	0.0	1.0	-2.1	-3.6	-0.3
Manuf.	1.7	1.3	-4.4	-2.3	1.6	-3.6	-7.2	1.4
Durables	1.2	0.9	-7.2	-4.4	0.5	-4.4	-6.6	1.4
Nondurables	3.7	3.2	1.3	1.0	3.7	-2.3	-8.9	1.4
Hourly Wage Compensation:								
Nonfarm	1.0	3.4	3.8	2.5	6.8	10.8	11.6	7.2
Manuf.	1.0	4.5	4.1	3.0	6.5	13.4	14.3	7.7
Durables	0.5	5.0	4.6	2.7	6.9	13.4	14.7	7.5
Nondurables	1.9	5.6	4.1	3.9	7.0	13.7	15.0	8.9
Unit Labor Costs:								
Nonfarm	0.3	2.7	3.0	2.9	5.7	13.2	15.6	7.5
Manuf.	-0.7	3.2	8.6	5.2	4.9	17.6	23.1	6.2
Durables	-1.0	3.9	12.8	7.5	6.2	18.5	22.9	6.0
Nondurables	-1.5	1.9	3.2	2.7	3.2	16.5	25.9	7.4
Real Hourly Wage Compensation:								
Nonfarm	3.1	2.5	0.4	1.2	1.0	-0.5	-2.1	2.2
Manuf.	3.2	3.8	0.6	1.3	0.8	1.9	-0.4	2.6
Durables	2.6	3.9	1.2	1.2	1.1	1.7	0.4	2.5
Nondurables	4.5	4.6	0.9	2.1	1.2	2.0	0.0	3.7

periods of expansion, in Table 1, and periods of contraction (or recession) in Table 2. The rows cover the nonfarm business sector, which can be interpreted as the appropriate indicator for the general economy ("cleaned up" by eliminating housing and farming activities), the manufacturing sector, and its subdivision into durable goods and nondurable goods.

Deindustrialization, if it were eroding our basic industrial capacity, would show up as an unusually slow recovery in output, employment, and productivity in the general economy, but even more clearly in manufacturing and durable goods industries.

The growth of output and the growth of manhours in the nonfarm sector, as well as in the manufacturing sectors, has been about as strong as during any completed business cycle expansion of the post-World War II period. More strikingly, the growth of productivity in manufacturing and durable goods manufacturing sectors is running at rates far surpassing prior completed expansions.

Disinflationary monetary policy has worked to lower the average annual rate of growth of hourly wages to only 4.9 percent from the last quarter of 1982 to the first quarter of 1984. When combined with an average annual rate of growth of productivity of 8.1 percent during this period, the rate of decline in unit labor costs has been 2.9 percent - a rate dramatically lower than any seen in the period covered. Indeed, the 1958-60 expansion is the only other time unit labor costs dropped during a completed expansion period.

The expansion currently under way is not complete, of course, and economic performance normally is best in the early phases. Nevertheless, the initial expansion has been so exceptionally strong, whether measured by the growth of output, hours, or productivity, that when the current expansion is over, it is very likely to be one of the best on record.

How Do You Spell Disinflation: P-A-I-N

Are there unusually perverse signs in the earlier periods? Yes, indeed, there are. But the extraordinary thing one notices is not in the body of Table 2, which shows normal behavior during recent recessions. The unusual evidence lies in the column headings. The last two recession periods shown in the column headings of Table 2 include a brief but sharp recession compressed entirely into the first half of 1980, followed by the recession of 1981-82, a deliberately triggered recession that lasted longer than any other recession since the Great Depression. Expansions during the post-World War II period were never as short as the twelve-month "recovery" sandwiched between these recessions. In fact, using the index of industrial production as a guide, one can argue that the disinflation period ran intermittently from early 1979 through late 1982.

We Choose Terrible Economic Performance in 1980-1982 over the Alternative

We effectively choose recessions to stop inflation. Not surprisingly, few policy makers will actually acknowledge, even today, that this exceptional, long, painful period of economic decline was preferred over the alternative of still greater acceleration of inflation.

Perhaps two recessions were worth the benefits of dramatically lower inflation, perhaps not. The rate of unemployment of the labor force hit 11 percent, a postwar record, and capacity utilization in manufacturing dropped below 70 percent, also a postwar record. But whether disinflation cost too much or not, the relevant point is that stopping an inflation that had been building for fifteen years was likely to stop economic growth in general, and manufacturing output growth especially. Notice also that monetary policy authorities choose to fight inflation first and worry about unemployment of labor and capital second. In this crucial sense, the recent bad performance in the U.S. economy was not due to "losing our competitive edge" or "deindustrialization." We could have kept real growth going for a while longer, but only at the clear risk of losing control of inflation to an extent never witnessed in U.S. peacetime history.

All advocates of industrial policy cite recent poor economic performance as evidence for their case. To be persuasive, however, they must: (1) blame bad industrial policy for inflation; or (2) argue that industrial policy would have permitted us to stop inflation without a recession; or (3) predict that the current recovery will be exceptionally slow. Neither of the first two propositions is credible, and the third is growing increasingly unlikely.

A graphic presentation of the business cycle data in Tables 1 and 2 is provided in Figures 1 and 2. Figure 1 shows the four-quarter percent change of output in the nonfarm business sector in the dotted line, and the similar change in the output of the durable goods manufacturing sector in the solid line. The recent growth of nearly 21 percent in durable goods manufacturing is unrivaled in the period since 1967. If data were only available through 1982, however, one could wrongly conclude that a secular downward trend was operating, and that recovery would be weak at best. Figure 2 is similar except that it shows four-quarter percent changes in productivity in the nonfarm business and durable goods manufacturing sectors in the dotted line and solid line, respectively. The recovery in productivity in durable goods manufacturing has been one of the strongest on record.

International Comparisons Do Not Support the Deindustrialization Theory

A thorough rebuttal to the international aspects of the deindustrialization theory has been presented by Robert Z. Lawrence ("The Myth of U.S. Deindustrialization," **Challenge,** Vol. 26, No. 5 (Nov/Dec 1983), pp. 12-21). He shows that the relative performance of the U.S. economy, and manufacturing in particular, improved during the period 1973-80. The United States was weak compared with Japan during the period 1960-73, when Japan was able to grow at double-digit compound rates for more than a decade. The OPEC crude-oil price shocks, global recessions, and disinflation policies produced a far more dramatic slowing in Japan's growth than in the growth of the United States, United Kingdom, Germany, or France.

Several other international comparisons by Lawrence are quite revealing in view of the al-

Figure 1

Output in the Nonfarm Business Sector
(dotted line) and Output in the Durable Goods
Manufacturing Sector (solid line)
(four-quarter percent change)

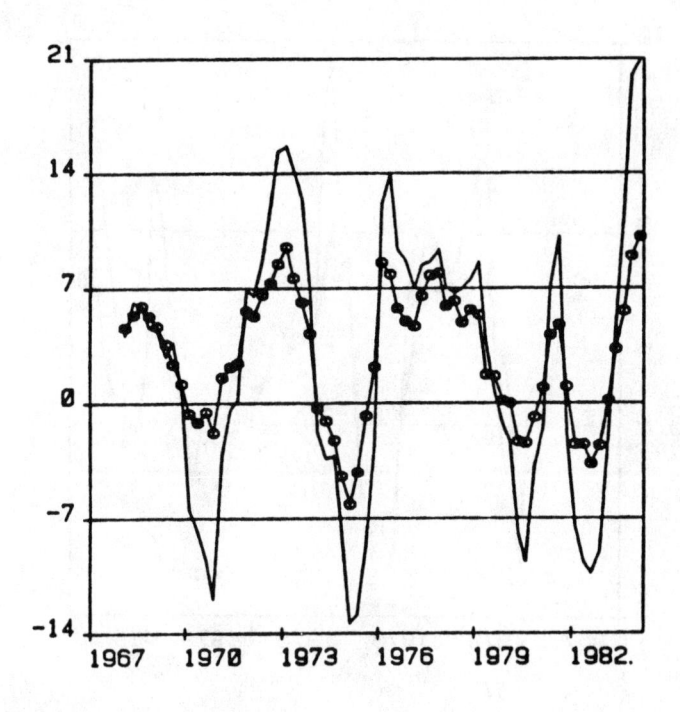

Figure 2

Productivity in the Nonfarm Business Sector (dotted line) and Productivity in the Durable Goods Manufacturing Sector (solid line) (four-quarter Percent Change)

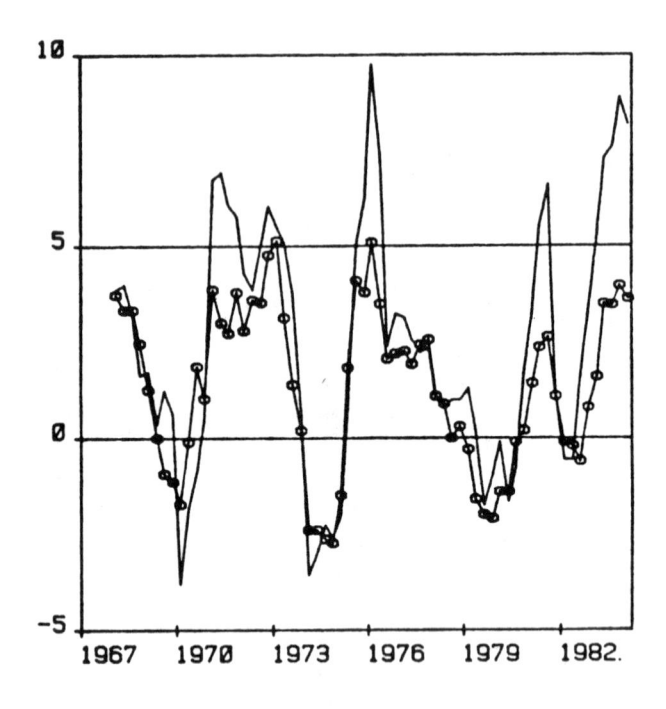

leged U.S. deindustrialization:

- Employment in manufacturing grew more rapidly in the United States from 1973 to 1980 than in any other major industrial country, including Japan.

- In 1977, spending on research and development in U.S. manufacturing was equal to about 6.5 percent of the domestic U.S. output, significantly greater than the 3.7, 5.0, and 4.0 percents spent by Japan, the United Kingdom, and Germany, respectively.

- U.S. output growth from 1973 to 1980 for food, textiles, apparel, chemicals, glass, and fabricated metals products was more rapid than that of either Germany or Japan.

Regional Evidence is Unpersuasive as Well

The regional evidence cited by Bluestone and Harrison is also highly dependent on the years selected. Their lamentations for California, cited above, are completely misplaced. From 1978, before the second OPEC price shock and the disinflation pain, until 1984, California will add over one million additional jobs, a gain in excess of 10 percent. Manufacturing will add about 150,000 more jobs. The vigorous recovery under way now has made up for the extended period of "bump and grind" from 1979 through 1982.

To summarize: First, consciously adopted monetary policies slowed and almost stopped inflation. In the process, these policies caused great pain as they brought on two recessions back-to-back. As usual, these recessions slowed manufacturing output by a much greater percentage than the general economy. Add the fact that the economy was adjusting to two unprecedented crude oil price shocks, and bad economic performance from 1973 to 1982 was entirely to be expected.

If deindustrialization were an ongoing process, (perhaps masked by the recessions), it should emerge in a lackluster recovery after inflation is slowed. But, even though the recovery from disinflation policies is not over, recent performance has been exceptionally strong, contrary to the secular deindustrialization theme developed by Bluestone and Harrison.

International comparisons lend further support to the view that U.S. economic performance is no more disappointing than the still more pronounced slowdown suffered in Japan and especially in Europe.

The radicals' critique may have had wider appeal when their book was first published in 1982, in the midst of the longest recession of the postwar era. Their long recitation of the real traumas caused by plant closings does and should attract our sympathy for people who lost their jobs and may not ever be reemployed in jobs with comparable wages. But their facts are wrong, their diagnosis is not persuasive, and they fail utterly to establish a credible basis for their version of "industrial policy," not to mention their implied call for more radical change in our capitalist system.

Negotiating Leverage Through Financial Incentives - the Rohatyn Version of Industrial Policy

Felix G. Rohatyn is a senior partner at the investment banking firm of Lazard Freres. He was chairman of the Municipal Assistance Corporation (MAC), which helped guide New York City through its near-bankrupcty in 1975. His experience with the New York City fiscal crisis convinces him that the private capital markets cannot impose the austerity and other concessions that are sometimes required of workers (and other suppliers, such as bankers) to reach a viable long-term solution to a financial crisis. Government financial leverage, in the form of temporary loans and reschedulings of existing debt payments, can provide the fulcrum for forcing unions, financiers, suppliers, and other involved participants to make concessions that avoid bankruptcy. Eventually, he argues, there need not be any net subsidy, since the loans made during restructuring may be paid back in full.

Rohatyn cites the government guaranteed loans to Lockheed and Chrysler as other successes where reorganization would have been the free market solution, but where government intervention was effective in avoiding the disruption of bankruptcy.

Another area where "free market" solutions are inadequate, according to Rohatyn, is renegotiating the debt burden of the Third World. He argues that the United States must take the lead in an effort to stabilize the world's monetary system and to provide economic breathing room by restructuring much of the Third World's debt. The alternative he sees is not attractive; in his words:

> If mature Western democracies are to become the locomotives to move the rest of the world, the rest of the world has to cooperate, and long-term debt restructuring ought to be the first step. There is a real danger that the unintended result of certain of the IMF's current programs would be populist, anti-American governments emerging in Brazil, Argentina, and other Latin American countries, ultimately including Mexico. That is not an acceptable risk. (p. 19)

"Populist, anti-American governments" is a euphemism, of course, for a Cuban-style communist dictatorship.

The central theme that Rohatyn develops for why the U.S. government should actively intervene in credit market arrangements affecting industries', regions', and nations' policies is that free market solutions, although often efficient, can be unfair, leading to social pressures that are not "politically tolerable."

This "prevent-the-revolution" diagnosis leads Rohatyn to urge the creation of a new credit agency, modeled after the Reconstruction Finance Corporation which was created by President Herbert Hoover in the Depression of the 1930s. It would be guided by a tripartite board made up of business, labor, and government representatives. Help would be available only if: (1) labor accepted reduced wages and relaxed work rules, permitting increased pro-

1. American banks lack enough control over borrowing firms:

   > [W]e prohibit U.S. banks from developing an intimate and even forceful relationship with the companies to which they lend, with the result that they remain at arm's length from their corporate borrowers. At arm's length, no one can manage a long-term financial relationship properly. (p. 65)

2. American banks face great risks in making business loans:

   > Thus neither market, bureaucratic, nor clan governance is possible between borrower and lender. The consequence is that the bank faces great risk in making business loans and thus must charge a higher risk premium or rate of interest and is unwilling to allow a corporate borrower to rise to a debt ratio as high as is commonplace in Japan. (p. 69)

3. American equity markets are dominated by poorly informed or passive investors:

   > Equity markets work well only if the equity owners are well informed about the company. The major equity holders must know the company well, know its executives personally, and be able to provide wise and farsighted guidance to the managers of the company. Our current equity markets do not make this possible. (p. 68)

4. Capital markets are "...vastly imperfect":

Capital markets in the United States are vastly imperfect. They are imperfect because the structures of U.S. law prevent the providers of capital from being well informed and from exercising governance over the users of capital. This happens because those who provide capital are well aware of their inability to be well informed and to protect their interests, and thus withhold capital while simultaneously charging a high-risk premium for the capital they provide....The assertions are strong, but the evidence is compelling. (p. 69)

A Critique of Ouchi's Japanese-Cooperative-Paradigm Thesis

The key features of the Japanese industrial policy system as presented by Ouchi, are:

1. There exists in Japan an extraordinarily sophisticated consensus-developing network, consisting of many firms in industry trade associations, broader aggregations of these trade associations, with the government, through many agencies including but not limited to MITI, interacting almost daily with one another.

2. Firms cooperate closely with their employees, who are represented effectively by "company" unions.

3. The banking system in Japan helps management take a long-term perspective, and our system, in contrast, is very short-sighted.

The Japanese industrial policy system so described by Ouchi is clearly quite different from the American way. This system is also obviously far removed from a system of purely competitive markets and laissez faire government policy.

One clear limitation of Ouchi's suggestions for industrial policy is that changes in our economic organization, law, politics, and, indeed, culture, would be necessary if we were to adopt the Japanese approach.

I can believe that the Japanese system is intensely competitive in its own way, and that it achieves cooperative goals, especially regarding aggressive export promotion, by a closely intertwined set of behaviors on the part of Japanese business, labor, and government. But I am persuaded that transplanting the Japanese social and economic decision-making system to the United States would be difficult and risky.

Most Other Industrial Policy Advocates Wrongly Depict MITI as a Soviet Central Planning Agency

Ouchi is persuasive that most industrial policy advocates who view MITI as the central authority simply do not understand what actually goes on in Japan. Clearly, the actual decision processes are far more sophisticated and flexible than commonly depicted. Thus, he shows persuasively that key Japanese institutions are in an important sense far more democratic than often represented. The more common depiction of "MITI-the-almighty" connotes an all-powerful agency that is not unlike the Soviet central planning agency. Ouchi's careful scholarship refutes this misunderstanding, since he documents the several cases when MITI has failed completely in getting its way.

Ouchi's Japanese-cooperation-paradigm thesis is clearly a major clarification for all who aspire to understand what made Japan successful in international competition.

Ouchi's critique of U.S. capital markets is, as he acknowledges, at odds with prevailing views among finance scholars. Indeed, some of his assertions are contrary to the most carefully researched and established scientific propositions in the field of finance. The counter argument to Ouchi's imperfect American capital market presumption is as follows:

One essential service provided by a reasonably efficient capital market is precisely that most investors need not spend any of their own time learning about the details of the products or financial strategies of the companies in which they invest, since any information they are likely to dig up by themselves lies so close to the surface that it was almost certainly well known, "long before," to a handful of other key, marginal investors.

An efficient market does not remotely require that every investor be informed, and it certainly is bizarre to suggest, as Ouchi does, that equity investors cannot possibly be well informed unless bankers have equity interests in the firms. Aren't any firms successful that are financed entirely through equity? Do bankers have a monopoly on wisdom?

For Ouchi to be persuasive, he must first argue that virtually no American investor has any incentive to be well informed. To top that off, he must then argue that if banks could hold equity interests in firms, then all would be well. Neither argument is persuasive.

In summary, Ouchi's Japanese-cooperative-paradigm thesis should be studied carefully when he describes the sophisticated and flexible institutions which assist MITI to develop a consensus industrial (and international) trade strategy. I am afraid that their system is too interdependent and subtle to be transplanted easily to the United States, but Ouchi's suggestions in this regard are worthy of careful consideration.

APPENDIX

TABLE 1. PART A. SUMMARY OF THE UCLA NATIONAL BUSINESS FORECAST (QUARTERLY DATA)

	1983:2	1983:3	1983:4	1984:1	1984:2	1984:3	1984:4	1985:1	1985:2	1985:3	1985:4
Growth in Monetary Aggregates, Velocity and GNP—% change
Money Supply (M1)	12.1	9.8	4.9	7.4	4.9	6.1	4.6	7.3	5.4	6.1	7.3
Money Supply (M2)	11.0	7.1	8.7	7.0	8.4	9.3	8.3	7.9	7.3	10.2	10.5
Velocity (M1)	1.0	1.5	4.0	5.1	3.2	2.1	2.8	0.2	1.2	1.8	1.8
Velocity (M2)	2.1	4.1	0.3	5.4	-0.2	-0.8	-0.9	-0.4	-0.6	-2.0	-1.1
Gross National Product	13.3	11.5	9.1	12.8	8.2	8.4	7.4	7.5	8.6	8.0	9.3
Real GNP	9.7	7.8	5.0	8.8	4.1	3.8	2.4	1.8	1.2	2.3	2.8
GNP Deflator	3.3	3.8	3.9	3.7	4.0	4.5	4.9	5.6	5.4	5.6	6.3
Interest Rates (%) on:
Treasury Bills	8.4	9.1	8.8	9.2	9.8	9.4	9.3	9.4	9.6	9.4	9.3
Prime Bank Loans	10.5	10.8	11.0	11.1	12.3	12.8	12.5	12.8	12.7	12.4	12.2
New Corporate AAA Bonds	10.8	12.0	12.4	12.9	13.3	13.4	13.6	13.7	13.6	13.2	12.8
Mortgage Commitments	13.0	13.5	13.3	13.1	13.6	14.0	14.0	14.1	14.2	14.3	14.1
Prime Rate Less Inflation	5.9	6.8	8.4	7.5	8.3	8.0	7.7	7.6	7.4	7.0	6.5

250

Federal Fiscal Policy

Effective Federal Tax Rates (%) on:									
Personal Income	13.4	12.4	12.4	12.2	12.3	12.4	12.4	12.8	12.7	12.9
Corporate Profits	29.4	29.1	29.1	29.9	30.1	30.1	30.0	29.9	29.1	30.1
Wages & Salaries (Soc.Sec.)	14.1	14.0	14.0	14.8	14.8	14.5	14.5	14.9	14.8	14.8
Total Federal Purchases—% change										
Current $	0.3	8.8	-6.8	-2.5	48.1	9.4	8.7	9.5	8.9	12.4
Constant $	-2.7	4.5	-8.1	-9.3	42.1	5.2	4.2	4.4	3.8	2.2
Defense Purchases—% change										
Current $	10.7	3.7	10.5	14.1	11.0	10.8	9.3	9.7	9.5	13.3
Constant $	7.5	0.0	7.8	5.7	7.3	6.5	4.8	4.5	4.2	3.1
Other Federal Expenditures—% change										
Transfers to Persons	7.0	-4.0	4.3	2.8	1.1	3.2	4.0	5.4	5.4	5.4
Grants to S&L Gov't	4.3	2.3	-3.8	19.8	13.4	10.8	5.1	5.8	4.8	3.2
Net Interest	18.3	48.5	15.0	13.8	23.8	15.2	13.0	17.8	13.5	12.2
Total Revenues (bil $)	852.8	845.2	657.5	687.4	700.8	714.5	726.0	745.0	758.8	773.4	797.0
as Share (%) of GNP	19.9	19.2	19.1	18.4	19.4	19.4	19.3	19.5	19.5	19.7
Total Expenditures (bil $)	818.7	832.5	847.3	858.3	877.2	890.5	908.8	932.0	950.8	968.2	988.8
as Share (%) of GNP	25.0	24.8	24.7	24.2	24.3	24.2	24.4	24.5	24.5	24.4
Federal Deficit (bil $)	-168.1	-187.3	-189.8	-170.9	-178.6	-175.9	-180.6	-187.0	-192.0	-194.8	-191.8

Table 1. Part A. (con't)

Details of Real GNP—% change

Real GNP	9.7	7.8	5.0	8.8	4.1	3.8	2.4	1.8	1.2	2.3	2.8
Final Sales	8.8	5.1	3.7	3.2	8.7	3.3	2.7	2.4	2.4	2.6	2.9
Consumption	10.0	2.2	6.5	6.9	2.9	2.9	2.6	2.5	2.2	2.1	2.4
Business Fixed Investment	8.0	18.6	27.4	14.7	11.4	7.5	5.0	4.8	4.2	5.5	8.3
Producers Durable Equipment	19.8	22.0	36.5	12.0	11.3	7.9	5.7	5.3	5.0	6.1	6.9
Structures	-14.9	11.1	6.8	21.8	12.0	6.3	3.3	2.8	2.4	3.9	4.9
Residential Construction	78.6	36.0	-6.9	25.8	15.3	-2.9	-3.8	-7.6	-5.7	-1.3	4.9
Exports	-3.2	13.9	-0.3	7.3	8.3	5.7	8.0	5.6	6.0	6.0	5.7
Imports	28.6	18.2	29.4	54.0	10.2	8.7	7.3	4.9	5.0	5.1	5.2
Federal Purchases	-2.7	4.5	-8.1	-9.3	42.1	5.2	4.2	3.5	4.4	3.8	2.2
State & Local Purchases	0.0	4.2	-0.9	2.5	3.2	4.2	3.4	2.4	2.0	2.3	1.4

Billions of 1972 Dollars

Real GNP	1525.1	1553.4	1572.5	1606.0	1622.3	1637.3	1647.1	1654.3	1659.4	1668.8	1680.3
Final Sales	1530.5	1549.7	1563.7	1575.9	1601.6	1614.5	1625.2	1635.1	1644.7	1655.4	1667.1
Inventory Change	-5.4	3.8	8.7	30.1	20.7	22.8	21.9	19.3	14.6	13.4	13.2

TABLE 1. PART B. SUMMARY OF THE UCLA NATIONAL BUSINESS FORECAST (QUARTERLY DATA)

	1983:2	1983:3	1983:4	1984:1	1984:2	1984:3	1984:4	1985:1	1985:2	1985:3	1985:4
Industrial Production and Resource Utilization
Production—% change	18.4	21.8	10.2	11.8	10.4	8.1	2.2	2.8	1.3	1.9	3.1
Capacity Util. Manuf.(%)	73.9	77.4	78.9	80.8	82.8	83.7	83.8	83.7	83.4	83.3	83.4
Real Business Fixed Investment as % of Real GNP	10.7	11.0	11.5	11.8	11.8	11.9	12.0	12.1	12.2	12.3	12.4
Employment (mil)	100.0	101.5	102.5	103.7	104.8	105.8	106.3	106.7	107.1	107.5	107.9
Unemployment Rate (%)	10.1	9.4	8.5	7.9	7.6	7.5	7.4	7.5	7.8	7.7	7.8
Inflation—% change
Consumer Price Index	4.3	4.2	4.4	5.0	4.7	5.4	5.3	5.5	5.8	5.7	5.9
Consumption Deflator	4.8	4.2	2.8	3.6	3.9	4.6	4.8	5.2	5.3	5.5	5.6
GNP Deflator	3.3	3.6	3.9	3.7	4.0	4.5	4.9	5.6	5.4	5.6	6.3
Producers Price Index	0.9	4.2	3.7	3.0	3.9	5.8	5.9	8.0	8.9	8.8	6.8

253

Table 1. Part B. (con't)

Factors Related to Inflation—% change

Nonfarm Business Sector										
Wage Compensation	4.8	3.7	4.5	5.9	5.5	5.9	6.2	7.6	6.4	7.0	7.7
Productivity	7.3	2.3	2.7	2.3	2.5	1.4	1.4	1.5	1.5	1.1	1.3
Unit Labor Costs	-2.8	1.5	1.5	3.8	3.0	4.4	4.7	8.0	4.8	5.9	6.3
Farm Producers Price Index	6.2	10.7	17.7	8.9	-6.2	4.5	4.5	4.8	4.7	4.9	5.1
Natural Gas Deflator	12.4	3.1	-7.4	-0.3	1.4	2.8	3.7	5.7	6.5	7.1	6.7
Imported Crude Oil ($/bbl)	28.57	29.27	29.35	29.00	29.32	29.65	29.97	30.30	30.84	30.98	31.32
New Home Price ($1000)	75.0	77.7	75.9	78.0	78.8	79.8	80.8	82.2	83.7	85.3	87.1

Income, Consumption and Saving—% change

Disposable Income	8.2	11.0	11.0	13.9	8.0	7.7	7.0	8.3	6.7	7.3	8.1
Real Disposable Income	3.5	6.5	8.0	10.1	1.9	2.9	2.1	2.9	1.4	1.7	2.4
Real Consumption	10.0	2.2	6.5	8.9	2.9	2.9	2.8	2.5	2.2	2.1	2.4
Savings Rate (%)	4.0	4.9	5.2	5.8	5.6	5.6	5.5	5.7	5.5	5.4	5.4

Housing and Automobiles—millions of units

| Housing Starts | 1.890 | 1.782 | 1.699 | 1.962 | 1.857 | 1.773 | 1.687 | 1.638 | 1.613 | 1.635 | 1.675 |
| Retail Auto Sales | 9.2 | 9.3 | 9.9 | 10.8 | 10.8 | 10.5 | 10.5 | 10.5 | 10.4 | 10.4 | 10.4 |

Corporate Profits—billions $

Before Taxes	203.3	229.1	228.2	240.6	245.8	250.6	252.1	252.6	252.7	251.6	254.5
After Taxes	127.2	144.1	142.9	148.5	151.5	154.5	155.8	156.1	156.8	157.1	155.9
Retained Earnings	55.2	70.4	67.0	70.2	70.3	71.1	70.3	68.8	67.2	65.6	62.4
S&P 500 Stock Price Index	182.7	185.5	165.7	160.4	160.2	163.2	166.5	168.1	189.0	171.3	174.1

International Trade

Trade Weighted Exchange Rate of											
U.S. Dollar—% change	7.3	10.5	0.9	3.1	3.4	-1.0	-1.0	-2.0	-2.0	-2.0	-2.0
Industrial Production: Major Trading Partners											
Canada—% change	12.3	20.0	12.5	4.7	8.3	3.7	3.3	3.3	2.8	2.7	2.4
Japan—% change	8.4	14.8	9.0	14.0	9.0	8.0	7.0	7.0	7.0	7.0	5.0
OECD Europe—% change	0.0	4.5	5.4	4.7	2.8	3.1	3.9	2.0	2.0	1.5	2.2
Real Exports—% change	-3.2	13.9	-0.3	7.3	8.3	5.7	8.0	5.6	6.0	6.0	5.7
Real Imports—% change	28.6	18.2	29.4	54.0	10.2	8.7	7.3	4.9	5.0	5.1	5.2
Net Exports (bil. 72$)	12.3	11.4	2.8	-10.3	-11.3	-12.6	-13.3	-13.1	-13.0	-12.8	-12.8

TABLE 2. PART A. SUMMARY OF THE UCLA NATIONAL BUSINESS FORECAST (ANNUAL DATA)

	1977	1978	1979	1980	1981	1982	1983	1984	1985	1986
Growth in Monetary Aggregates, Velocity and GNP—% change									
Money Supply (M1)	7.6	8.2	7.7	8.3	7.1	8.6	11.0	6.7	8.0	8.4
Money Supply (M2)	12.7	8.5	8.3	8.0	9.5	9.5	12.6	8.2	8.5	8.8
Velocity (M1)	3.7	4.2	3.8	2.4	4.8	-2.4	-3.0	3.3	1.6	2.4
Velocity (M2)	-1.0	3.9	3.2	0.8	2.6	-5.0	-4.4	1.8	-0.8	0.1
Gross National Product	11.7	12.8	11.7	8.8	12.2	4.0	7.7	10.2	7.7	8.9
Real GNP	5.5	5.0	2.8	-0.3	2.6	-1.9	3.4	6.1	2.3	2.6
GNP Deflator	5.8	7.4	8.7	9.2	9.4	6.0	4.2	3.9	5.2	6.2
Interest Rates (%) on:									
Treasury Bills	5.3	7.2	10.1	11.4	14.0	10.6	8.6	9.4	9.4	8.9
Prime Bank Loans	6.8	9.1	12.7	15.3	18.9	14.9	10.8	12.1	12.5	11.4
New Corporate AAA Bonds	8.1	8.9	9.9	12.5	15.0	13.9	11.6	13.3	13.3	12.1
Mortgage Commitments	9.0	9.7	11.3	14.0	16.7	16.6	13.3	13.7	14.2	13.5
Prime Rate Less Inflation	1.0	1.1	3.2	5.0	11.4	9.9	7.4	7.9	7.1	5.4

Federal Fiscal Policy

Effective Federal Tax Rates (%) on:									
Personal Income	13.0	13.1	13.7	14.0	14.4	14.0	12.9	12.3	12.7	13.8
Corporate Profits	31.8	31.1	29.4	29.9	29.7	28.7	29.1	30.0	29.7	29.9
Wages & Salaries (Soc.Sec.)	12.1	12.4	12.9	12.8	13.7	13.9	14.1	14.6	14.9	15.1
Total Federal Purchases—% change										
Current $	11.0	7.1	9.8	17.0	18.3	12.8	6.3	8.3	12.5	9.3
Constant $	3.8	-0.1	1.8	4.2	3.8	5.8	1.1	4.0	5.9	2.8
Defense Purchases—% change										
Current $	8.0	8.0	11.5	17.3	17.4	16.5	11.8	10.8	11.4	10.4
Constant $	0.7	0.4	2.8	3.9	5.2	7.0	6.9	5.8	4.8	4.1
Other Federal Expenditures—% change										
Transfers to Persons	8.8	7.2	12.7	20.1	14.1	12.0	7.8	2.3	6.5	7.1
Grants to S&L Gov't	10.8	14.4	4.2	10.2	-0.9	-4.5	3.1	8.7	8.2	3.8
Net Interest	8.7	20.8	20.5	28.0	37.0	18.1	13.8	19.8	15.2	11.8
Total Revenues (bil $)	375.2	431.8	483.7	540.9	627.0	617.4	644.8	707.1	768.6	875.0
as Share (%) of GNP	19.8	19.9	20.4	20.5	21.2	20.1	19.5	19.4	19.6	20.5
Total Expenditures (bil $)	421.1	461.1	509.7	602.1	689.2	764.5	826.3	883.2	959.9	1034.2
as Share (%) of GNP	21.9	21.3	21.1	22.9	23.3	24.9	25.0	24.2	24.4	24.2
Federal Deficit (bil $)	-45.9	-29.5	-16.1	-61.3	-62.2	-147.1	-181.6	-176.0	-191.3	-159.2

Table 2. Part A. (con't)

Details of Real GNP—% change

Real GNP	5.5	5.0	2.8	-0.3	2.6	-1.9	3.4	6.1	2.3	2.6
Final Sales	5.1	4.9	3.5	0.5	1.8	-0.7	2.8	4.4	2.9	2.7
Consumption	5.0	4.5	2.7	0.5	2.7	1.4	4.2	4.9	2.5	2.0
Business Fixed Investment	11.7	12.9	7.4	-2.4	5.2	-4.7	1.4	14.7	5.6	8.4
Producers Durable Equipment	15.9	13.8	8.3	-3.1	4.2	-7.5	5.3	16.8	6.2	8.9
Structures	2.4	10.5	10.0	-0.7	7.5	1.8	-6.9	10.0	4.1	5.0
Residential Construction	18.8	2.8	-6.2	-20.3	-6.2	-15.3	39.4	14.6	-3.1	5.2
Exports	2.5	12.2	15.4	8.8	0.4	-7.8	-5.8	5.9	6.0	5.4
Imports	7.4	13.0	8.2	-0.2	7.3	1.4	7.2	25.0	8.2	4.9
Federal Purchases	3.8	-0.1	1.8	4.2	3.8	5.6	1.1	4.0	5.9	2.8
State & Local Purchases	0.2	3.3	1.1	1.0	-1.0	-0.5	0.1	2.3	2.7	1.5

Billions of 1972 Dollars

Real GNP	1369.7	1438.5	1479.4	1475.0	1513.8	1485.4	1535.3	1628.2	1665.7	1708.3
Final Sales	1356.4	1422.5	1472.1	1479.3	1505.3	1494.8	1537.4	1604.3	1650.6	1694.9
Inventory Change	13.3	16.1	7.3	-4.3	8.5	-9.4	-2.1	23.9	15.1	13.4

TABLE 2. PART B. SUMMARY OF THE UCLA NATIONAL BUSINESS FORECAST (ANNUAL DATA)

	1977	1978	1979	1980	1981	1982	1983	1984	1985	1986
Industrial Production and Resource Utilization										
Production—% change	5.9	5.8	4.4	-3.6	2.8	-8.1	6.4	11.6	3.4	2.9
Capacity Util. Manuf.(%)	82.2	84.7	86.0	79.8	79.4	71.1	75.2	82.7	83.4	83.4
Real Business Fixed Investment										
as % of Real GNP	10.2	11.0	11.5	11.2	11.5	11.2	11.0	11.9	12.2	12.7
Employment (mil)	92.0	96.0	98.8	99.3	100.4	99.5	100.8	105.1	107.3	108.9
Unemployment Rate (%)	7.0	6.1	5.9	7.2	7.6	9.7	9.8	7.6	7.6	7.9
Inflation—% change										
Consumer Price Index	6.5	7.6	11.3	13.5	10.3	6.2	3.2	4.7	5.5	6.0
Consumption Deflator	5.8	7.0	9.0	10.2	8.4	5.8	3.9	3.8	5.1	5.8
GNP Deflator	5.8	7.4	8.7	9.2	9.4	6.0	4.2	3.9	5.2	8.2
Producers Price Index	6.1	7.8	12.5	14.1	9.1	2.0	1.3	3.9	6.1	7.1

Table 2. Part B. (con't)

Factors Related to Inflation—% change

Nonfarm Business Sector								
Wage Compensation	7.8	8.8	9.0	10.4	9.7	7.9	5.5	5.2	6.7	7.9
Productivity	2.3	0.8	-1.5	-0.7	1.9	0.0	3.1	2.8	1.5	1.5
Unit Labor Costs	5.1	8.0	10.7	11.2	7.7	7.9	2.3	2.6	5.2	8.3
Farm Producers Price Index	0.8	10.4	13.8	3.4	2.1	-4.9	2.5	8.8	4.0	5.2
Natural Gas Deflator	19.1	9.9	16.0	18.9	13.0	20.8	18.8	0.4	5.1	6.6
Imported Crude Oil ($/bbl)	14.55	14.59	21.53	33.97	37.07	33.59	29.35	29.48	30.81	32.20
New Home Price ($1000)	48.0	55.8	62.7	84.7	88.8	89.3	75.5	79.3	84.6	92.1

Income, Consumption and Saving—% change

Disposable Income	10.0	12.2	12.0	10.8	12.0	8.3	7.3	9.9	7.4	7.1
Real Disposable Income	4.0	4.9	2.7	0.8	3.2	0.5	3.2	5.8	2.2	1.2
Real Consumption	5.0	4.5	2.7	0.5	2.7	1.4	4.2	4.9	2.5	2.0
Savings Rate (%)	5.9	8.1	5.9	6.0	6.8	5.8	4.9	5.8	5.5	4.8

Housing and Automobiles—millions of units

Housing Starts	1.982	2.001	1.717	1.300	1.098	1.058	1.704	1.820	1.640	1.767
Retail Auto Sales	11.0	11.2	10.6	9.0	8.5	8.0	9.2	10.5	10.4	10.4

Corporate Profits—billions $

Before Taxes	194.7	229.1	252.7	234.8	228.9	174.2	207.8	247.2	252.8	270.7
After Taxes	122.0	145.9	185.1	149.8	144.1	115.1	130.6	152.8	158.5	165.8
Retained Earnings	81.2	98.9	112.4	91.2	79.5	48.4	57.3	70.5	65.9	67.6
S&P 500 Stock Price Index	98.2	96.0	103.0	118.8	128.0	119.7	160.4	162.6	170.6	180.9

International Trade

Trade Weighted Exchange Rate of

U.S. Dollar—% change	0.8	-6.0	-1.0	-0.1	8.9	9.4	3.7	3.1	-1.4	-2.8

Industrial Production: Major Trading Partners

Canada—% change	2.8	3.6	3.1	-1.4	0.9	-10.7	5.9	8.8	3.4	2.4
Japan—% change	4.2	6.2	8.2	3.6	1.1	0.4	3.5	10.5	7.1	5.4
OECD Europe—% change	2.0	1.7	4.7	-1.2	-2.3	-1.4	0.7	3.9	2.5	2.2
Real Exports—% change	2.5	12.2	15.4	8.8	0.4	-7.8	-6.8	5.9	6.0	5.4
Real Imports—% change	7.4	13.0	8.2	-0.2	7.3	1.4	7.2	25.0	6.2	4.9
Net Exports (bil. 72$)	22.0	24.0	37.2	50.3	43.0	28.9	11.8	-11.8	-12.9	-12.8

Table 3

Shares of Industrial Countries' Manufactures Exports, 1970-84 [1]
(In percent)

	United States Total	United States Hi-Tech	Canada Total	Canada Hi-Tech	Japan Total	Japan Hi-Tech	EC [2] Total	EC [2] Hi-Tech
1970	21.3	32.2	1.8	1.5	8.9	7.9	e57.1	49.2
1971	19.6	31.2	1.4	1.3	9.9	8.4	59.9	50.0
1972	18.3	28.2	1.3	1.3	10.2	9.6	60.8	51.6
1973	17.9	27.9	1.1	1.0	10.4	9.7	60.8	51.8
1974	18.7	28.6	1.1	1.0	11.9	9.8	59.0	51.3
1975	19.1	28.4	1.1	1.0	11.4	9.6	58.7	51.3
1976	18.8	27.7	1.1	1.0	12.0	11.1	58.5	51.0
1977	17.3	26.1	1.0	0.9	12.6	12.0	59.8	51.8
1978	17.0	26.0	1.0	0.9	12.4	12.5	59.8	51.2
1979	17.3	26.1	1.0	1.1	10.8	11.6	61.4	52.3
1980	18.3	27.2	1.2	1.2	11.9	12.5	59.6	50.8
1981	20.6	30.3	1.2	1.3	14.5	14.7	54.9	e45.4
1982	19.8	29.6	1.2	1.2	13.9	e13.6	56.5	e47.2
1983	19.4	e30.1	1.0	NA	14.8	e14.7	56.1	NA
1984	NA	NA	NA	NA	NA	NA	NA	NA

1983:1......	18.8	NA	1.0	NA	14.5	NA	57.1	NA
2......	19.0	NA	1.1	NA	14.4	NA	56.6	NA
3......	19.8	NA	1.0	NA	14.8	NA	55.4	NA
4......	19.9	NA	1.1	NA	14.9	NA	55.2	NA
1984:1......	19.3	NA	1.0	NA	15.2	NA	55.5	NA
2......	20.1	NA	1.1	NA	15.3	NA	54.6	NA
3......	NA	NA	NA	NA	NA	NA	NA	NA
4......	NA	NA	NA	NA	NA	NA	NA	NA

e = estimate.
1/ Shares of exports of 15 major industrial free-world countries, excluding shipments to the United States. Quarterly data are seasonally adjusted.
2/ Based on exports of Belgium, Denmark, France, West Germany, Italy, Netherlands, and United Kingdom.

Source: U.S. Department of Commerce. Office of Trade and Investment Analysis.

Bibliography

Bluestone, Barry, and Bennett Harrison. **The De-Industrialization of America: Plant Closings, Community Abandonment, and the Dismantling of Basic Industry.** New York: Basic Books, 1982.

Eckstein, Otto et al. **The DRI Report on U.S. Manufacturing Industries.** New York: McGraw-Hill Book Company, 1984.

Economic Report of the President. Washington, D.C.: Government Printing Office, 1984.

Hart, Gary. **A New Democracy.** New York: Quill, 1983.

Heenan, David D. **The Re-United States of America,** Reading. Mass.: Addison-Wesley Publishing Company, 1983.

Lawrence, Robert Z. "The Myth of U.S. Deindustrialization." **Challenge,** Vol. 26, No. 5 (Nov/Dec 1983): 12-21.

Magaziner, Ira C., and Robert B. Reich. **Minding America's Business.** New York: Vintage Books, 1983.

McKenzie, Richard B. **Fugitive Industry.** Cambridge, Mass.: Ballinger Publishing Company, 1984.

Ouchi, William G. **The M-Form Society.** Reading, Mass.: Addison-Wesley Publishing Company, 1984.

Reich, Robert B. **The Next American Frontier.** Middlesex, England: Penguin Books, 1983.

Rohatyn, Felix G. **The Twenty-Year Century.** New York: Random House, 1983.

Stein, Herbert. **Presidential Economics.** New York: Simon and Schuster, 1984.

Thurow, Lester C. **The Zero-Sum Society: Distribution and the Possibilities for Economic Change.** Middlesex, England: Penguin Books, 1981.

Reginald H. Alleyne, Jr.

9

Illusory Shrinkage of Employer Discretion to Discipline

> All [employers] may dismiss their employees at-will, be they many or few, for good cause, for no cause, or even for cause morally wrong without being thereby guilty of legal wrong.
> - Tennessee Supreme Court, 1884.[1]

> It shall be an unfair practice for an employer...to discharge or otherwise discriminate against an employee except for just cause.
> - House of Representatives Bill, U.S. Congress, 1980.[2]

More so than their counterparts in the world's industrial democracies, employers in the United States have had discretion to disci-

---

[1] Payne v. Western & Atlantic R.R. Co., 81 Tenn. 507 (1884).

[2] HR 7010, 95th Cong. (1980). The bill carried the popular title, Corporate Democracy Act. It was referred to seven committees of the House of Representatives. It failed to gain a majority vote in any committee and died at the end of the 96th Congress, no action on it having been taken. **The Employment-At-Will Issue, A BNA Special Report,** p. 9 (1983). (Hereafter cited as BNA **Special Report.**)

pline employees.[3] But that discretion has been slowly and incrementally narrowed by a growing number of court decisions and some delimiting statutes. Limits have been placed upon what was once the complete discretion of American employers to discipline and discharge employees for any reason, fair or foul. Until recently, though, the encroaching limitations were never viewed as having established a trend in the direction of zero discretion to discipline arbitrarily. As early as fifty years ago, it was possible to identify a period of complete freedom of American employers to discipline and discharge, for any reason, with impunity. Today, the number of American workers who are wholly unprotected by law from all arbitrary employer discipline may be on the verge of shrinking to nearly zero. But the range of legal protection from arbitrary discharge remains very narrow in the United States and promises to remain narrow despite the new trend. This paper concludes that the trend away from the rule of employment-at-will merely appears to be dramatic because of its potential for sweeping changes in employment relations law in the United States; that a more qualitative-oriented analysis of the kinds of changes being made rather than the numbers of courts and statutes making them reveals little evidence that the potential will be realized.

What has prompted this potentially dramatic turnabout in the once untrammeled discretion of employers to discipline? What lies ahead in

---

[3]See Summers, "Individual Protection Against Unjust Dismissal: Time For A Statute," 62 **Va. L. Rev.** 481, 508 (1976).

the area of employer discretion to discipline? The answers seem inextricably linked with the question of how the discretion-encroaching law has developed over the last five decades.

In this discussion, "law" means not only the statutes of Congress and the various states, but the decisions of courts in their formulation of judge-made, nonstatutory "common law." Indeed, the most recent developments in the area of employer discretion to discipline have been those produced by courts without the aid of statutes.

The First "Encroachment"

The "Discrimination" Provisions of NLRA

Until the union movement produced the Railway Labor[4] and National Labor Relations Acts[5] in 1926 and 1935, respectively, private sector employers in the United States enjoyed complete freedom to discipline employees for any reason. As explained by the Tennessee Supreme Court in 1884, in restating about a century of law in the United States, moral wrong in discharging an employee did not make the employer guilty of "a legal wrong."[6] The common law rule of termination at-will was based on a principle of mutuality of obligation: if the employee was free to terminate his or her employment at any time and for any reason, the

---

[4] 45 U.S.C. 151-163 (1926).

[5] 29 U.S.C. 151-169 (1935).

[6] Note 2 **supra**.

employer was also free to terminate the employee and the employment relationship at any time and for any reason.[7] The rule was applied without qualification or exception of any kind when no written contract of employment for a fixed term existed.

That the law would not intervene in discipline cases of any kind before unions won protection from "discrimination on account of union activity" is illustrated by the language of a United States Court in a 1943 National Labor Relations Act case. The issue was whether Section 8(a)(3) of the NLRA had been violated by the discharge of an employee. Section 8(a)(3) of NLRA makes it an unfair practice for an employer to "discriminate because of union activity." Weighing the evidence in **Edward G. Budd Mfg. Co. v. NLRB**,[8] the United States Court of Appeals for the Third Circuit noted:

> An employer may discharge an employee for a good reason, a poor reason or no reason at all so long as the provisions of the National Labor Relations Act are not violated.

As the court's statement connotes, lawful discharge (or other discipline) for any reason was at that time the general rule. The NLRA made a discharge because of union activity an exception to the general rule of "employment at

---

[7] See Adair v. United States, 208 U.S. 161, 174-5 (1908). Adair has been repudiated by the Supreme Court. See, e.g., Phelps Dodge Corp. v. NLRB, 313 U.S. 177 (1941), NLRB v. Jones & Laughlin Steel Corp., 301 U.S. 1 (1937).

[8] 138 F.2d 86 (3rd Cir. 1943).

will." That the discretion of employers to discipline for any reason had been infringed by the NLRA was not a very startling proposition. The NLRA's limitations on discretion to discipline were largely overshadowed by the larger and overarching principle that the NLRA compelled employers to bargain with unions when majority employee support for the union could be demonstrated.[9] Compulsory bargaining could not work if employers were free to discharge employees who triggered the events designed to bring about compulsory bargaining. Thus, the unlawful discharge because of union activity was somewhat incidental to the NLRA's grand design of making unionism and collective bargaining work. A job-protection concern as a primary objective of Congress would more likely have prompted Congress to enact a statute placing greater-than-NLRA-restrictions on employer discretion to discipline.

The limits the NLRA placed on employer discretion to discipline were very narrow, as illustrated by the multi-element nature of NLRA Section 8(a)(3). The required elements of proof are: union activity by the disciplined employee; knowledge of such by the employer, and what amounts to incriminating timing by the employer in disciplining the union-active employee in relation to the time of the employee's union activity.[10] Failure of proof on any

---

[9] 29 U.S.C. 158(a) (5).

[10] See, e.g., Lakes Concrete Industries, Inc., 172 NLRB 896 1968); McKinnon Services, Inc. 174 NLRB 1141 (1969); Technitrol, Inc. 174 NLRB 1234 (1969).

one element wins the case for the employer.[11]

Take the hypothetical example of an NLRB proceeding in which a nonunion employer in the midst of a union organizing drive is charged with a violation of NLRA Section 8(a)(3) for discharging employee Poe because of Poe's union activity. Assume that there is a persuasive evidence of Poe's deep involvement in union activity and that the discharge of Poe immediately followed the peak period of Poe's union activity. Assume further that there is no persuasive proof of the employer's knowledge of Poe's union activity and that there is evidence suggesting that Poe was discharged because he drove a foreign manufactured automobile. (The employer has claimed that Poe was not a productive worker.) The employer would very likely win this hypothetical NLRB case. Lacking proof of the employer's knowledge of Poe's union activity, the NLRB would not find a violation of NLRA Section 8(a)(3). If the NLRB were persuaded that Poe was discharged because he drove a foreign manufactured automobile, an antiunion motive would be negated rather than supported. Accordingly, the employer's defense against a Section 8(a)(3) violation would be strengthened rather than weakened. Though the NLRA did not itself directly limit employer discretion to discharge, except for the restrictions of NLRA Section 8(a)(3), it did authorize collective bargaining, which in turn led to collective bargaining agreements containing, among other things, restrictions on employer disciplinary action. Collective bargaining agreements typically provide that discipline shall be for "just cause," and that

---

[11]Ibid.

disputes over their meaning will be resolved by the grievance-arbitration procedures created by the collective bargaining agreement.

Contractual "Just Cause"

Take the same hypothetical case as that described, alter the facts to make the employer party to a collective bargaining agreement, make the forum arbitration rather than the National Labor Relations Board, and the result would inevitably be quite different. In a labor arbitration proceeding under a "just cause" clause in a collective bargaining agreement, the union representing Poe would win the case on proving the very facts that would defeat the union's Section 8(a)(3) claim in the NLRB proceeding. A discharge for driving a foreign manufacture automobile, though not an unfair labor practice under NLRA Section 8(a)(3) (for lack of an anti-union motive), would not be regarded by many arbitrators as a discharge for "just cause." Contractual "just cause" includes but is by no means limited to discrimination prohibited by NLRA Section 8(a)(3). "Just cause" embraces all forms of arbitrary disciplinary action[12] and not merely the ex-

---

[12] It is uniformly acknowledged that there is a "common law" of just cause developed by the collective body of decisions of labor arbitrators. Summers relies upon it in his article, note 3 **supra,** in arguing for a wrongful discharge statute. His suggestion is that the existence of a common law of just cause would make it unnecessary for courts to develop a new body of law in a vacuum. Numerous arbitration decisions on discharge and discipline are collected and discussed in Elkouri and Elkouri, **How Arbitration Works,** pp. 610-666 (3rd ed., 1978).

treme kinds of employer arbitrariness so far addressed by courts finding common law wrongful discharges.

As a standard, contractual "just cause" is virtually impossible to define in the abstract. Its identifying strands are discernible only in the context of concrete cases decided by labor arbitrators.[13] The developing common law of wrongful discharge appears to be indicative of sweeping changes in the law of the subject. The appearance is based in part on the unsupportable, but sometimes prevailing assumption that contractual just cause is now or will become the standard used by judges in common law wrongful discharge cases. As will be developed later in this paper, courts have in the main shown no such inclination. Thus, NLRA has not had more than a minor impact on employer discretion to discipline, either directly, through its own terms, or indirectly, through the collective bargaining agreements it authorizes. The same may be said of Title VII of the Civil Rights Act of 1964.

The Second Encroachment

Title VII of the Civil Rights Act became effective on July 2, 1965. It was the second Congressional encroachment on employer discretion to discipline with impunity. Thirty years intervened between the time of its effective date and that of the National Labor Relations

---

[13]Discipline and discharge cases cover a wide range of fact patterns. They are also the largest class of cases going to arbitration. See Elkouri, **id.**, at 610, n. 1.

Act. Title VII prohibits employment discrimination on the basis of race, religion, national origin, and sex.[14] Unlike the discrimination aspect of the NLRA, Title VII's discrimination provisions are the heart of the statute, which has no overarching objective beyond ending the prohibited forms of discrimination.

Like proof of a violation of Section 8(a)(3) of the NLRA, proof of a violation of Title VII requires satisfactory proof of several essential elements. That is the only close similarity between the two statutes. NLRA reaches a comparatively narrow constituency, one that grows narrower as the unionized work force shrinks. The Title VII constituency has always been large in comparison with that of the NLRA. Thus, if limitations on employer discretion to discipline are measured by the number of persons protected by a discretion-limiting statute, Title VII has more of an impact on employer discretion than does the NLRA. Title VII's sex discrimination provisions would alone support that proposition, given the roughly half of the adult-age population that is female.

But even with a comparatively large Title VII constituency, Title VII's impact on employer discretion may be viewed as narrow. The appropriate yardstick is not the number of persons covered by the statute in relation to the size of the work force, but the nature of the conduct Title VII prohibits. Employer discre-

---

[14]42 U.S.C. 2000e-703(a). The prohibitions of Title VII also run against unions, 42 U.S.C. 2000e-703(c).

tion is substantially affected by Title VII because the statute's mere existence, in addition to encouraging violation-avoiding employer conduct, also encourages employer behavior that is designed to avoid the appearance of having violated its prohibitory terms.

Take the example of an employer seeking to fill a position requiring moderate skills. Two persons apply for the job, one black, one white. Assume that but for the enactment of Title VII, the employer in good faith would reject both candidates in hopes of finding a candidate more qualified than both, even though both candidates have the minimum skills required to do the job. Here, concern for a possible charge of violating Title VII may prompt the employer to hire the black candidate. Indeed, many would argue that that is precisely the effect Title VII was intended to have on employer discretion.

Taking that more or less qualitative analysis of Title VII's potential effect and linking it with the quantitative factor of constituency size, the statute's effect on employer discretion becomes somewhat clearer. The ease with which an employer may avoid consideration of the effects of NLRA or Title VII depends upon the size of the portion of the work force the statute protects generally and the size and nature of the work force from which the employer draws employees. For example, an employer who operates a manufacturing plant in an area uninhabited by blacks or other groups protected by Title VII (excluding females, who cannot be hypothesized out of any area) would not have the same concerns about avoiding the appearance of Title VII violations as would an employer operating in a city with a large multi-ethnic population. Thus, any measurement of limitations on employer discretion must consider numbers of persons affected by the discretion-limiting law, the type of conduct the law prohibits, and the tandem effect of both factors. Discrimination statutes like NLRA and Title VII are self-limiting because discrimination means treating similar groups differently, to the detriment of one group and the benefit of another.

Treating all employees unfairly and arbitrarily, across the board, and without distinction among groups of any kind is valid employer conduct under a discrimination statute, but invalid when the governing prohibitions go beyond discrimination and ban - as do just-cause clauses in collective bargaining agreements - arbitrary employer action. Just-cause clauses in collective bargaining agreements are very limiting of employer discretion, but only in terms of the kind of employer conduct such clauses prohibit (particularly when compared with pure "discrimination" limitations). Measured by the numbers of workers who are covered by them,[15] contractual just-cause clauses are not very limiting of employer discretion. Not until the beginning of a developing common law just-cause standard did it become necessary to consider the implications of a discretion-limiting standard that combined breadth of numbers of employees covered **and** breadth of restraints on employer discretion.

---

[15] See Mitchell, Chapter 12 below, and Craver, "The Vitality of the American Labor Movement in the Twenty-First Century," **Univ. of Ill. L. Rev.** 633 (1983).

Common Law Exceptions

Either on grounds of "public policy" or breach of an implied contract of employment, courts have begun to extend to employees a common law of wrongful discharge. The beneficiaries of the new rule are those employees not otherwise protected by law or collective bargaining agreement. Not surprisingly, employers have opposed the new trend. Possibly because of concerns for the effect of the new common law on their ability to organize employees, unions have been ambivalent in their reaction to the developing wrongful discharge common law.[16] Thus, the institutional support

---

[16] In a "Special Report" prepared by Bureau of National Affairs staff members, union and employer officials were interviewed and asked their views on the wrongful-discharge trend. The report provides in part: "Most labor officials contacted by BNA asserted that statutory 'just cause' would enhance organizing efforts. However, while labor verbally supports such legislation, it is clearly not actively crusading for it. The report quotes Martin Gerber, United Auto Workers' Vice President for Organizing, as follows: "Our mission is to improve the lot of working people, and this can be established through statutory relief as well as collective bargaining." The report also notes Gerber's admission that just-cause legislation "is not a priority of the union at this time." See **BNA Special Report,** pp. 17-19.

Whatever the concerns of unions on the relationship between just-cause legislation and the success of their organizing efforts, it seems evident that unions could play a helpful role in the implementation of just-cause legislation, once enacted. Acquiring adequate representation is a problem for many individuals who pursue wrongful discharge actions. Unlike the

that unions provided for passage of the NLRA,

---

common law decisions permitting recovery in tort, and hence the possibility of damages above a mere "make-whole" amount, wrongful discharge legislation will no doubt limit recovery to make-whole sums. The limited recovery may make statutory just-cause cases unattractive for lawyers, unless attorney fees are liberally allowed. Employees represented by unions would have the possible advantage of union representation. However, the same limitations on resources that prevent a union from taking all grievances to arbitration would limit the number of wrongful discharge actions a union could file. The costs of the wrongful discharge action, though, would be less than the costs of the same or similar case brought to an arbitration forum. Arbitrators' fees and transcript costs are the main costs the union would not have to expend in a statutory wrongful discharge action.

A bill pending in the California legislature during the 1983-84 regular session provides for the repeal of an at-will provision in the State Labor Code, Cal. Labor Code Section 2922. The bill would substitute for statutory at-will a wrongful discharge statute. It would require both the employee and the employer to deposit $500.00 with the California State Mediation and Conciliation Service to cover the costs of resolving the dispute. Mediation followed by arbitration would be the means of resolving wrongful-discharge issues. See Assembly Bill No. 3017, 1983-84 Regular Session). The $500.00 deposit requirement illustrates the difficulties of regulating by law employee discharges. Obviously, many employees (already out of work for having been discharged) would find it difficult to make the required deposit. Further, the bill provides that "All costs of the [arbitration] procedures shall be shared equally by the employee and the employer." **Id.**, at Art. 3.7, Section 2888 (b)(3). The employee would thus be responsible for one-half of the arbitrator's fees and court reporter fees, if any.

and that civil rights organizations provided for passage of Title VII of the Civil Rights Act, has not been a factor in the development of common law wrongful discharge. It also partially explains the singular lack of success enjoyed by proponents of wrongful discharge statutes, a subject treated subsequently in this paper.

An examination of early cases making at-will exceptions suggests that the new common law on the subject has evolved from early cases involving extreme examples of arbitrary discharges. Once the courts began to make exceptions to the employment-at-will rule, it seemed inevitable that less extreme employer conduct would also be considered to be within the exception to the general rule of employment at-will. It might well be, though, that in the absence of statutes creating a just-cause standard, courts will apply the exception only in cases of extreme employer conduct. At this juncture in the development of a common law on wrongful discharge, it is by no means certain that courts will eventually employ the more sweeping standard of "just cause" that is used in collective bargaining agreements. It is not even certain now that courts will depart from the current practice of narrowly applying the at-will exception to cases of extreme employer arbitrariness.

Successful recovery for wrongful discharge not based on statutory violations like those of Title VII and NLRA, or contractual just cause, have so far been limited to those in violation of public policy and those in breach of an implied contract of employment. The public policy exception so far remains limited to extreme forms of employer conduct; the implied contractual just-cause standard has so far been limited to rather clear indications of employer promises not to terminate arbitrarily.

The "Public Policy" Exception

An example of extreme employer arbitrariness is the discharge of an employee for refusing to violate the law. In a California Court of Appeal case,[17] a union business agent was discharged for refusing his employer's request that he testify falsely before a committee of the California Legislature. Conceding that "public policy" is a vague expression, the Court of Appeal attempted nonetheless to define it as "a principle which makes unlawful that which has a tendency to be injurious to the public or against the public good."

Because a discharge for failing to give perjured testimony would discourage truthful sworn testimony, and the public has a strong interest in truthful testimony, the discharge was determined to be wrongful. Similar reasoning was later used by the California Supreme Court in **Tameny v. Atlantic Richfield Co.**,[18] where a retail sales representative for a major oil company was discharged for refusing to take part in an illegal price-fixing scheme. The court approved the employee's recovery of damages from the employer for tortious conduct. What was vindicated in that case was not a

---

[17]Petermann v. International Brotherhood of Teamsters, 174 Cal. App. 2d 184, 344 P.2d 25 (1959).

[18]27 Cal. 3d 167 (1980).

breach of a contractual promise but an employee's interest in "freedom from various kinds of harm."

Courts in at least twenty states have made public-policy exceptions to the employment-at-will rule.[19] In each of the cases, the courts identified some interest extending beyond that of the plaintiff employees, such as the interest of the public in avoiding criminal conduct. In none of these cases is there much in the way of suggestion that courts were influenced by anything more than the gross arbitrariness of the employer's conduct. "Public policy" is a convenient supporting rationale. When some overarching interest of the public cannot be identified by a plaintiff in a wrongful discharge action, courts have been reluctant to find for the employee on a public-policy ground.[20]

---

[19] See **BNA Special Report,** note 16 **supra,** at p. 8.

[20] See, e.g., Lampe v. Presbyterian Medical Center, 41 Colo. App. 465, 590 P.2d 513 (1978). A nurse claimed that she was discharged for performing her job in accordance with governing statutory standards for professional nursing. Her discharge was upheld by the Colorado Court of Appeals. The Court left open the possibility of applying a public-policy exception in future cases. The Court also distinguished cases from other jurisdictions: a discharge for serving on a jury, Nees v. Hocks, 72 Ore. 230, 536, P.2d, 512 (1975), and a discharge for filing a workmen's compensation claim in Frampton v. Central Indiana Gas Co., 260 Ind. 249, 297 N.E. 2d, 425 (1973). Distinguishing those cases, the Colorado Court of Appeals said:

> ...Frampton and Nees relied on a specifically enacted right and a

If public policy remained the single exception to the at-will rule, the exception would have a minimal effect on employer discretion. Discharges for refusals to commit crimes are undoubtedly rare. The number of potential victims of discharges for refusals to commit crimes is almost certainly small compared to the number of potential victims of discharges in violation of Title VII of the Civil Rights Act. In this rather limited area of possible violations of wrongful discharge law, employers need not engage in substantial cost efforts to avoid the appearance of a wrongful termination. Even though "public policy," as an exception to termination at-will, remains an amorphous term, its meaning is narrowed if the crime-refusal exception is viewed as a kind of benchmark standard. But at-will exceptions are not limited to matters of public policy.

The Implied Promise to Terminate for Cause

Except in collective bargaining agreements in the United States, express contractual obli-

---

> duty....In contrast, the plaintiff in this case relies on a broad, general statement of policy contained in a statute which creates the State Board of Nursing and which gives that Board the authority to discipline....Given the general language used in the statute...we cannot impute to the General Assembly an intent to modify the contractual relationships between hospitals and their employees in such situations. (41 Colo. App. at 468)

In Geary v. United States Steel Corp., 456 Pa. 171, 319, A.2d, 174 (1974), the Pennsylvania Supreme Court adhered to the at-will rule, though an employee had been discharged for calling his employer's attention to a defective product and objecting to its marketing.

gations to discharge and discipline only for just cause are very rare. But courts in the United States are beginning to avoid the absence of express "just-cause" clauses by finding implied promises to terminate for cause. How readily courts may find an implied just-cause clause is the key question in determining how employer discretion may ultimately be circumscribed by wrongful-termination law. For example, in the following hypothetical case, it seems reasonably evident that no wrongful discharge would be found by a court: Employer hires employee Doe as a salesman working for salary plus commissions. There is no written contract and no oral understanding of how long Doe is to remain employed. Doe is discharged for "lack of productivity." Doe argues that her work was productive and, indeed, evidence reveals that she was at least as productive as all other salesmen working for the employer. She makes no claim of sex discrimination (the employer having similarly treated male salesmen); she does bring a wrongful-discharge action, claiming that her discharge breached an implied employment contract containing an implied promise to terminate for cause. There are no personnel manual or other company standards outlining the conditions under which an employee might be terminated or otherwise disciplined.

On these facts, a finding that there was an implied contract of employment would effectively do away with distinctions between the protection afforded employees covered by just-cause clauses in collective bargaining agreements and those who are not. Courts have not gone that far, and so far show few signs of drawing such unwarranted inferences of just-cause promises. Courts have found implied just-cause promises on the basis of a combination of the duration of employment, promotions received, employer assurances of permanent employment and employer personnel policies, including the employer's adoption of specific procedures for the adjudication of disputes.[21] These decisions might be viewed as the precursor to a rolling trend in the direction of a general law of implied just-cause promises. But the better view is that they are revolutionary only in the sense that they make exceptions to what was once the unqualified termination-at-will rule. Indeed, so long as implied contractual promises are relied upon as rationale for wrongful termination decisions, employers may simply make clear in contracts of hire that employment is at-will and not subject to just-cause standards. The truly revolutionary court decision would be one holding that an employer's insistence on a contract of employment that expressly negated employment at-will would be void as against public policy. Then,

---

[21]The leading case is Pugh v. See's Candies, Inc., 116 Cal. App. 3d (1981). See Cleary v. American Airlines, Inc. 111 Cal. App. 3d 443 (1980), recognizing an implied covenant of good faith and fair dealing in employment contracts, and Note, 34 **Stan. L. Rev.** 153 (1981). The breach of the covenant of good faith and fair dealing theory was formulated by the New Hampshire Supreme Court in Monge v. Beebe Rubber Co., 114 N.H. 130, 316 A.2d 549 (1974). Plaintiff in the case, a married female, claimed that she was fired for refusing to date her foreman. The implied covenant of good faith is sometimes recognized as being separate and distinct from implied-cause rationale. The covenant theory is based on an implied-in-law covenant, Monge v. Beebe Rubber Co., **supra**; implied cause is premised on implied-in-fact doctrine. In the latter, inferences are drawn from the conduct of the contracting parties; in the former, inferences are drawn from law.

the unseemly state of the law would be that inferences of just-cause terminations may be drawn from certain employer conduct, but express negations of such inferences are against public policy and void.

Legal restraints on employer discretion to discipline merely appear to be close and confining because of the drama associated with any departure from the long-standing and once unqualified rule of termination at-will. When the degree of departure from the old rule is closely examined, it reveals a wide area in which employers may exercise discretion to terminate. At this time there is little evidence that courts will chip away at the at-will rule, case-by-case and incrementally, until all arbitrary discharges are deemed unlawful at common law. There seems to be little room in the at-will-exceptions rationale to support its expansion to a standard of contractual just cause. When just-cause clauses appear in collective bargaining agreements or in statutes (all hypothetical so far), their appearance alone leaves open to question only the manner in which they ought to be interpreted by arbitrators or courts. Common law wrongful termination findings on the other hand require a search for rationale in support of justification for a "cause" standard and in support of the manner in which "cause" is defined. The so far articulated judicial rationale of public policy and implied cause barely support what is tantamount to the creation of a special and limited standard of cause. It is doubtful that any conceivable kind of common law rationale could support the expansion of common law wrongful discharge doctrine beyond the limits now supported by "public policy" and implied-cause rationale.

Standing alone, the comparison of numbers of valid reasons for discharging employees with numbers of invalid reasons is not a fair measure of employer discretion. It places no value on the degree of care employers must take to avoid the appearance of a law violation, and the attendant costs. By that standard, neither the public policy nor the implied contractual just-cause standard offers serious challenges to the fair exercise of employer discretion to discipline.

Statutory Just Cause

Passage of the Corporate Democracy Act of 1980[22] would drastically have changed the rule of employment at-will. The turnabout would have represented a complete abrogation of the common law rule. A covered employer would not have been able to escape coverage by anything along the lines of negating implied promises with express conduct and language. "Just cause," as used in the not successful bill, would have meant what "just cause" means in collective bargaining agreements: a restraint on discharges for arbitrary reasons, including restraints on discharges for no readily apparent reason. The law would have had nationwide coverage. It would have amended the National Labor Relations Act to include "just cause" along with "union-activity" discrimination as standards governing the employment relationship monitored by the National Labor Relations Board.[23] Its passage would have created a

---

[22]See note 2 **supra**.

[23]Section 401 of the proposed Corporate Democracy Act, note 2 **supra**.

nearly impossible administrative burden for the NLRB, which for many years now has had a rising caseload that threatens the NLRB's ability to perform its statutory function. The Board now handles a total of nearly 45,000 unfair practice cases per year.[24] At the same time, about 50,000 employment grievances are taken to arbitration each year,[25] about half of which are discipline-related grievances arising under contractual just-cause clauses. They originate with the roughly 20 percent of workers who are covered by collective bargaining agreements. If the Corporate Democracy Act had become law, at least four times as many workers would have been protected by a just-cause standard. It seems evident that the NLRB's caseload would

---

[24]**NLRB, Forty-Sixth Ann. Report** (1981), p. 8. For recent reports on the NLRB's backlog of cases see **Wall Street Journal**, March 13, 1984, p. 1, col. 5, and May 15, 1984, p. 1, col. 5, quoting NLRB Chairman Dotson's prediction that "It could take up to three years to cut the [Board's] huge caseload to the acceptable level of the late 1970s."

[25]The exact number of arbitration decisions per year is almost impossible to determine because of the large number of unreported cases that do not originate as American Arbitration Association or Federal Mediation and Conciliation Service cases. FMCS alone closed 8,094 grievance arbitration cases in 1981. **FMCS Ann. Rpt.** (1981) (latest available data). In 1983, the American Arbitration Association handled 17,516 labor arbitration cases. Telephone conversation with Gerald Murase, Regional Director, American Arbitration Association, Los Angeles, quoting from as yet unpublished internal AAA, data. Many arbitration cases arise through "ad hoc" selections of arbitrators, that is, without requesting a list of arbitrators from FMCS, AAA, or other such agency. There is also a growing practice of parties including the names of a group of arbitrators in their agreements and selecting one such arbitrator on a rotating basis.

have increased by a minimum of 100,000 cases. Quite likely, the increase in the NLRB's caseload would have exceeded 100,000 cases. Unions screen grievances and take but few of the total filed to arbitration. With no restraints of that kind and the free services of the NLRB available to employees, there might easily have been a 200,000 case increase in NLRB filings.[26]

Nonetheless, the mere existence of any statutory just-cause standard, even one not capable of being expeditiously enforced, would have the effect of inducing employers to govern their conduct with thoughts of the statute in mind. Under the Corporate Democracy Act, or similar statute, the range of violation-avoiding conduct and the range of conduct designed to avoid appearances of violations would have been much larger than those created by NLRA, Title VII of the Civil Rights Act, or the common law decisions in favor of limitations on employment at-will.

The prospects for passage of federal legislation like the Corporate Democracy Act of 1980 are, at this writing, almost nonexistent. The ambivalence of unions with respect to any wrongful discharge legislation is easily understood when the interests of unions are considered. The promise of protection from arbitrary discipline is an effective weapon in a union's arsenal of organization campaign arguments. When employees are already protected by a wrongful discharge statute, the argument for

---

[26]NLRB unfair practice charges are exclusively prosecuted by the NLRB's General Counsel (42 U.S.C. 153) who has complete discretion to prosecute or withhold prosecution. A charging party may gain representation by General Counsel at the trial, NLRB, U.S. Court of Appeals, and U.S. Supreme Court levels.

union representation is weakened.[27] However, it is quite likely that unions would devise a way to make wrongful discharge legislation work to their advantage, by providing unions with the opportunity of representing employees before statutory agencies empowered to resolve wrongful terminations claims.[28] Employer groups are beginning to show support for wrongful discharge legislation.[29] They now tend to view some form of wrongful discharge as an acceptable alternative to excessive jury awards in common law termination cases. Legislation on the subject would undoubtedly follow the example of the National Labor Relations Act, most other discrimination statutes, and arbitration practice, by limiting monetary awards in discharge cases to make-whole amounts. Employer backing should sharply heighten the possibilities for the enactment of some form of unfair-dismissal legislation. That support may be essential, for in the labor-management legislation arena in the United States, the argument that "other countries do it" does not have the persuasive force required to overcome long-standing practice and tradition, irrespective of the argument's validity on the underlying

---

[27]In England, for example, under the Employment Protection Act of 1975, unrepresented employees are less successful in pursuing unfair dismissal claims made to Industrial Tribunals than are employees with representation before the tribunals. Represented employees are successful in 40 percent of cases filed; unrepresented employees are successful in 30 percent of cases filed. See Dickens et al., **Dismissed,** 89, Table 4.2 (1985).

[28]E.g., Summers, n. 3. **supra.**

[29]For example, Assembly Bill No. 1400, California Legislature (1985).

merits. Labeling employment-at-will as "anachronistic"[30] is not enough to carry the day in favor of legislation that does not identify and remedy something immediately harmful to the economy or contribute to the maintenance of peace and order.

Some arguments in support of wrongful discharge legislation are based on a principle of inequity: union-represented employees are protected from arbitrary discipline, nonunion employees are not;[31] therefore, nonunion employees should similarly be protected, by statute. It seems doubtful, though, that an unjustifiable inequity exists solely for the reason that union employees have something that nonunion employees do not. It would be irrational to suggest, for example, that a statute should provide nonunion employees with a wage stipend making up the difference between their nonunion wages and union wages in enterprises whose employees perform similar kinds of work. Even assuming, for the sake of argument, that "inequity" is a fair characterization in comparing union and nonunion employees as regards protection from arbitrary discharges, nonunion employees have the means of removing the inequity: they may become union employees. The decline in the number of representation elections won by unions[32] suggests that employees are now engaging in a kind of cost-benefit analysis with respect to how they should vote in a union representation election. More often than not,

---

[30] Summers, n. 3 **supra,** at 484.

[31] **Id.,** at 532. The theme of inequality as between union and nonunionized employees runs throughout Professor Summers' article.

[32] See Craver, n. 15 **supra,** at 634-635 and n. 3.

they are concluding that the costs of union representation outweigh the benefits of union representation,[33] including the benefits of protection from arbitrary discipline. Whether this is a temporary low side of the cycle for union interests or part of a permanent decline leading to the end of unionism as it has existed for the last half century is now a subject of debate.[34] What is critical in this discussion is that the fate of the union movement is mainly in the hands of employees in the exercise of their votes in representation elections.[35]

---

[33]Unions are now losing slightly more than 50 percent of the representation elections in which they take part. In fiscal year 1981, unions took part in 6,439 representation elections in which they sought to become exclusive bargaining representative. A total of 395,573 employees voted in the elections. Unions won 46.2 percent of the elections conducted by the NLRB. See NLRB, **Forty-Sixth Annual Rpt.** (1981), p. 205. In 1950, unions won 74.5 percent of all representation elections conducted by the NLRB. See Seeber and Cooke, "The Decline in Union Success in NLRB Representation Elections," 22 **Ind. Relations** 34 (1983).

[34]Note 29 **supra,** at 636, n. 17, 18. Professor Craver cites authorities on both sides of the issue, but the sources for the optimistic view (from the union perspective) were written in 1970 and 1963: Forsey, "Trade Unions in 2020," in **Visions, 2020** 94 (S. Clarkson ed. 1970), and Taft, "Is There a Crisis in the Labor Movement?" No. 350 **The Annals** 10 (1963). The beginning of a precipitous decline in union fortunes is of much more recent origins. Professor Craver's article is valuable in its recreation of a wide range of demographic and industrial-system changes that have gradually affected union fortunes over a long term.

[35]Under the National Labor Relations Act, a union may seek to demonstrate its majority status in a representation election conducted by the National Labor Relations Board. If the union wins the election, the NLRA obligates the

The arguments in favor of wrongful discharge legislation run against the American labor relations tradition of unions sharing in employee relations governance through the collective bargaining agreement. The manner in which unions represent their employees in the United States has always differed from that of their European counterparts, who play a more political role in gaining through enacted legislation what American unionists gain through collective bargaining.[36] Discretion to discipline is one of those employment relations matters, among many others, that have long remained uncontrolled by legislation in the United States. The exceptions are those certain areas in critical need of direct legislative control, like the already noted discrimination on the basis of the relatively narrow but important grounds prohibited by the 1964 Civil Rights Act. Statutory authorization for collective bargaining may fairly be viewed as a fair compromise substitute for unchecked corporate power,[37] on the one hand, and, on the other, a corporate environment as closely controlled by legislation as are employers in other industrial democracies. That calculus may fairly be regarded as including discretion to discipline and the avoidance of costs asso-

---

employer to bargain in good faith with the union in an effort to reach a collective bargaining agreement. See NLRA Sections 9 and 8(a) (5), 42 U.S.C. 159, 158(a) (5).

[36] See Bok and Dunlop, **Labor and the American Community** 210-212 (1970).

[37] See Blades, "Employment at Will vs. Individual Freedom: On Limiting the Abusive Exercise of Employer Power," 67 **Colum. L. Rev.** 1404 (1967).

ciated with governing employer conduct in a manner that avoids both violations of **and** the appearance of having committed violations of wrongful discharge legislation. It also includes the costs of defending against the vast numbers of wrongful discharge cases that would ultimately be revealed as having no merit. Currently in the unionized work force, the costs of arbitration force unions to be selective in determining which employee grievances to arbitrate. These are all factors a legislature might fairly take into account in determining that the time for enactment of wrongful discharge legislation has not yet arrived in the United States.

Conclusion

Notwithstanding a contrary practice in other industrial democracies, the long-standing practice of permitting American employers wide discretion in disciplining employees is not very close to termination. Public policy exceptions to employment at-will are used in extreme cases of employer arbitrariness; implied promises of terminations for cause are rare and, in any event, controllable by employers. Statutory just-cause standards, by comparison, would narrowly limit employer discretion to discipline, but the chances of passage of such legislation are not very high because of the absence of institutional support for its passage and the existence of some not irrational arguments in favor of leaving protection from arbitrary discipline to the unionized sector.[38]

---

[38]See Catler, "The Case Against Proposals to Eliminate the Employment At Will Rule," 5 **Ind.**

Any inequity in the treatment of nonunion and unionized employees as regards protection from wrongful discharge is scarcely less unjustifiable than the "inequity" of wage and some other collective bargaining based differences between union and nonunion employees. Any inequity, however characterized, has some rational basis in the availability of the union option for nonunion employees. American employers' discretion to discipline is shrinking, but not very rapidly and, so far, not very much.

Rel. L.J. 471 (1983); Getman, "Labor Arbitration and Dispute Resolution," 88 **Yale L.J.** 916 (1979), criticizing Professor Summers' views; and n. 3 **supra** on grounds of workability: "Although the goals of the proposal are worthy, the obstacles to their achievement would be formidable" (**id.,** at 934).

Benjamin Aaron

10

Trends in Labor Relations Law: Past and Future

The content of this chapter is more limited in scope than the title might suggest. The past I intend to review extends no further back than 1977, and the future about which I shall speculate is only the 1980s. Moreover, I shall concentrate almost exclusively on trends in labor-management relations under the National Labor Relations Act (NLRA).

The Watershed of 1977-78: Defeat of the Labor Reform Act

As Professor Mitchell makes clear in his paper prepared for this conference, the dominant factor in the bargaining process in the private sector during the period 1979-83 was the depressed state of the economy. That circumstance explains not only the phenomenon of "concession bargaining," but also the "hard line" towards unions taken by many employers. We must look to the years 1977-78, however, to see the beginning of a major shift in the pattern of contemporary labor-management relations. It was during those two years that organized labor and its allies in the Congress sought and failed to obtain enactment of the proposed Labor Reform Act,[1] consisting of a handful of amendments to the NLRA designed primarily to give added protection to employees and unions against the more flagrant types of employer unfair labor practices. A few of the provisions of the proposed statute, such as the one authorizing the National Labor Relations Board (NLRB) to determine the amount of a wage increase to be paid to its employees by an employer found guilty of refusing to bargain over the terms of an initial agreement, seemed to me to be seriously flawed; but for the most part, the bill was quite modest in its objectives and constituted no significant threat to any employer willing to abide by the terms of the law as it then stood.[2]

Unions and many neutral observers were taken completely by surprise, therefore, by what can be described only as a savage, all-out assault on the bill by a solid phalanx of the major firms in business and industry. This effectively organized campaign against the bill

---

[1] H.R. 8410 was passed by the House of Representatives on Oct. 5, 1977, by a vote of 257 to 163, but a companion bill, S. 2467, was killed in the Senate on June 22, 1978, when attempts to end a filibuster failed and the bill was sent back to committee.

[2] The principal provisions of the proposed law would have speeded up substantially the holding of representation elections by the NLRB; expanded board membership from five to seven; required an employer who had unlawfully refused to bargain with a union over the terms of an initial agreement to compensate employees for lost wages; required double back pay for workers unlawfully discharged for union organizing activities; and barred employers found guilty of willful and repeated violations of Board orders from obtaining federal contracts.

simply overwhelmed the unions and their supporters, and the bill was eventually defeated.

The attack on the proposed statute was joined by some major corporations with long-established collective bargaining relationships with unions; not one publicly supported it. Organized labor was thus forced again to confront the bitter truth that in the United States, to a degree unknown in any other Western industrial country, employer resistance to the very idea of unionism remains strong; it may subside during cyclical "eras of good feeling," when the economy is relatively stable and healthy, but it becomes resurgent whenever employers sense a weakness in organized labor that can be exploited to their advantage. The defeat of the bill profoundly and adversely affected relations between the leaders of organized labor and the spokesmen for large industry.[3] Following the defeat of the reform bill, a labor-management policy group that had been patiently nursed along during the Carter administration by Professor John T. Dunlop, Secretary of Labor in the Ford administration, ceased to function, and Lane Kirkland, who was shortly thereafter to succeed George Meany as president of the AFL-CIO, spoke for most unions when he declared that he was no longer willing to discuss the future of industrial society with "convivial Dr. Jekylls of corporate enterprise, while their Mr. Hydes are busy at work in Washington preserving the power of certain companies to add to their profits while breaking the law...." He added that although a

---

[3]For an informative account of these and related events, see Raskin, "A Reporter at Large/Unionist in Reaganland," **The New Yorker,** Sept. 7, 1981, pp. 50 ff.

"certain amount of hypocrisy...helps to make the world go round," he "would not know how to carry on a serious and constructive dialogue with split-level, double-breasted management."[4]

But organized labor had not yet drained the dregs of its cup of bitterness, for it had not yet encountered Ronald Reagan. His landslide electoral victory in 1980 exposed deep divisions within the house of labor. Although only a small number of unions - the Teamsters, some maritime and building trades unions, and, ironically, the professional Air Traffic Controllers Organization (PATCO) - openly endorsed his candidacy, workers voted for him in large numbers. The Reagan juggernaut in the Congress rolled over the labor lobby with ease in the subsequent orgy of budget cutting, which dealt severe blows to some of those programs previously thought to be untouchable. Moreover, individual members of the Congress, especially in the Republican-controlled Senate, have since fixed their sights on the modification or repeal of such sacred cows as the federal minimum wage law and various social security benefits. Perhaps the most widely perceived indication of the new government labor policy and the collapse of organized labor as an effective political force against hostile action by the executive branch was the crushing of PATCO and the outright discharge, on orders from the president, of over 11,000 air traffic controllers.[5]

---

[4]Bureau of National Affairs, **Daily Labor Report** No. 104:D-1, 2 (May 30, 1978).

[5]To be sure, PATCO did everything possible to insure its own downfall. See, e.g., Northrup, "The Rise and Demise of PATCO," 37 **Ind. & Lab. Rel. Rev.** 167 (1984).

Developments Under the National Labor Relations Act

The New National Labor Relations Board

The foregoing events received a good deal of attention in the news media and are more or less common knowledge. Less well known, perhaps, are the significant shifts in the interpretation and application of the NLRA since Mr. Reagan became President. The majority of the present NLRB (which is still short one member, an acceptable substitute for former member Howard Jenkins, Jr., not having yet been found) reflects the ideology of the Reagan administration. The sole dissenting voice is that of Don A. Zimmerman, a survivor of the Carter administration, whose term expires in December of this year.

The new NLRB majority has, in a relatively short time, overturned a number of important policies enunciated by its predecessors. In some instances the new policies have been prompted by adverse decisions by the courts; in others the changes have merely reflected the triumph of a different ideology from that reflected in earlier rulings. Whether or not one agrees with these recent changes, it is clear that they are almost uniformly adverse to unions.

Transfer of Work Out of the Bargaining Unit

One of the most controversial of the recent Board decisions is **Milwaukee Spring Division, Illinois Coil Spring Co.**[6] During the

---

[6] 268 N.L.R.B. 601 (1984).

life of a collective agreement with the United Auto Workers, the employer sought unsuccessfully to persuade the union to accept substantial reductions in pay and benefits in order to reduce labor costs to the level of those in one of its nonunion plants. At length, the employer unilaterally moved the assembly operation of the Milwaukee Spring plant to the unorganized McHenry Spring plant; this resulted in the layoff of over 30 employees at Milwaukee Spring. The union then filed unfair labor practice charges against the employer, alleging that the latter had interfered, restrained, or coerced its employees in the exercise of their Section 7 rights, in violation of Section 8(a)(1) of the NLRA; had discriminated in regard to tenure of employment to discourage membership in a labor organization, in violation of Section 8(a)(3); had refused to bargain over a mandatory subject, in violation of Section 8 (a)(5); and had unilaterally modified the terms of a collective bargaining agreement in violation of the procedural requirements set forth in Section 8(d) of the Act. It was conceded that the employer's actions had been prompted solely by its desire to reduce the labor costs required by the agreement, rather than by antiunion animus, and that it had bargained over the decision to relocate the assembly operation and was willing to bargain over the effects of that decision.

The case was first considered (**Milwaukee Spring I**) in 1982 by a panel of the Board, consisting of Chairman Van de Water, Mr. Reagan's first appointee to the NLRB, who subsequently failed to be confirmed by the Senate, and Members Fanning and Jenkins. Relying upon an earlier decision, **Los Angeles Marine Hardware**

Co.,[7] the Board unanimously held that the employer had acted in derogation of its bargaining obligation under Section 8(d), and hence had violated Sections 8(a)(1), (3), and (5) of the Act. The Board found a violation of Section 8(a)(1) and (3), even in the absence of an antiunion motive, on the ground that the employer's termination and refusal to reinstate employees was "inherently destructive of employee rights."[8] It found a violation of Sections 8(a)(5) and 8(d) because, in its view, the unilateral modification of the collective agreement was not excused either by subjective good faith or economic necessity. Finally, it concluded that the employer's reliance on the management rights clause in the agreement was misplaced, because the clause did not specifically grant the employer the right to move, transfer, or change the location of part of its operations to another facility to reduce labor costs.[9]

The employer petitioned the Court of Appeals for the Seventh Circuit for review, and in August 1983, that court, at the Board's request, remanded the case to the Board for further consideration. Thereafter, in **Milwaukee Spring II**, a wholly reconstituted Board, consisting of Chairman Dotson, Members Hunter and Diaz Dennis (all Reagan appointees), and Member

---

[7]235 N.L.R.B. 720 (1978), **enforced** 602 F.2d 1302 (9th Cir. 1979).

[8]See NLRB v. Great Dane Trailers, 388 U.S. 26 (1967).

[9]Milwaukee Spring Div., Illinois Coil Spring Co., 265 N.L.R.B. 206 (1982).

Zimmerman, who dissented, overruled the previous decisions in **Los Angeles Marine Hardware** and in two other cases, holding that reassignment of bargaining-unit work impermissibly modified a union recognition clause in the collective bargaining agreement;[10] it also reversed its earlier ruling in **Milwaukee Spring I**. The new majority held that neither the wage and benefit provisions nor the recognition clause in the agreement had the effect of preserving bargaining-unit work at the Milwaukee Spring plant for the duration of the contract, and that the employer had not modified those contract terms when it relocated its assembly operation. It followed, therefore, that there had been no violation of Sections 8(a)(5) or 8(d), or of Sections 8(a)(1) or (3).

The majority in **Milwaukee Spring II** argued that under its decision:

> an employer does not risk giving a union veto power over its decision regarding relocation and should therefore be willing to disclose all factors affecting its decision. Consequently, the union will be in a better position to evaluate whether to make concessions.[11]

The same argument has been stressed by management spokesmen generally, most of whom hail the decision as a return by the Board to a reason-

---

[10] Boeing Co., 230 N.L.R.B. 696 (1977), **enforcement denied** 581 F.2d 793 (9th Cir. 1978); University of Chicago, 210 N.L.R.B. 190 (1974), **enforcement denied** 514 F.2d 942 (7th Cir. 1975).

[11] 268 N.L.R.B 601 (1984).

able and balanced approach toward construction of collective bargaining agreements and of the Act. Union representatives take the opposite position and view the decision in **Milwaukee Spring II** as a major setback. As one union lawyer put it, the decision "renders wage agreements meaningless and will promote a kind of blackmail," because the parties can negotiate a contract, but management is free to seek a wage cut a few months later while threatening to move the work elsewhere, and the union is bound by a no-strike clause.[12]

More recently, in **United Technologies, Otis Elevator Co.,**[13] the Board, reversing an earlier ruling in the same case,[14] unanimously held that the employer was not obligated to bargain with the union before deciding to transfer bargaining unit work to other facilities, because the decision was based on the need to take advantage of "technological advances" and to become more competitive. This time, Member Zimmerman concurred in the result, on the ground that there was "no concession proposed by the Union that could reasonably be expected to alter the Respondent's concerns."[15] Over Zimmerman's dissent, the other three members of the Board also held that the union was not entitled to information relevant to the decision to transfer work, because that deci-

---

[12]Bureau of National Affairs, **Daily Labor Report** No. 19: A-3 (Jan. 30, 1984).

[13]269 N.L.R.B. 891 (1984).

[14]255 N.L.R.B. 235 (1981).

[15]269 N.L.R.B. at 901.

sion was not a mandatory subject of bargaining, and that the issue whether the employer unlawfully refused to bargain over the effects of the decision must be remanded to the administrative law judge.

Thus the Board seems to have come almost full circle since its landmark decision in **Fibreboard Paper Products Corp. v. NLRB,**[16] in 1962. In that case it held that an employer's decision to subcontract maintenance work for economic reasons without first bargaining with the union representing the affected employees constituted an unlawful refusal to bargain. That ruling was ultimately sustained by the Supreme Court, which specifically affirmed that the decision to contract out is a mandatory subject of bargaining. But Justice Stewart, in a separate opinion concurring in the result, which has since been deferred to almost as much as has the majority opinion by Chief Justice Warren, imposed the following gloss on the Court's decision:

> In many...areas the impact of a particular management decision upon job security may be extremely indirect and uncertain, and this alone may be sufficient reason to conclude that such decisions are not...[subject to mandatory bargaining.] Yet there are other areas where decisions by management may quite clearly imperil job security, or indeed terminate employment entirely. An enterprise may decide to invest in labor-saving machinery. Another may resolve to liquidate its assets and go out of business. Nothing the Court holds today should be under-

---

[16]138 N.L.R.B. 550 (1962), **enforced** 322 F.2d 411 (D.C. Cir. 1963), **affirmed** 379 U.S. 203 (1964).

stood as imposing a duty to bargain collectively regarding such managerial decisions which lie at the core of entrepreneurial control....[17]

In 1966 the Board held unanimously, in **Ozark Trailers, Inc.**, that it was an unfair labor practice for an employer to shut down one of several facilities in an integrated enterprise without bargaining first with the union over both the decision to shut down and the impact of that decision on the affected employees. Disagreeing with the decisions denying enforcement of Board orders in two similar cases by the Third and the Eighth Circuit Courts of Appeals,[19] the Board held that **Ozark Trailers** was governed by **Fibreboard**, and declared:

> [W]e do not believe that the question whether a particular management decision must be bargained about should turn on whether the decision involves a commitment of investment capital, or on whether it may be characterized as involving "major" or "basic"

---

[17] 379 U.S. at 223.

[18] 161 N.L.R.B. 561 (1966).

[19] NLRB v. Royal Plating and Polishing Co., 350 F.2d 191 (3d Cir. 1965) (decision to shut down one of employer's two plants involved a "management decision to recommit and reinvest funds in the business" and a "major change in the economic direction of the Company"; no need to bargain); NLRB v. Adams Dairy, Inc., 350 F.2d 108 (8th Cir. 1965), **cert. denied** 382 U.S. 1011 (1966) (employer's decision to subcontract distribution of its product was a "partial liquidation and a recoup of capital investment"; no need to bargain).

change in the nature of the employer's business.[20]

In **Milwaukee Spring II**, however, the majority hinted that the Board's conclusion in **Ozark Trailers** "may not...survive the Supreme Court's analysis"[21] in **First National Maintenance Corp. v. NLRB**,[22] a case I shall discuss below.

Board Deferral to Arbitration Awards

Another Board policy recently overturned by the Reagan Board concerns deferral to arbitration awards. Section 10(a) of the NLRA empowers the NLRB "to prevent any person from engaging in any unfair labor practice... affecting commerce," and declares that this power "shall not be affected by any other means of adjustment or prevention that has been or may be established by agreement, law, or otherwise." Taken literally, this provision would authorize the Board to assume jurisdiction over any meritorious unfair labor practice charge, even though the conduct on which the charge was based also arguably violated the terms of a collective bargaining agreement. In 1955, however, the Board adopted a policy limiting the scope of its jurisdiction over issues that had already been arbitrated and then were submitted to the Board by unsuccessful grievants in the form of unfair labor practice charges. In **Spielberg Mfg. Co.**[23] the Board declared that it

---

[20] 161 N.L.R.B. at 566.
[21] 268 N.S.R.B. 601, 603 (1984).
[22] 452 U.S. 666 (1981).
[23] 122 N.L.R.B. 1080 (1955).

would defer to an arbitrator's award, but only if the arbitration procedures had been fair and regular; all parties had agreed to be bound by the arbitrator's award; and the award was not repugnant to the provisions and policies of the Act. A few years later, the Board announced that it would refuse to defer to an arbitrator's award in so-called pretext cases - i.e., those in which it was alleged that a discharge ostensibly for just cause was actually prompted by an employer's antiunion motive - unless the arbitrator knew of and dealt with the allegation of an unfair labor practice.[24] In **Raytheon Co. v. NLRB**,[25] however, an appellate court held that in such cases the Board must enforce the arbitrator's award unless it affirmatively finds an improper reason for the discharge.

In succeeding years, and under different administrations, the Board's policy on this issue went through several incarnations. In **Electronic Reproduction Service Corp.**[26] the Board, overruling several earlier decisions to the contrary, deferred to an arbitral award sustaining a discharge although the union did not introduce available evidence of unlawful discrimination at the arbitration hearing. In

---

[24] Montsanto Chemical Co., 130 N.L.R.B. 1097 (1961). The Court of Appeals for the District of Columbia Circuit went even further in Banyard v. NLRB, 505 F.2d 342 (D.C. Cir. 1974), holding that to justify Board deferral the arbitrator's award must have addressed the identical issue that would be raised in an unfair labor practice proceeding, and that the arbitrator's construction of the agreement must not depart from the Board's construction of the same language in the statute.

[25] 326 F.2d 471 (1st Cir. 1964).

[26] 213 N.L.R.B. 758 (1974).

Suburban Motor Freight, Inc.,[27] however, Electronic Reproduction was itself expressly overruled, the Board holding that no deference would be given to an arbitration award that did not deal with the statutory issue of discrimination in determining the propriety of the discipline involved, and that the party seeking deferral would have the burden of proving that the issue of discrimination was litigated before the arbitrator. In 1982 a majority of the Board, Chairman Van de Water and Member Hunter dissenting, refused to defer to an arbitration award sustaining a discharge, even though the arbitrator affirmatively found that the discharge was not for activity protected by the NLRA, because no evidence of discrimination by the employer had been submitted to the arbitrator.[28]

Earlier this year, however, in **Olin Corp.**,[29] a majority of the Board, Member Zimmerman dissenting in part, adopted a new standard for deferral to arbitration awards. Until further notice, the Board will "find that an arbitrator has adequately considered the unfair labor practice if (1) the contractual issue is factually parallel to the unfair labor practice issue, and (2) the arbitrator was presented generally with the facts relevant to resolving the unfair labor practice."[30] In addition, the

---

[27] 247 N.L.R.B. 146 (1980).

[28] Professional Porter & Window Cleaning Co., Division of Propoco, Inc., 263 N.L.R.B. 136 (1982).

[29] 268 N.L.R.B. 573 (1984).

[30] Id. at 574.

majority declared that it will not require an arbitrator's award to be totally consistent with Board precedent, so long as the award is susceptible to an interpretation consistent with the Act. Finally, overruling **Suburban Motor Freight** to that extent, the Board will now place the burden of proof on the party seeking to show that deferral should not be granted.

It would be manifestly unfair to single out the Reagan appointees for criticism because they reversed earlier policies on the deferral issue; appointees of other Presidents have done the same thing. Moreover, there are tenable arguments in favor of the Board's latest stance on that question. I have called attention to this series of cases for two reasons. First, it presages a similar about-face by the Board on another aspect of the deferral problem: whether to defer to the grievance and arbitration procedures of a collective bargaining agreement when an employer's conduct arguably violates both the NLRA and the agreement, and the employee files an unfair labor practice charge with the Board instead of using the contract procedures.[31] Second, whether or not one agrees with the most recent decisions of the Reagan Board, it is clear that they are consistent with the prevailing pattern of policies inimical to the objectives of organized labor.

---

[31]Successive combinations of Board members have waffled even more on this issue than on that of deferral to an arbitrator's award. See Collyer Insulated Wire, 192 N.L.R.B. 837 (1971); Roy Robinson Chevrolet, 228 N.L.R.B. 828 (1977); General American Transportation Corp., 228 N.L.R.B. 808 (1977).

Defining "Concerted Activity"

Further evidence of this pattern is to be found in the reversal by the Reagan Board of still another well-established NLRB policy relating to the definition of "concerted activity." Section 7 of the NLRA guarantees to employees, among other things, the right "to engage in...concerted activities for the purpose of...mutual aid or protection." Since 1975 the Board has consistently followed its decision in **Alleluia Cushion Co.**,[32] which held that an employee in an unorganized plant who was discharged for complaining about unsafe working conditions was engaged in protected concerted activity, even though there was no evidence that he acted with the prior or subsequent approval of fellow employees. In the words of the Board,

> ...where an employee speaks up and seeks to enforce statutory provisions relating to occupational safety designed for the benefit of all employees, in the absence of any evidence that fellow employees disavow such representation, we will find an implied consent thereto and deem such activity to be concerted.[33]

In **Meyers Industries, Inc.**,[34] decided earlier this year, the Board, Member Zimmerman dissenting, overruled **Alleluia Cushion Co.** and held that an over-the-road truck driver who

---

[32] 221 N.L.R.B. 999 (1975).

[33] Id. at 1000.

[34] 268 N.L.R.B. 493 (1984).

was discharged because he refused to drive a patently unsafe truck and reported its condition to state safety authorities was not engaged in concerted activity protected by the Act. Uncharacteristically emphasizing that its powers are limited, the Board majority stated:

> Outraged though we may be by a respondent who - at the expense of its driver and others traveling on the nation's highway - was clearly attempting to squeeze the last drop of life out of a trailer that had just as clearly given up the ghost, we are not empowered to correct all immorality or even illegality arising under the total fabric of Federal and state laws.[35]

The Board majority distinguished **Meyers Industries** from other cases involving individual protests against violation of provisions in collective bargaining agreements.[36] In so doing, however, it gave no indication whether it would deem that distinction decisive in future cases.

A few months after deciding **Meyers Industries**, a Board panel consisting of the three Reagan appointees unanimously held, in **Alcan Cable**,[37] that an employee who was discharged for contacting a state workers compensation

---

[35] Id. at 499.

[36] E.g., Interboro Contractors, 157 N.L.R.B. 1295 (1966), **enforced** 388 F.2d 495 (2d Cir. 1967). The **Interboro Contractors** doctrine was expressly approved by the United States Supreme Court in NLRB v. City Disposal Systems, Inc., 104 S.Ct.1505 (1984).

[37] 269 N.L.R.B. 184 (1984).

agency to assert his right to medical treatment and for filing a pay claim under an unorganized employer's internal complaint procedure had not engaged in protected concerted activity and was thus not protected by the Act.

This group of decisions on concerted activity may have one unintended result, namely, to spur efforts to provide statutory protection to unorganized employees who, under prevailing common law principles, may be discharged at will for any reason or no reason. Even in the absence of a statute, and even when, as in California, the employment-at-will doctrine is embodied in the Labor Code,[38] dismissals based on an employee's refusal to violate a law or on his exercise of a constitutional or statutory right have been held by some courts to be unlawful[39]. Under present California law, for

---

[38]Cal. Labor Code §2922 (Deering) provides in relevant part: "An employment, having no specified term, may be terminated at the will of either party on notice to the other...." But see Tameny v. Atlantic Richfield Co., 27 Cal.3d 167, 610 P.2d 1330 (1980) (dismissals of employees that violate public policy create a cause of action in tort; violation of public policy may be established through reference to either statute or "sound morality").

[39]See, e.g., Peterman v. Teamsters Local 396, 174 Cal. App. 2d 184, 344 P.2d 25 (1959) (discharge for refusal to commit perjury at a state legislative committee hearing); Frampton v. Central Indiana Gas Co., 260 Ind. 249, 297 N.E.2d 425 (1973) (discharge for filing workers compensation claim); Monge v. Beebe Rubber Co., 114 N.H. 130, 316 A.2d 549 (1974) (discharge for refusal to go out with foreman); Tameny v. Atlantic Richfield Co., 27 Cal. 3d 167, 610 P. 2d 1330 (1980) (discharge for refusal to participate in illegal scheme to fix prices).

example, the facts in **Meyers Industries** and **Alcan Cable** would support tort actions for unjust dismissal and claims of punitive damages.

Decisions of the Supreme Court

Unilateral Termination of Collective Agreements by Employers

Turning now from the NLRB to the Supreme Court, we find that most of the Court's decisions have reflected a more neutral attitude toward the rights of employees and unions than have the Board's. Nevertheless, within the past few years, in a few of its decisions, from which I have chosen only two examples, the Court has dealt damaging blows to unions. The first of these was the decision in **First National Maintenance Corp. v. NLRB**,[40] to which I referred earlier.[41] In that case an employer, without bargaining with the union representing all affected employees, terminated a contract with a customer and discharged the employees who had been working under that contract. A majority of the Court held that although the employer has a duty to bargain in good faith with the union representing its employees over the effects of the decision to terminate the contract, it has no duty to bargain over the decision itself. The majority proposed a balancing test that would not "serve either party's individual interest, but...[would] foster in a neutral manner a system in which the conflict between these interests may be resolved."[42]

---

[40] 452 U.S. 666 (1981).

[41] See text at note 22 supra.

[42] Id. at 680-81.

Taking for granted "the employer's need for unencumbered decision-making,"[43] the majority concluded that "bargaining over management decisions that have a substantial impact on... continued...employment should be required only if the benefit, for labor-management relations and the collective bargaining process, outweighs the burden placed on the business."[44]

The majority conceded that the union had a legitimate concern about job security, but declared that the union's practical purpose in participating in a decision whether to close a particular facility would be "largely uniform: it will seek to delay or halt the closing."[45] In so doing, the majority continued, the union would "doubtless be impelled...to offer concessions, information, and alternatives that might be helpful to management or forestall the termination of jobs."[46] But the majority thought it unlikely that requiring bargaining over the decision itself would "augment the flow of information and suggestion."[47]

In deciding **First National Maintenance** the Court "intimate[d] no view as to other types of management decisions, such as plant relocations, sales...subcontracting, automation, etc., which are to be considered on their particular facts."[48] Given the thrust of the deci-

---

[43]Id. at 679.
[44]Ibid.
[45]Ibid.
[46]Id. at 681.
[47]Ibid.
[48]Id. at 686, n. 22.

sion in **First National Maintenance,** however, that statement can provide no comfort to unions.

It is clear that in purporting to effect a balance between the competing interests of employers and unions the Court had its thumb on the scale. It noted that if the employer were required to listen to union counterproposals before making a final decision, it would seek concessions permitting it to continue operations; but this consideration was outweighed, in the Court's judgment, by the employer's probable need for "speed, flexibility and secrecy."[49] Moreover, the Court said, "[T]he publicity incident to the normal process of bargaining may injure the possibility of a successful transition or increase the economic dammage to the business."[50] It is no wonder, then, that the Court concluded:

> The harm likely to be done to an employer's need to operate freely in deciding whether to shut down part of its business purely for economic reasons outweighs the incremental benefit that might be gained through the union's participation in making the decision, and we hold that the decision itself is **not** part of ..."terms and conditions"...over which Congress has mandated bargaining.[51]

The Bankruptcy Code and the National Labor Relations Act

The second damaging blow dealt by the Supreme Court to labor unions was its decision

---

[49]Id. at 682.

[50]Ibid.

[51]Id. at 686 (italics in original).

in **NLRB v. Bildisco & Bildisco, Debtor-in-Possession,**[52] a case involving the effect of the Bankruptcy Code on an employer's duty to bargain under the NLRA. Section 365(a) of the Bankruptcy Code provides that, with certain exceptions, the trustee, subject to the bankruptcy court's approval, may reject any "executory contract" of the debtor, i.e., a contract under which acts remain to be performed. In **Bildisco** the employer, a building supplies distributor, filed a voluntary petition in bankruptcy for reorganization under Chapter 11 of the Code, and was subsequently authorized by the bankruptcy court to operate the business as debtor-in-possession. At the time the petition was filed, the employer had a collective bargaining agreement with a union representing its employees. After defaulting on payments due under that agreement, the employer requested and received permission from the bankruptcy court to reject the agreement, and the union was given 30 days in which to file a claim for damages for breach of contract. The District Court upheld that order, and the union appealed. Thereafter, the union filed charges with the NLRB, accusing the employer of unilaterally changing the terms of the collective agreement without first bargaining with the union. The Board found in the union's favor and ordered the employer to make the payments to the union on which it had defaulted.

The Court of Appeals for the Third Circuit consolidated the union's appeal from the decision of the District Court and the Board's petition for enforcement of its order. It ruled that the debtor-in-possession's right to seek rejection of the agreement was not affected by

---

[52] 104 S.Ct. 1188 (1984).

Section 8(d) of the NLRA, which forbids unilateral termination or modification of a collective bargaining agreement without satisfying certain procedural requirements, none of which had been observed in this case. The court refused to enforce the Board's order, holding that the debtor-in-possession was a new entity, not bound by the debtor's prior agreement. The court held that in order to obtain permission to reject an executory contract the debtor-in-possession must show not only that the contract burdens the estate, but also that the balance of equities favors rejection.

While **Bildisco** awaited a final decision by the United States Supreme Court, several large employers either sought refuge under Chapter 11 of the Bankruptcy Code and repudiated their collective bargaining agreements, or threatened to take such action unless the unions party to those agreements granted them immediate and substantial concessions in respect of wages, fringe benefits, and work rules. Perhaps the most notable exemplar of this tactic was Continental Airlines, which, after unsuccessfully demanding that the three unions representing the bulk of its employees acquiesce in immediate major concessions, sought the protection of Chapter 11 and then repudiated the collective bargaining agreements, cut wages by 50 percent, and abolished existing work rules. Subsequently, a bankruptcy court sustained the legality of this action; its decision is currently being appealed.[53]

The Supreme Court handed down its long-awaited decision in **Bildisco** in February 1984.

---

[53] In re: Continental Airlines Corp., 99 CCH Lab. Cas. ¶10,748 (Bankruptcy Court, S.D. Tex. 1984).

It unanimously affirmed the Court of Appeals holding that the language of Section 365 (a) of the bankruptcy Code relating to executory contracts includes collective bargaining agreements subject to the NLRA, and held that the rejection of such agreements may be permitted by the bankruptcy court if the debtor can show that the agreement burdens the estate and that the balance of equities favors rejection. Four members of the Supreme Court dissented, however, from the majority's conclusion that the NLRB may not find a debtor-in-possession guilty of an unfair labor practice for unilaterally terminating or modifying a collective bargaining agreement, even when such action is taken **before** the bankruptcy court has formally approved it. Conceding that there is some tension between the policies underlying the Bankruptcy Code and a holding that Section 8(d) of the NLRA remains applicable after a bankruptcy petition has been filed, the dissenters argued that the majority had ignored the problem instead of trying to resolve it in a way that accommodates the policies of both federal statutes. Speaking for the dissenters, Justice Brennan remarked, perhaps prophetically:

> Holding §8(d) inapplicable in these circumstances...strikes at the very heart of the policies underlying that section and the NLRA, and will, I believe, spawn precisely the type of industrial strife that NLRA §8(d) was designed to avoid.[54]

For reasons not pertinent to this discussion, Congress is obliged to amend the 1978 bankruptcy law.[55] Many members of Congress,

---

[54]104 S. Ct. at 1211.

[55]In Northern Pipeline Construction Co. v. Marathon Pipeline Co., 458 U.S. 50 (1982), the United States Supreme Court struck down as a violation of Article III of the Constitution

shocked by the Supreme Court's decision in **Bildisco** and heavily lobbied by representatives of organized labor, are supporting an amendment sponsored by Representative Peter Rodino of New Jersey, Chairman of the House Judiciary committee, which would require a hearing before a bankruptcy court prior to rejection of a collective bargaining agreement, and would forbid the court to permit such rejection unless the employer met the strict standards laid down by the Court of Appeals for the Second Circuit in **Brotherhood of Railway, Airline and Steamship Clerks v. REA Express,** [56] namely, that rejection should be authorized "only where it clearly appears to be the lesser of two evils and that, unless the agreement is rejected, the [employer] will collapse and the employees will no longer have their jobs."[57] This test, of course, was specifically rejected by the Supreme Court in **Bildisco.**

Ever since the Rodino bill was introduced, both Houses of Congress have been considering a number of compromise proposals; the situation has been further complicated by divisions within the ranks of both the proponents and opponents of legislative relief for the unions. Because Congress, sooner or later, must amend the bankruptcy law by replacing its unconstitu-

---

the 1978 bankruptcy law because it provided for independent bankruptcy judges who lacked lifetime tenure. Pending enactment of remedial legislation by Congress, the bankruptcy judges are governed by interim rules promulgated by the Administrative Office of the United States Courts. Among other things, those rules require that decisions of bankruptcy courts in Chapter 11 cases be approved by the appropriate federal district courts.

[56]523 F.2d 164 (2d Cir. 1975).

[57]**Id.** at 172.

tional features, and because the fight over the labor provision threatens to delay passage of the amendment indefinitely, the situation obviously calls for a compromise. It is indicative of the present climate of labor-management relations, however, that a representative of the U.S. Chamber of Commerce, the self-styled "principal spokesman for American business," was quoted in the **Wall Street Journal** as saying, "The defeat of the labor provision is our No. 1 priority - it's that simple."[58] But, perhaps, it is not that simple; for some big retailers, credit lenders, and the American Bankers Association are reported in the same **Journal** article as opposing the Chamber and favoring a compromise. If the major lobbying groups on the other side - AFL-CIO, Air Line Pilots Association, and Teamsters - can compose their differences, organized labor may yet salvage something from the disaster wrought by the **Bildisco** decision.[59]

---

[58]**Wall Street Journal,** Apr. 26, 1984, p. 33, col. 3.

[59]After this paper was presented, a legislative compromise was reached and a new provision - section 1113 - was added to the Code to deal specifically with rejection of collective bargaining agreements in Chapter 11 cases. It provides that after filing its bankruptcy petition and **before** applying to a bankruptcy court for permission to reject an agreement, a debtor-in-possession (DIP) must make a proposal to the union setting forth "the necessary modifications in the employees' benefits and protections that are necessary to permit the reorganization of the debtor and assures that all creditors, the debtor and all of the affected parties are treated fairly and equitably." The DIP is also obligated to furnish the union with the most complete and reliable information then available to assist the latter to evaluate its proposal, subject to such a protective court order as may be necessary to prevent disclosure of the information to the DIP's competitors.

The Current Climate of Labor-Management Relations

There is little doubt that, as previously mentioned, the present climate of labor-management relations in this country is characterized by considerable belligerence on the part of many employers and their advisers. Hardly a week goes by that I do not receive in the mail announcements of conferences or seminars designed to show employers how to avoid unionization of their employees or to get rid of unions with which they presently deal. At a recent hearing before a New York State legislative committee, union witnesses complained that the economic strike, i.e., a legal strike not caused by an employer's unfair labor practices, is being used as a "union-busting tool" by employers who provoke strikes so that they can

---

Thereafter, the DIP must meet and confer in good faith with the union in an effort to reach mutually satisfactory modifications of the agreement. The court may approve the DIP's application for rejection only if it finds (1) that the DIP's proposal for modifications is necessary and fair; (2) that the union has refused to accept it "without good cause"; and (3) that "the balance of equities clearly favors rejection of such agreement." The court must schedule a hearing on the DIP's application within 14 days (which may be extended to 21 days "in the interests of justice"), and all interested parties have a right to appear and be heard. Following the hearing, the court must rule on the application within 30 days from the commencement of the hearing, unless the parties agree to an extension of time. If the court fails to rule within the allotted time, the DIP may unilaterally terminate or alter the agreement, pending the court's final determination.

hire permanent replacements for the strikers.[60] At a recent meeting of the National Lawyers Guild in Chicago, attorneys reported that the filing of libel charges against unions or dissident employee groups is proving to be an effective tool to discourage employee criticism of management policies.[61] The Postal Service's Board of Governors, a policy-setting group appointed by the President, and now controlled by Reagan appointees, which has never before played an active role in contract negotiations, has recently hired its own attorney to advise the Postal Service management on bargaining strategy, and has publicly ordered the negotiators to roll back wages and benefits for any classification of postal workers whose pay exceeds that for comparable workers in private industry.[62] In the coal industry even some members of the Bituminous Coal Operators Association (BCOA) are critical of its chief spokesman's bargaining style, which they characterize as "pugnacious, macho, cowboy."[63] Both BCOA and the United Mineworkers are getting set for a strike in the forthcoming negotiations over the terms of a new agreement.

Inevitably, this belligerence has resulted in similar muscle-flexing on the union side. Among workers in the automobile industry, which

---

[60]Bureau of National Affairs, **Daily Labor Report** No. 58:A-8 (Mar. 26, 1984).

[61]Id., No. 55:A-4 (Mar. 21, 1984).

[62]**Wall Street Journal,** Apr. 23, 1984, p. 7, col. 1.

[63]Id., p. 31, col. 3.

has made at least a temporary recovery from its previously depressed state, a popular slogan is "restore and more" - a demand that all previous wage and fringe concessions be restored and that substantial increases be granted. This sentiment has been fueled by announcements of record-breaking company profits and generous bonuses being granted to automobile company executives. Even the spokesmen for the postal unions, whose members cannot legally strike, are warning that if pushed too far, their members may walk out anyway.[64]

On the other hand, one hears increasingly the call for industry and labor to abandon their "confrontational" policies in favor of mutual cooperation for their joint benefit. Thus, Paul W. McCracken, a former chairman of the Council of Economic Advisors, wrote recently in the **Wall Street Journal:**

>The main reason for hope that the cost inflation, which so bedeviled the economy during the 1970s, will not automatically return with economic expansion is a growing conviction that the old confrontational relationships between management and employees will not work out well for anyone. A major change in our philosophy about these relationships seems to be emerging....
>
>Whether this emergent view will last...remains to be seen, but in the inscrutable ways of these processes in a free society, they may be nudging us into an era when we will less prone to shoot ourselves in the foot

---

[64]**Ibid;** Bureau of National Affairs, **Daily Labor Report,** No. 72:A-6 (Apr. 13, 1984).

through self-imposed cost inflation.[65]

The public expression of such sentiments is a recurring phenomenon in American life. As in the present case, they reflect hopes rather than reality. In the words of the late Professor Sir Otto Kahn-Freund, "conflict between capital and labour is inherent in an industrial society and therefore in the labour relationship. Conflicts of interest are inevitable in all societies."[66] In some segments of American industry there are signs of increased cooperation between management and employees; but such cooperation tends to take the form of implementing decisions unilaterally made by management. There is neither a widespread effort by unions to participate actively in the making of basic managerial decisions, through membership on boards of directors, nor any apparent willingness on the part of management to consider this form of participation. Among unorganized firms, which are generally the most vociferous advocates of greater employer-employee cooperation, the major incentive appears to be the avoidance of unions, and in many cases the so-called participation in decision making by employees is nothing more than a form of sophisticated manipulation of consent.

As is also customary, there are those who seek to import to the United States aspects of foreign systems they find agreeable. The apparent absence of serious conflict in Japanese

---

[65]McCracken, "On the Inflation Watch," **Wall Street Journal,** Apr. 11, 1984, p. 26, col. 4.

[66]O. Kahn-Freund, **Labour and the Law** 17 (2d ed. 1977).

labor-management relations has led to suggestions that we accept the Japanese system as an appropriate model for ourselves. Such naive proposals lack merit, not because we cannot learn from others, but because institutional devices cannot be separated from the total culture from which they emerged and be transplanted into a totally alien environment. The most important lesson we can learn from the Japanese is how to recognize useful new ideas and then adapt them to our own culture. Inasmuch as our society is founded on the belief in competition and a free market, however, it is idle to suppose that we can preserve those ideals and somehow eliminate competition between capital and labor.[67]

Outlook for the Near Future

Developments in labor-management relations, even in the near term, are likely to be heavily influenced by events that have not yet taken place. The trends I have mentioned in the decisions of the NLRB will be accelerated, as the administration imposes its ideology more firmly on that agency; but that is only part of the picture. One may also expect a continuation and enhancement of the policy of a relaxed governmental enforcement of labor protective legislation such as the Occupational Safety and Health Act (OSHA), renewed efforts to lift the ban on home work in the garment industry, and the like.

Whether the economy, and the society as a whole, will be better off if these events actually occur, is, of course, a matter of indivi-

---

[67]Aaron, "Plant Closings: American and Comparative Perspectives," 59 **Chi-Kent L. Rev.** 941 (1983).

dual opinion. Unions and their supporters, under the best of circumstances from their point of view, however, face an immediate future that is rather bleak. The percentage of union membership in the labor force, now hovering around 20 percent, continues to decline. Moreover, much of the substance of collective bargaining has been preempted by federal or state legislation, which is applicable to all workers, regardless of union membership. I refer to such laws as OSHA, various statutes, executive orders, and administrative regulations prohibiting employment discrimination on the basis of race, religion, sex, national origin, age and handicap, the Employee Retirement Income Security Act (ERISA), and many others. The emerging remedy against unjust dismissal may perhaps also diminish the attractiveness of unions for the unorganized; for the promise of unions to defend individual employees against arbitrary and invidious treatment by employers has traditionally been perhaps their most persuasive appeal.

Robert J. Flanagan

11

Labor Compensation and Labor Costs

Introduction

It is tempting to suggest that changes in the level and structure of compensation are subject to three general influences: inflation, the tax system, and Adam Smith's durable observations on the role of nonpecuniary attributes of work in job choice. This view is a trifle simple - labor unions and statutory wage regulation can exert an independent influence on compensation, for example - but it remains a fairly powerful organizing principle for the analysis of the major compensation developments during the 1970s and the likely behavior of compensation in the near future.

During the 1970s, inflation was an influence on the general pattern of pay changes; the tax laws continued to stimulate an increase in the importance of nonwage compensation; and social legislation altered the risks associated with many jobs and job environments in ways that may influence the structure of compensation. In addition, institutional influences can be found in the growth of the union-nonunion wage differential and in periodic increases in the federal minimum wage.

My purpose in this paper is **not** to add to the long list of studies that have shown how responsive compensation changes are to unemployment (or some other indicator of the tightness of labor markets) and changes in prices. The factors influencing aggregate changes in wages are fairly well understood. Instead, I shall focus on certain changes in the composition of aggregate pay that were important in the 1970s and are likely to be of concern throughout the 1980s. With this in mind, the first section below decomposes the growth of compensation during the 1970s into its main elements and explores the implications of compensation growth for changes in the international competitiveness of the United States.

The second section examines the sources and future prospects for two of the most notable recent changes in the structure of compensation - the growth of the union-nonunion pay differential and of the share of nonwage benefits in total compensation. I find little evidence of important structural changes in wage-setting procedures, and hence little reason to believe that the response of pay to a given set of economic stimuli would be any different in the future than it was in the 1970s. This observation leads to the concluding section of the paper, which addresses the problems confronting possible future attempts to use incomes policy to restrain the growth of compensation.

Growth of Compensation

The role of some of the basic elements in the growth of labor compensation in the 1970s is illustrated by the data in Table 1. The growth rate of average hourly earnings reported in the first line of the table is notable largely for the extent to which it exceeded the trend rate of growth of labor productivity, generally estimated to have been less than one percent per year since 1973. The well-known result of this gap was a substantial increase in unit labor costs (to be discussed more extensively below). During this same period prices increased at an average annual rate of 7.8 percent per year, so that real wage gains were quite modest.

A comparison of the first two lines of Table 1 indicates that fringe benefits, including legally required payments by employers for social insurance, increased more rapidly than wages during the 1970s. (This trend will be explored in more detail in the next section). Hourly compensation includes payment for time not worked, including vacations, holidays, wash-up time and the like, so that hours paid for (the general concept used in wage and compensation data) typically exceed hours worked. In the third line of Table 1, the hourly compensation data have been adjusted (by Daniel S. Hamermesh) to correct for the fraction of time not worked and to include certain irregular payments to workers (e.g., bonuses).[1] Largely

---

[1] Daniel S. Hamermesh, "New Measures of Labor Cost: Implications for Demand Elasticities and Nominal Wage Growth," in Jack E. Triplett, (ed.), **The Measurement of Labor Cost** (Chicago: University of Chicago Press, 1983), pp. 287-305.

Table 1

Growth of Alternative Labor Cost Series,
1970-1980[a]
(average annual percent change)

	Manufacturing	Private Business
Annual hour earnings	8.3	7.9
Hourly compensation	8.8	8.5
Cost per hour worked	9.0	8.7
Cost per hour worked, adjusted for taxes	9.1	8.7

Source: Daniel S. Hamermesh, "New Measures of Labor Cost: Implications for Demand Elasticities and Nominal Wage Growth," in Jack E. Triplett, ed., **The Measurement of Labor Cost** (Chicago: University of Chicago Press, 1983), Appendix C.

[a]Fourth quarter to fourth quarter.

because of increases in paid holidays and vacations, labor cost per hour worked grew more rapidly than hourly compensation during the 1970s.

It is well-recognized that the tax system can drive a wedge between payments made by employers and payments received by employees. Wages and fringe benefit contributions are deductable expenses for corporations, and the deductions are worth more when the corporation tax is high than when it is low. Declines in the corporation income tax, as occurred during the 1970s, effectively increased the cost of labor to employers. The bottom line in Table 1 adjusts for the effect of the declining corporate income tax on labor costs by multiplying the cost per hour worked by one minus the maximum marginal tax rate on corporations. The effect on the general growth of labor costs was modest. Nevertheless, it will become apparent below that the impact of taxes on the **structure** of compensation can be of considerable importance.

One element of labor compensation is not reflected in Table 1. This element is the (net) nonpecuniary benefits of jobs that economists have recognized as an influence on the allocation of labor since the days of Adam Smith. Smith's basic point was that unlike other factors of production, labor receives positive or negative utility from various nonmonetary aspects of a job, including degree of risk, discretion, exertion, etc., and this utility should be included in the definition of compensation that is relevant for the job choices made by workers. Jobs that differ in their nonmonetary aspects will tend to have offsetting differences in wage rates in order to be equally attractive, so that the wage structure becomes a set of "equalizing" or "compensating" wage differentials.[2] During a period in which nonpecuniary benefits increase, therefore, wages should increase less rapidly than they would otherwise. Something like this may have occurred during the 1970s as a result of legislation aimed at improving health and safety conditions at the workplace. To the extent that the legislation succeeded in improving the nonmonetary aspects of some jobs (at a cost to affected employers), wages should have grown less rapidly than they would have otherwise. In this sense, the data in Table 1 may **understate** the growth of compensation and employer labor costs in the 1970s.

Both the general growth of hourly compensation and labor costs during the 1970s discussed above and the dramatic deceleration of wages and compensation in the early 1980s, to 4 to 5 percent annual growth rates in 1983, are of interest in part for their implications for

---

[2]The effects of labor unions or wage legislation may alter the compensatory aspects of the wage structure somewhat, but in fact there is considerable empirical evidence of exactly the kinds of tradeoffs between wages and other job characteristics anticipated by Smith. For example, wages vary to offset the costs of human capital investments and the risk of death associated with a job. See Gary Becker, **Human Capital**, 2nd ed. (New York: National Bureau of Economic Research, 1975); Jacob Mincer, **Schooling, Experience and Earnings** (New York: National Bureau of Economic Research, 1974); Robert S. Smith, "Compensating Wage Differentials and Public Policy: A Review," **Industrial and Labor Relations Review**, Vol. 32 (April 1979), pp. 339-52. Evidence is mixed on the relation between wages and risk of injury on the job.

the international competitive position of the United States. Some illustrative data on this are provided in Table 2. Despite the aggregation, several interesting central tendencies are revealed by the data.

First, it is obvious that during the 1970s compensation was generally increasing at a more rapid rate abroad than within the United States. In terms of national currencies, compensation increased 230 percent over the decade in the U.S. manufacturing sector, in comparison to 264 percent in West Germany and 359 percent in Japan.

Second, in comparison to Germany and Japan, the development of labor **costs** during the 1970s in the United States was just the opposite of the comparative development of compensation. The compensation data in panel A of Table 2 do not provide a reliable guide to the comparative development of labor costs until they are adjusted for the growth of labor productivity, which varies considerably among countries. Panel B of the table presents comparative data on the growth of unit labor costs (hourly compensation divided labor productivity) since 1970. Despite the relatively slow growth of hourly compensation in the United States, the growth of labor productivity was slower still in comparison to West Germany and Japan, so that relative unit labor costs in U.S. manufacturing increased. The U.S. unit labor cost story is more favorable in relation to the trade-weighted average of eleven foreign countries (including Germany and Japan). Nevertheless, the depreciation of the U.S. dollar during the 1970s effectively **reversed** the disadvantageous position of the United States re-

Table 2

Comparative Compensation and Unit Cost in
Manufacturing, 1970-1983
(annual percent changes)

	United States	West Germany	Japan	Eleven Foreign Countries[a]
Hourly Compensation in Manufacturing (in national currency)			
1970-1980				
1980	8.7	10.2	13.6	13.4[b]
1981	11.7	8.8	7.9	11.7
1982	9.9	7.6	6.3	12.0
1983	8.5	5.5	3.4	9.3

Unit Labor Costs in Manufacturing, 1970-1983

	National Currency	U.S. Dollar	National Currency	U.S. Dollar	National Currency	U.S. Dollar	National Currency	U.S. Dollar
1970-1980								
1980	6.0	6.0	5.4	13.1	5.5	10.5	8.9[b]	9.9[b]
1981	11.5	11.5	7.3	8.3	-1.5	-4.7	9.3	10.0
1982	6.1	6.1	5.1	-15.3	0.5	3.1	8.1	-5.8
1983	7.2	7.2	3.8	-3.7	-0.7	-12.2	7.1	-4.6

Sources: U.S. Bureau of Labor Statistics, Office of Productivity and Technology, "Output Per Hour, Hourly Compensation, and Unit Labor Costs in Manufacturing, Twelve Countries, 1951-1981," unpublished paper (January 1974); and Donato Alvarez and Brian Cooper, "Productivity Trends in Manufacturing in the United States and Eleven Other Countries," **Monthly Labor Review** (January 1984), pp. 52-58.

[a] Trade-weighted average of Canada, Japan, and nine European countries.

[b] 1973-1979.

lative to Germany and Japan in unit labor cost growth.

Third, the relative labor cost position of the United States has apparently worsened since 1980, despite the deep recession and sharp deceleration in compensation that included significant wage concessions in some parts of the union sector. However dramatic the behavior of domestic compensation, it is clear from Table 2 that in a comparative sense, the U.S. labor cost position has continued to deteriorate. Compensation did decelerate more in the United States than it did on average in a group of eleven foreign trading partners (although compensation increases in Germany and Japan fell considerably more than in the United States). Moreover, a comparison of the estimates in terms of national currencies in panel B shows that after accounting for productivity growth, unit labor costs decelerated more in the United States than on average in eleven foreign countries. (Again, however, there was a more rapid deceleration in Germany and Japan). The powerful influence on international labor cost comparisons in the early 1980s, however, has been the appreciation of the dollar. Once the effects of the appreciation have been taken into account (compare the national currency and U.S. dollar estimates in panel B), there has been a **decline** in unit labor costs abroad since 1970, while the increase was merely slowed within the United States.[3]

---

[3]The same point can be made when attention is restricted to production workers in manufacturing. Between 1980 and 1983, hourly compensation costs in Germany declined from 125 to 84 percent of the comparable costs in the United

Structure of Compensation

The steady march of aggregate compensation sometimes obscures important changes in the structure of pay. This section addresses developments and prospects in two aspects of the structure of compensation in which there have been significant changes - union-nonunion differences and nonwage benefits.

Union-Nonunion Compensation Differences

One of the developments with the most far-reaching consequences was the sustained growth of the union-nonunion wage differential since 1970. Prior to 1970, the relation between the union and nonunion wage levels was substantially influenced by the difference in the duration of employment contracts in the two sectors. On average, formal employment contracts are longer in the union sector than in the nonunion sector in the sense that the time period between dates at which wages can be adjusted in response to **all** relevant contingencies is longer for union workers. Therefore, union wage growth tended to lag behind nonunion wage growth in the early stages of periods of unexpected slowdowns in growth. The result was a tendency toward a countercyclical movement in the ratio of union to nonunion wage rates, but no real trend to the relative wage advantage of unionism once a union was established.

States. The decline in Japan was from 57 to 51 percent (U.S. Bureau of Labor Statistics, Office of Productivity and Technology, "Hourly Compensation Costs for Production Workers in Manufacturing, 22 Countries, 1975-83," [Xerox], Janurary 1974).

This pattern of relative wage behavior was broken in the 1970s as inflation in combination with the spread of cost-of-living adjustment (COLA) clauses increased union wages relative to nonunion wages (and increased the wages of union workers with COLA clauses relative to union workers without COLA clauses). Because COLA clauses are more prevalent in (and are often a quid pro quo for) long duration contracts, the union-nonunion differential grew more rapidly in manufacturing (where long-term contracts are relatively frequent) than in nonmanufacturing (where contracts are shorter and COLAs less prevalent). As a result, the union-nonunion wage differential in manufacturing increased by over 13 percentage points between 1969 and 1982.[4] Wage developments in 1983 only just began to reverse the 13-year growth in the differential. Indeed, it would take another decade of the differences in union and nonunion wage growth of the size observed in 1983 to restore the relative union wage in manufacturing to its 1969 level. The union-nonunion wage gap in nonmanufacturing was more variable during the 1970s, but widened substantially in the early 1980s. Union and nonunion wage channels in nonmanufacturing only returned to equality

---

[4]The growth in the union-nonunion **compensation** differential may have been even greater. There is evidence that the level of fringe benefits is higher in union firms than in nonunion firms, reflecting differences in the preferences of average and marginal workers. The same factors may raise the relative growth fringes for union workers. See Richard B. Freeman, "The Effect of Trade Unions on Fringe Benefits," **Industrial and Labor Relations Review,** Vol. 34 (July 1981), pp. 489-509.

in 1983. There will obviously have to be a more substantial deceleration in order to move the gap back toward where it was in the late 1970s.

What are the prospects for a continuation of the recent reversal of the union-nonunion wage gap into the future? Since much of the growth of the gap during the 1970s is related to the spread of inflation and COLAs, it is obvious that a continued reduction in the wage gap depends in part on the behavior of inflation. This is particularly so because the concession bargaining of the early 1980s did not lead to a widespread abandonment of COLAs either generally or in the industries under the greatest economic pressure.[5]

A second hope for a reduction of the union-nonunion wage gap would be to mitigate the rigidity of fixed, deferred increases in pay in long-duration collective bargaining agreements. The fixed annual improvement factor (AIF) was originally grounded in developments in labor productivity. With the decline in the productivity growth trend in the United States during the late 1960s and 1970s, however, the AIF was not in general revised downward. Sustained progress in reducing the union-nonunion wage gap would appear to depend upon the ability to establish collective bargaining agreements that trade at least some of the former AIF for profit sharing or other plans that link pay to firm performance. This

---

[5]For details on this point, see Robert J. Flanagan, "Wage Concessions and Long-Term Union Wage Flexibility," **Brookings Papers on Economic Activity**, 1:1984, pp. 183-216.

is all the more important because the weight of the recent evidence on the recovery of productivity is not very encouraging.[6]

Unfortunately, the prognosis for this type of change is not great given the incidence and the features of the negotiated plans to date. Since 1980, the coverage of profit-sharing plans has increased from 1 percent to 8 to 10 percent of workers under major collective bargaining agreements. The new plans have basically been negotiated in those industries in which the product market pressures have been greatest.[7] This is quite consistent with the view that union policy is likely to be dominated by the views of the median (voting) union member. Under seniority arrangements, the median voter is not susceptible to layoff under normal economic fluctuations. A fixed-wage policy is a fixed-income policy and is preferred to the more uncertain income stream offered by performance-based compensation. When layoffs

---

[6]A recent econometric exploration concludes that the recovery of productivity and profits is about in line with the cyclical turnaround, but no more than that. See Peter K. Clark, "Productivity and Profits in the 1980s: Are They Really Improving?" **Brookings Papers on Economic Activity,** 1:1984, pp. 133-67.

[7]Interestingly, profit-sharing plans are not widespread in the nonunion sector either. A Bureau of Labor Statistics Survey of medium and large size firms indicates that about 13 percent of production workers were eligible to participate in profit sharing and 24 percent were eligible to participate in various stock ownership plans (U.S. Bureau of Labor Statistics, **Employee Benefits in Industry, 1980,** Bulletin 2107 [Washington, D.C.: U.S. Government Printing Office, 1981], p. 31).

threaten the employment of the median union voter, as they have in some industries in the early 1980s, compensation proposals that index pay to performance become more possible. But this incentive does not apply to all industries and even within an industry or union, not all firms have adopted such plans.[8]

Some of the plans have first-year guarantees that effectively convert them into fixed wage increases much like an annual improvement factor, because the profit rates that would be necessary to generate the payments in the absence of the guarantee are unrealistically high under present conditions. Others, e.g., those that distribute profits on the basis of a worker's share of total hours compensated rather than total compensation, are proportionately more beneficial to low-wage than high-wage workers. Such formulae may generate internal disagreement over the value of maintaining performance-based compensation as a large component of compensation in the future. One attraction of such plans to management, but a detriment from the union's point of view, is that profit-sharing payments ordinarily do not go into the base wage rate. They have to be "earned all over again" in each pay period. Perhaps more importantly, payments that do not go into the base rate do not trigger automatic increases in employer payments into certain

_____

[8]For example, GM and Ford have profit sharing, but Chrysler does not; some smaller steel companies have plans, but a proposal recommended by the leadership of the United Steelworkers for the Big Eight steel companies was turned down by the bargaining council of local union presidents.

fringe benefits (e.g., pensions).[9] The gloomy conclusion of all this is that progress in reducing the union-nonunion wage gap is likely to be slow in the next decade, and what progress occurs will be largely dependent on a lower inflation rate.

Nonwage Benefits

Discussions of inflation and its control inevitably focus on wages, but it is important to note that nonwage (fringe) benefits have increased on average twice as fast as wages during the postwar period and by 1980 constituted about 37 percent of the payroll of private industry. (Fringes increased from about 31 to 37 percent of payrolls during the 1970s alone.) In this section we consider the components of the increase, some determinants of the increase, and the prospects for the future behavior of fringe benefits.

What types of fringe benefits are mainly responsible for the declining share of wages in compensation? The data in Table 3 describe the share of the **increase** in total fringe benefit payments by employers from 1951-71 and 1971-80 accounted for by several major categories of benefits along with their share in the **level** of benefits in 1980. There are no major changes between the two periods and for present purposes it is more useful to focus on the more recent period. It is clear from the table that over a third of the increase in fringes result-

---

[9]For a more detailed discussion of the incentives embedded in recently negotiated profit-sharing plans, see Flanagan, "Wage Concessions and Union Wage Flexibility," pp. 201-09.

Table 3

Shares and Shares of Growth in Total Employer Fringe Benefit Payments, 1951-1980

Type of Benefit	Share of Growth of Total Employee Benefits (percent) 1951-1971	1971-1980	Share of Total Employee Benefits 1980 (%)
Legally required payments[a] (employee's share)	21.2	26.1	23.8
Agreed-upon payments for pensions, insurance, etc.	33.6	35.1	34.0
Pensions	14.7	13.7	14.6
Premiums for medical, hospital, & life insurance	16.9	16.4	15.6
Paid lunch and rest periods	11.4	8.4	9.5
Payments for time not worked[b]	28.6	24.6	26.7
Other[c]	5.2	5.8	6.0

Source: Survey Research Center, U.S. Chamber of Commerce.

[a]OASDI (FICA) taxes, unemployment compensation, workers' compensation, railroad benefits.

[b]Paid vacations, holidays, sick leave, etc.

[c]Including payments for profit sharing, thrift plans, special bonuses, and employee education.

ed from premiums for pension plans, medical plans, life insurance, and smaller items that are not legally required of employers. Next in importance are legally required payments for programs such as social security, unemployment insurance, workers compensation, etc., which account for about a quarter of the increase in fringe benefit costs during the seventies. (Some of this increase reflects an overindexation of social security payments to inflation in the early part of the 1970s.) Increased payments for time not worked (e.g., vacations, holidays and sick leave) accounted for another quarter of the increase.

Some fringe benefit contributions are computed on the basis of an individual's earnings and hence have a technical relationship to wages that produces parallel movement over time. Several types of fringe benefits also increased their **share** of total compensation and contributed to the growth in the importance of fringes in the total payroll during the 1970s, however. (None of the categories of fringes decreased significantly relative to wages during the period). Table 4 points to this by showing the change in employer contributions as a percent of payroll for several individual categories of fringe benefits. It is clear that most of the expansion in the role of fringes came from legally required payments (particularly social security) and the health and life insurance contributions.

Why has the income elasticity of demand for some fringe benefits been greater than one, producing an increased shared of fringes in compensation over time and across income groups? Economic analysis suggests that em-

Table 4

Employer Fringe Benefit Payments as Percent of Payroll, 1951-1980

Type of Benefit	1971 (%)	1980 (%)	Change 1971-80 (%)
Total employee fringe benefits	30.8	37.1	6.3
Legally required payments	6.3	8.9	2.6
OASDI	4.5	5.8	1.3
Unemployment compensation	0.7	1.4	0.7
Workers' compensation	1.0	1.6	0.6
Agreed-upon payments	10.0	12.6	2.6
Pensions	4.9	5.4	0.5
Premiums for medical, life insurance, etc.	4.5	5.8	1.3
Paid lunch and rest periods	3.4	3.5	0.1
Payments for time not worked	9.2	9.9	0.7
Vacations	4.8	4.9	0.1
Holidays	3.0	3.4	0.4
Sick Leave	1.0	1.3	0.3
Other	1.9	2.2	0.3

Source: Survey Research Center, U.S. Chamber of Commerce.

ployees should be schizophrenic about nonwage benefits. On the one hand, there is the well-worn result that under most circumstances greater satisfaction can be achieved with cash (which can be allocated across alternatives in accord with one's tastes) than with income in kind. Arrayed against this incentive is the role of tax incentives. Employees facing higher marginal tax rates should prefer an increasing fraction of compensation in nontaxable (or deferred tax) form. To the extent that fringe benefits are not taxed or are effectively taxed at lower rates than income, higher income groups should prefer a larger proportion of their income in this form. Under an income tax system that is not indexed to inflation, the demand for fringes will increase relative to wages over time as inflation moves workers into higher marginal tax brackets.[10]

For employers, the tax incentives are somewhat different. The effect of the corporate tax is neutral with respect to the form in which compensation is paid, since both wage and fringe payments are deductible. However, some legally required employer payments (e.g., those for social security and workers' compensation) are computed as a fraction of the earnings base, so that each dollar of wage compensation

---

[10]This general idea may even have some application to legally required payments through constituent pressure on political representatives. In addition, there is a less visible way in which rising marginal tax rates influence the structure of compensation. High marginal tax rates should increase the demand for nonpecuniary benefits compensation, which also are untaxed.

"costs" an employer more than a dollar of nonwage compensation. With the growth in the OASDHI tax rate from 4.8 percent to 6.05 percent during the 1970s, an increase in employer preferences for nonwage compensation is understandable.

What does the taxation explanation of the past growth of the share of fringes in total compensation imply about the future development of the share during the 1980s? Three factors pertaining to taxation raise the possibility of a slowdown in the growth. First, under the Economic Recovery Tax Act of 1981, marginal tax rates at the highest income levels have fallen. Second, that legislation provides for indexation of the federal income tax brackets and exemptions beginning in 1985. The first of these changes reduces the incentive to increase the share of compensation taken as nontaxable fringe (or nonpecuniary) benefits directly. The second reduces the incentive to increase the share as a result of bracket creep during periods of rapid inflation. Third, OASDHI tax rate on the wage base is expected to increase more slowly during the 1980s than during the 1970s.

These developments may have little to do with the growth of nonwage compensation during the last half of the 1980s, however. In the face of sizeable federal budget deficits projected for the next several years, it seems likely that Congress will be driven to consider tax reforms that will generate more revenue, and none of the alternatives currently under discussion are likely to leave the incentives for nonwage compensation unaltered. Because different proposals have different effects on the incentives for nonwage (and nonpecuniary) benefits, the implications of some of the main alternatives are reviewed below.

First, Congress could repeal the indexation provisions of the Economic Recovery Tax Act. Employee demand for nonwage benefits would then continue to be a fraction of inflation, due to bracket creep, but the effect of a given amount of inflation would be muted in relation to the 1970s because the brackets have been widened.

Second, Congress could retain the concept of an income tax but broaden the income base that is subject to taxation in order to raise revenues. One leading version of this approach, the Bradley-Gephart proposal, contains a list of changes that would broaden the taxbase, including termination of the exclusion form taxable income of some fringe benefits (e.g., employer-purchased health insurance).[11]

Third, Congress could produce a more farreaching revision of the tax system by moving from the concept of taxing income to the concept of taxing expenditure. The latter approach is variously referred to as a consumption tax, a cash flow tax, or a lifetime income tax (to emphasize the idea that it is the time path of taxes rather than the total lifetime taxes paid that differs between the income and

---

[11]Other changes under this proposal include elimination of the 60 percent exclusion for long-term capital gains, repeal of or limitations on many tax credits, and lengthening the depreciable lives of many investments.

expenditure tax approaches).[12] However, in each case the principle is basically the same - income would be taxed when it was spent rather than when it was earned. Taxable income would be computed by subtracting amounts saved from income earned in the course of a year. Progressivity could be built in by increasing the marginal tax rate with the level of expenditure. Since distinctions between various forms of income are irrelevant to the tax base, taxation would not influence preferences toward the form in which compensation was earned, and employee demand for nonwage remuneration would decline.

Finally, Congress could adopt the value added tax (VAT) version of an expenditure tax. Under this approach, which is currently used in several European countries, a tax is applied to the value added at each stage of production (hence, it is often described as a national sales tax). If progressivity is desired, it must be approximated by varying tax rates by category of expenditure so as to apply relatively high rates to goods and services consumed mainly by the rich. Since both wages and

---

[12]Recent proposals and discussions include Henry Aaron and Harvey Galper, "Reforming the Tax System," in Alice Rivlin (ed.), **Critical National Choices** (Washington, D.C.: The Brookings Institution, 1984); Peter Mieskowski, "The Advisability and Feasibility of an Expenditure Tax System," in Henry J. Aaron and Michael J. Boskin (eds.), **The Economics of Taxation** (Washington, D.C.: The Brookings Institution, 1980), pp. 179-201; and Robert E. Hall and Alvin Rabushka, **Low Tax, Simple Tax, Flat Tax** (New York: McGraw-Hill, 1983).

fringes are part of value added, they would be treated symmetrically under a VAT, and the tax system would be neutral with respect to the choice between wage and nonwage forms of compensation.

In summary, it would seem that most of the main alternatives for revenue-raising tax reforms that will be under consideration following the 1984 election would reduce or remove tax-induced preferences for fringe benefits relative to wage income, presumably slowing the future growth of fringes relative to wages.

Future Wage Inflation and Its Control

Over the past twenty years the United States has experienced considerable annual variation in the extent of wage inflation and three efforts by the federal government to use income policies to restrain wage and price increases (the Kennedy-Johnson guideposts, Nixon's phases, and Carter's stages). None of the incomes policy episodes were notably successful, and it is hard to find examples of important success among the many incomes-policy experiments that have been conducted in Europe over the past twenty years. On the other hand, the deep recession of the 1980s has demonstrated that the drastic use of market forces can achieve a marked deceleration in wages. In the United States overall wage and compensation changes have fallen to the 4 to 5 percent per year change yielding unit labor cost changes of 2 to 3 percent. One must go back almost twenty years to find increases this low. This perspective poses two questions concerning wage behavior and policy for the next few years. First, have there been important structural changes in compensation arrangements during the wage deceleration of the early 1980s that would change the wage response of the economy to a future economic expansion? That is, if one were to rerun the general economic conditions of the 1970s, would the wage response differ? The answer to this first question also answers part of a ubiquitous second question: whether governments might be inclined to use incomes policies in the future. The rest of the second question - whether the policies are likely to be more effective than in the past - is more conjectural for reasons indicated below.

The wage deceleration of the early 1980s was a dramatic response to a dramatic set of economic circumstances. In contrast to the prior twenty years, union wages led the deceleration rather than acting as a drag on it (although in the early stages this was in part the result of fortuitous timing of the contract cycle). By 1983 a third of the workers covered by major collective bargaining agreements in manufacturing received wage **reductions** and another quarter received no fixed wage change. There was also a substantial decline in compensation from cost-of-living adjustments as consumer price inflation declined and as collective bargaining negotiations resulted in canceled, deferred, or diverted COLA payments. The fact that these dramatic concessions occurred during a period in which work stoppages were at the lowest levels since the late 1930s also indicates that they resulted from a scaling back of union bargaining objectives as well as employer pressure to reduce labor costs. As noted earlier, however, the concessions only just began to check and reverse the thirteen year growth in the union-nonunion wage gap in manufacturing.

Thus, while there has been a dramatic decrease in the size (and, in some cases, sign) of wage adjustments, there is little evidence that this was accompanied by alterations in compensation arrangements that portend a significant change in the response of wages to a given set of economic conditions. At least in the labor market, the economy would seem to be about as inflation prone as in the past. This conclusion, along with the speed of the recovery to date, resurrects the issue of government policy toward wage increases. Absent a structural change in wage determination, the probability that the government will at some date have to reconsider incomes policy as a policy instrument is high. The question, then, is whether there is any basis for thinking that the results of such an escapade would be any more successful than in the past.

The basic problem facing designers of any incomes policy is the **compliance risk** faced by workers considering compliance with the pay standard set forth by a government. Compliance risk arises because the benefits of compliance with incomes policy are a public good. The slower rate of inflation that results from lower wage increases benefits everyone, and there is no way to restrict the benefits to those who produce the benefit by complying with government pay standards. Indeed, since wage restraint produced by the compliance of any one group of workers will have a small impact on the **overall** rate of price increase, the group will collect only a small fraction of the total benefit that its action produces. At the same time other groups, knowing that any benefits produced by the compliance of workers elsewhere will accrue to all workers irrespective of their degree of compliance, may choose not to comply and to take a free ride on the benefits of the compliance by others. Overall price restraint from the policy will then be limited and groups of workers who comply with the program will suffer a lower increase in real pay and a lower wage level relative to those who do not comply. Small wonder that this prisoner's dilemma frequently defaults into limited compliance.

Income policies in the United States and Europe have not been notably successful in addressing the problem of compliance risk. The policies of the 1960s, which were often based upon pay and price guidelines announced by a government did not address the issue at all. Indeed, virtually all of the risks associated with the policies rested on the workers who were being asked to comply with them. Two general approaches to this problem emerged in the 1970s: the "social contract" and the tax-based incomes policy (TIP). The social contract approach, found almost exclusively in Europe, consists of multilateral negotiations between the government and the main economic interest groups in an effort to reach a bargaining solution that includes commitments on wages, prices, and tax and expenditure policy. The general approach is an advance conceptually over the older guideline approach in that it recognizes that the government may have to offer compensation (in the form of specific policy measures) to labor and other economic interest groups in exchange for their compliance and the risks that the compliance entails. This approach has at most cosmetic value in the United States (witness the National Accord of the Carter administration), for given the country's institutional setup, neither of the parties to bargaining are able to deliver on the commitments that the other is seeking in the negotiations.[13] For that reason, I put little stock in this approach.[14]

The TIP approach to incomes policy has received more talk than application thus far. Several different varieties of TIPs have been proposed. Some would offer rewards for compliance with pay and/or price standards. Others would impose penalties for noncompliance. In either case the incentives would be aimed at groups of workers at the firm level, so that the TIP approach may be more suited to economies, such as the United States, with relatively decentralized wage-setting. Yet, not all TIPs address the problem of compliance risk. Only the real wage insurance version, under which workers receive a tax rebate to indemnify them for greater-than-expected price increases, goes in this direction. Even this, however, would leave workers who comply with a lower re-

---

[13] As is widely appreciated, the AFL-CIO has little influence over the bargaining objectives of its affiliates, and the executive branch of the federal government cannot bind Congress to any commitments that it might make as part of social contract negotiations.

[14] For a detailed examination of European social contract experiments and the difficulties encountered in trying to apply the compensatory approach to incomes policy, see Robert J. Flanagan, David W. Soskice, and Lloyd Ulman, **Unionism, Economic Stabilization, and Incomes Policy: European Experience** (Washington: Brookings Institution, 1983).

lative wage than those who do not. Despite potential difficulties, the TIP approach (particularly the real wage insurance variant) seems better suited to the relatively decentralized wage setting institutions in both the union and nonunion sectors of the United States. If someone were to insist on another social experiment with incomes policy, this is where I would put my money.

Concluding Comments

A few themes emerge from the foregoing review of recent and prospective compensation growth. One is that some of the major influences on current compensation developments are quite remote from the labor market. Since 1970 the compensation prospects of workers in export and import-competing industries have first benefited from and then lost from changes in the exchange rate. The division of pay into wage and nonwage payments is strongly influenced by tax law. Clearly, the parties who establish compensation arrangements are not always responsible for their shape or consequence.

A second, less explicit, theme is that one should not confuse changes in the structure of compensation with changes in its level. The relatively rapid growth of fringe benefits implies nothing more than a relatively slow growth of wages. Competitive employers must trade one form of compensation for another if they are to survive. Sometimes the results of this proposition can be quite subtle, as when employers who incur (legally mandated) costs to improve the work environment subsequently increase monetary pay less rapidly.

A third theme has been that there have been few alterations in those aspects of union pay determination that most influence the aggregate flexibility of money wages.

Daniel J.B. Mitchell

12

Labor Relations Over the Past Five Years: Implications for the Future

In 1979, the Autoworkers Union, in recognition of the special economic difficulties then facing the Chrysler Corporation, separated that company's negotiations from those with Ford and General Motors. As a result, Chrysler received a less costly wage package than the other firms. This episode signaled the beginning of a period of "concession bargaining" in the union sector. By the end of 1983, a large fraction of the unionized work force had been covered by some form of concession contract.

Various developments might be cited to explain the concession movement. Obviously, there were legal and political developments which were unfavorable from the union point of view. Among those which might be noted were new appointments to the National Labor Relations Board (NLRB) by the Reagan administration, the firing of striking air traffic controllers by the President, a Supreme Court decision permitting employers to void union contracts in bankruptcy proceedings, and administrative changes with regard to the Davis-Bacon Act. However, although these developments have attracted considerable media attention, and although they may have long-run significance for unions, a major theme of this essay is that they had little to do with the concession bargaining which began in 1979.

Even if the question of the cause(s) of concession bargaining is put aside, another issue arises as to the long-term impact of the concessions themselves. Some observers of the industrial relations scene have asserted that the concessions represent an alteration in the fundamental style of collective bargaining. The argument is basically that collective bargaining has become - or is becoming - a completely different institution. But others - including this author - have argued that a more restrained position is warranted by the evidence.[1]

In what follows, four key points will be developed:

1) The key mover in the wage concessions made since 1979 has been the economy. Both macro and micro conditions and policies produced an atmosphere in which concessions became necessary for survival.

---

[1] In a previous paper, I have reviewed the literature on concession bargaining as it stood as of late 1982. See Daniel J.B. Mitchell, "The 1982 Union Wage Concessions: A Turning Point for Collective Bargaining?", **California Management Review,** Vol. 25 (Summer 1983), pp. 78-92. Two more recent sources are D. Quinn Mills, "When Employees Make Concessions," **Harvard Business Review,** Vol. 61 (May-June 1983), pp. 103-113, and Peter Cappelli, "Union Gains Under Concession Bargaining," **Proceedings** of the Industrial Relations Research Association, December 1983.

2) Management's "hard line" - basically the willingness to replace strikers and operate nonunion if management's bargaining objectives could not be met - did not develop because the President took a tough stance with the air traffic controllers. Rather, economic conditions enhanced the probabilities that a hardline approach would be successful and also put more pressure on management to restrict labor costs.

3) Although concession bargains have contained some novel features, the primary impact of the era of wage concessions has **not** been to alter the fundamentals of collective bargaining. Rather, the impact was to reduce the size of the union sector, probably on a long-term basis.

4) The novel features in some of the concession bargains are a mixed bag. Some may prove popular enough to outlast the concession era, others may fade away, and still others carry the seeds of potential future conflict.

I. Concession Bargains

Since collective bargaining is a give-and-take process under any circumstances, it is difficult to define a "concession" in a precise manner. In this paper, an operating definition is adopted that includes as concessions negotiations in which the basic wage is either frozen or reduced for the first year of the contract. Obviously, other definitions are possible. However, the operating definition has two virtues. First, it includes most of the negotiations which have generally been viewed as concessions in the media. Second, it has the practical virtue of being easily measurable.

There is a difficulty with the wage freeze or cut definition. Price inflation was considderably reduced after 1980. Hence, the significance of a nominal wage freeze or cut changed in real terms as the inflation rate decreased. It can be asked, therefore, whether wage freeze or cut contracts were "truly" abnormal developments.

One way of dealing with this question is to use the 1983 rate of consumer price inflation as a baseline against which wage settlements can be measured. An immediate measurement problem arises from this approach; there are two consumer price indexes published by the U.S. Bureau of Labor Statistics (BLS). These differ slightly in terms of weighting schemes. More importantly, in 1983 the two indexes differed in the treatment of the housing sector. One index - CPI-U - applied a rental approach to owner-occupied housing. The other index - CPI-W - used a different concept which is sensitive to mortgage interest rates. The latter index has been most frequently used for union escalator clauses and was at one time the only consumer price index published. But the former is probably a better measure of actual price inflation.[2]

---

[2]Discussion of this problem and other matters relating to the CPI can be found in Daniel J. B. Mitchell, "Should the Consumer Price Index Determine Wages?", **California Management Review,** Vol. 25 (Fall 1982), pp. 5-21.

Table 1 avoids this measurement problem by presenting data based on both indexes. Columns (1) and (2), respectively, show the inflation rate as measured by CPI-U (current definition) and CPI-W. As can be seen from the table, during the 1970s, CPI-W generally exceeded CPI-U due mainly to rising mortgage interest rates. By 1982, however, this relationship reversed as interest rates declined. Thus, in 1983, CPI-U rose by 3.8 percent and CPI-W rose by 3.3 percent. Put another way, a wage freeze in 1983 amounted to a real wage decrease in 1983 of 3.8 percent as measured by the former index and 3.3 percent as measured by the latter.

The BLS maintains data on private union contracts covering 1,000 or more workers. These major-contract data reveal that wage freezes have been rare - but not unprecedented - during the period prior to the concession era. In particular, a significant proportion of the workers under new major union agreements were subjected to first-year wage freezes in the early 1960s. Note, however, that price inflation was lower during that period than it was during the early 1980s. Yet the later period featured a high proportion of workers experiencing freezes or cuts in wages.

The major-contract data also show that wage cuts were virtually nonexistent until the early 1980s, even during the low-inflation period of the early 1960s. Obviously, instances of wage cutting can be found in isolated situations. And, of course, wage cuts can be found further back in history than the years covered by Table 1.[3] But nominal wage cutting is clear-

---

[3]For an analysis of the 1920s and early 1930s, see Daniel J.B. Mitchell, "Wage Flexibility: Then and Now," **Industrial Relations,** Vol. 24 (Spring 1985), pp. 266-279.

Table 1

Distribution of Workers Under Major Union Settlements, Private Sector, 1959-1983

Year	Annual Rate of Change[a] (%) CPI-U[b] (1)	CPI-W (2)	Proportion of Workers Under Major Settlements with: First-Year Wage Freeze or Cut (3)	First-Year Wage Cut (4)	First-Year Adjustment 3.8% Below CPI-U[b] (5)	First-Year Adjustment 3.3% Below CPI-W (6)
1959	—	1.5	3	0	—	0
1960	—	1.5	4	0	—	0
1961	—	0.7	7	0	—	0
1962	—	1.2	22	0	—	0
1963	—	1.6	25	0	—	0
1964	—	1.2	5	0	—	0
1965	—	1.9	4	0	—	0
1966	—	3.4	1	0	—	1
1967	—	3.0	1	0	—	0
1968	—	4.7	0	0	—	0
1969	5.2	6.1	1	0	1	1
1970	4.5	5.5	0	0	0	0
1971	3.5	3.4	1	0	0	1

1972	3.3	3.4	3	0	0	3
1973	8.5	8.8	1	0	21	41
1974	11.1	12.2	1	0	24	39
1975	6.6	7.0	4	0	8	9
1976	5.1	4.8	4	0	6	6
1977	6.3	6.8	2	0	7	9
1978	7.9	9.0	2	0	11	31
1979	10.8	13.4	4	0	42	52
1980	10.8	12.5	0	0	24	50
1981	8.5	8.7	8	5	12	13
1982	5.0	3.9	44	2	47	45
1983	3.8	3.3	37	15	37	37

- = Not available.

aDecember-to-December basis.

bCurrent definition CPI-U. CPI-U-X1 prior to 1982.

Note: Estimates in columns (3) to (6) are rounded to nearest whole number.

Source: Current Wage Developments, Monthly Labor Review, various issues.

ly a most unusual practice; the fact that 15 percent of the workers covered by major agreements in 1983 experienced wage cuts is dramatic evidence of atypical behavior.

It is possible to cut the real - as opposed to the nominal - wage during periods of positive inflation by simply granting wage increases below the rate of price increase. Thus, an interesting question is whether there have been previous episodes of wage cutting in real terms equal to 3.8 percent as measured by current definition CPI-U or 3.3 percent as measured by CPI-W, i.e., the rates that would have been experienced in 1983 by a worker whose nominal wage was frozen.

Columns (5) and (6) provide estimates of the proportion of workers who suffered real wage losses under newly negotiated settlements equivalent to 3.8 percent or 3.3 percent, using the two price indexes. Two periods can be identified prior to the concession era in which significant fractions of the workers under major settlements experienced such losses: 1973-74 and the late 1970s. Both periods differed from the concession era in that they were characterized by accelerating inflation. The real wage losses were in large part wage **lags** rather than deliberate cuts in worker purchasing power. In contrast, during the concession era, inflation was decelerating. If anything, wage lags ought to have produced above normal increases in real wages. By any measure, then, the concession era represents an unusual episode in union wage determination.

II. Concession-prone Industries and Unions

Tables 2 and 3 present the results of a tabulation of union wage agreements during 1982 and 1983, respectively, which resulted in first-year wage freezes or cuts. The tabulations were based on surveys appearing in the **Daily Labor Report** on a biweekly basis. Some evidence of the accelerating pace of concession bargaining is found in the number of contracts underlying the two tables. The 1982 results involved 160 contracts, while the 1983 tabulation is based on 444 settlements.

There is a considerable overlap of industries and unions in the two tables. Construction is the leading concession sector in both years. The construction industry has been historically recession-prone. In addition, nonunion competition has been capturing an increasing share of the marketplace. Unions have complained of "double breasted" operators in construction; unionized employers who have opened nonunion subsidiaries. Employers have complained of differential labor costs between union and nonunion contractors which put unionized contractors at a competitive disadvantage.

The unions that lead the concession listings of Tables 2 and 3 are those affiliated most closely with the concession-prone industries. In particular, the Teamsters have the misfortune to fall into several such industries including trucking, construction, and retail foodstores. Similarly, the Food and Commercial Workers find themselves in both meatpacking and retail food.

Table 2

Industry and Union Pattern of Wage Freeze and Cut Contracts, 1982

Industry	Teamsters	Autoworkers	Food and Commercial Workers	Transit Union	Rubber Workers	Carpenters	Machinists	Electrical Workers (IBEW)	Steelworkers	Plumbers	All Others	Percent of Total Wage Freeze or Cut Contracts	Wage Cuts as a Proportion of Wage Freezes and Cuts[c] (%)
Construction	x					x		x		x	x	24	18
Metals	x	x					x		x		x	9	21
Public transit[a]				x							x	9	0
Motor vehicles[b]		x									x	8	0
Retail foodstores	x		x									8	8

Rubber						X	7	0
Machinery	X				X	X	6	11
Meatpacking		X					6	11
Airlines	X					X	4	29
Trucking	X				X		3	0
All others	X				X	X	X	18	14
Percent of total wage freeze of cut contracts	13	9	8	6	5	5	4	4	32	100	12

Note: An "X" indicates one or more wage freeze or cut contracts were negotiated by union indicated in designated industry.

aIncluding intercity bus lines.

bIncluding motor vehicle parts.

cExcludes wage cuts affecting only new hires. Wage cut may not have affected all workers under the contract.

Source: Daniel J.B. Mitchell, "The 1982 Union Wage Concessions: A Turning Point for Collective Bargaining?" **California Management Review**, Vol. 25 (Summer 1983), pp. 80-81.

Table 3

Industry and Union Pattern of Wage Freeze and Cut Contracts, 1983

Industry	Union											Percent of Total Wage Freeze or Cut Contracts	Wage Cuts as a Proportion of Wage Freezes and Cuts[b] (%)
	Steelworkers	Food and Commercial Workers	Teamsters	Carpenters	Laborers	Operating Engineers	Autoworkers	Plasterers	Plumbers	Machinists	All Others		
Construction			x	x	x	x		x	x			x	45	24
Metals	x		x	x			x			x		x	12	38
Machinery	x						x			x		x	8	11
Retail foodstores		x	x									x	7	21
Lumber and paper				x								x	5	0

Printing and publishing			X				X	3	86
Meatpacking	X							3	0
Airlines			X			X	X	2	64
Aerospace					X	X	X	2	0
Motor vehicles[a]					X		X	2	0
All others	X	X	X		X		X	12	14
Percent of total wage freeze & cut contracts	9	9	7	6	6	5 4 4	36	100	24

Note: An "X" indicates one or more wage freeze or cut contracts were negotiated by union indicated in designated industry. Details need not add to totals due to rounding.

[a] Including motor vehicle parts.

[b] Excludes wage cuts affecting only new hires. Wage cut may not have affected all workers under contract.

Source: **Daily Labor Report**, various issues.

III. Characteristics of the Concession-prone Sector

BLS data on workers covered by major collective bargaining contracts can be conveniently broken down into forty-one industry classifications in the private, nonfarm sector. Those which were particularly concession-prone, as identified on Tables 2 and 3 can be separately analyzed.[4] Table 4 distinguishes the concession-prone industries from the others by various characteristics.

As can be seen from the table, concession-prone industries tended to pay higher wages than other sectors. They had a larger concentration of union represented workers and major contracts. And their unionization rate - measured by the ratio of workers under major con-

---

[4]Sixteen industries were identified as concession-prone, based on Tables 2 and 3. These were translated as closely as possible into the SIC (Standard Industrial Classification) codes used by BLS. The sixteen industries were construction (three industries: SIC 15, 16, 17), metals (two industries: SIC 33, 34), local transit (SIC 41), transportation equipment (SIC 37), retail foodstores (SIC 54), rubber manufacturing (SIC 30), machinery (SIC 35), food manufacturing (SIC 20), airlines (SIC 45), motor freight (SIC 42), lumber and paper (two industries: SIC 24, 26), and printing and publishing (SIC 27). The complete list of BLS industries (which account for most of the private, nonfarm sector) can be found in John J. Lacombe II and James R. Conley, "Collective Bargaining Calendar Crowded Again in 1984," **Monthly Labor Review,** Vol. 107 (January 1984), p. 30. The average hourly earnings figures of Table 4 are simple averages of the industry estimates. Average hourly earnings data were not available for airlines and water transportation. These industries are omitted from the earnings estimates of Table 4.

Table 4

Characteristics of Industries with High and Low Concession Rates, November 1979

	Characteristic	Industries with High Concession Rates[a] (1)	Industries with Low Concession Rates (2)
(1)	Average hourly earnings[b] ($)	7.59	6.42
(2)	Number of workers under major union contracts (millions)	5.6	3.8
(3)	Number of major union contracts	1,326	720
(4)	Unionized workers as percent of production and nonsupervisory workers[c]	34	9

[a] Comprises SIC 15, 16, 17, 20, 24, 26, 27, 30, 33, 34, 35, 37, 41, 42, 45, 54. All other industries from the BLS tabulation are in column (2).

[b] Simple average of industries. Production and nonsupervisory workers. Excludes water and air transport.

[c] Row (2) divided by production and nonsupervisory workers in column (1) or (2).

Source: *Employment and Earnings, Monthly Labor Review,* various issues.

tracts to production and nonsupervisory employees - was substantially higher.

Of course, since only union bargainers can make union wage concessions, it is not surprising that union workers were especially concentrated in the concession-prone industries. And, since union workers tend to be more highly paid on average than others, it is also not surprising that hourly earnings are higher in the concession-prone sector. However, Table 5 suggests that employment trends have diverged between the concession-prone industries and the other industries.

Employment trends are not inherent in the definition of concession-prone industries. Thus, the fact that the trends diverge suggests a causal factor in the concessions. Specifically, union employment appears to have declined substantially faster at an annual rate in concession-prone industries than in other industries during 1979-82. The same divergent trend appears if the measure of employment used is the number of production and nonsupervisory employees. In that case, the concession-prone sector shows a declining trend over 1979-83, while the other industries show an employment increase.

Table 5 does not explain why employment declined. However, a substantial loss of employment in a large sector over a brief span of years will occur only during a general economic decline. The shift in macroeconomic policy in 1979 toward a restrictive, anti-inflation stance is the culprit for much of what appears in Table 5. However, in certain industries, the macro forces were enhanced by special characteristics of the particular industries in the concession-prone sector.

Table 5

Employment Trends, 1979-1983

	Industries with High Concession Rates[a] (1)	Industries with Low Concession Rates (2)
Annual rate of change in number of workers under major union contracts(%)	-5.0	-3.3
Annual rate of change in number of production and nonsupervisory workers(%)	-2.4	+1.1

[a]See Table 4 for definition.

Source: See Table 4.

Some industries are especially sensitive to recession. The case of construction has already been noted above. But the same factor affects such industries as autos, metals, rubber, lumber, and trucking. In addition, the appreciation of the U.S. dollar after 1979 adversely affected the competitive position of a number of import-competing industries. Autos and metals also fall into this category. The dollar appreciation appears itself to have been the result of macro policy. Large, ongoing federal budget deficits apparently raised U.S. interest rates sufficiently to attract foreign financial capital, thus bidding up the dollar exchange rate.

There were also micro-level economic policy effects in certain industries. Deregulation in the transportation area affected union employment adversely in trucking and airlines. (Its effect was also apparent in the Greyhound dispute of 1983.) The policy of deregulation, it might be noted, had its roots in the Carter administration. Indeed, the Reagan administration appeared to be reluctant to move quickly in trucking, apparently in response to election support by the Teamsters.

All of these factors came together and combined with still another influence, prior relative wage growth, as discussed below. The impact on union wage bargaining far exceeded any specific labor relations policy mounted by the Reagan administration or the courts. For example, there is no doubt that Reagan administration appointments to the NLRB were unfavorable to unions. However, the NLRB is not much involved in specific contract negotiations. Unions were disappointed in the Board's **Milwaukee Spring** decision, a decision which made it somewhat easier for employers to close a plant during the life of a collective bargaining agreement.[5] But the plant closing issue becomes important only during a recession. Had there been no recession, the plant closing issue would have been much less significant as a determinant of wage outcomes.

The bankruptcy issue also falls into the category of a policy that matters only during a recession. In a 1984 ruling, the Supreme Court made it easier for employers to sever union contracts in the course of a bankruptcy action.[6] But bankruptcy is not a costless route for employers. Employers that have used the bankruptcy route - notably Continental Airlines and Wilson Foods - have been under prior distress due to background economic conditions.

The attitude of the administration, the NLRB, and the courts will have a long-term influence, however, on the growth or decline in the union sector. A more hostile environment makes organizing difficult. Unions need to organize new employers simply to hold their position in the labor market; hanging on to old employers by itself can only produce long-run

---

[5]For an analysis see "NLRB Okays Employer's Authority to Move Work to Nonunion Facility," **Daily Labor Report**, January 25, 1984, pp. AA1-AA2, G1-G9. The Board's decision was a reversal of its 1982 verdict on the same case. That earlier decision had been appealed to the courts, but was recalled by the NLRB after its membership had sufficiently altered. There will be further court challenges to the Board's 1984 decision.

[6]For an analysis of this case, see "Supreme Court Permits Unilateral Rejection of Contract by Financially Troubled Employer," **Daily Labor Report**, February 23, 1984, pp. AA1-AA3, D1-D12.

decline as the older industries which unions have traditionally organized (and the older employers within those industries) give way to new sources of employment.

IV. Trends in Union Membership

Since membership trends seem to be linked in the short run to concessions (as shown in Table 5), and since membership growth is needed by unions if they are to remain an influential force in society in the future, it is important to analyze these trends in detail. What was the record before the downturn in 1979? What happened to membership during the 1979-83 period?

Table 6 reports a tabulation based on major union contract coverage for the private sector. According to the table, during the period 1972-79, the number of workers covered by major union agreements fell by 734,000. Had no such loss occurred, the major unionization rate would have been 1.2 percentage points higher than it actually was in 1979. Yet most industries expanded their work forces during the period 1972-79. If unions had simply held their own on an industry-by-industry basis, not only should the number of workers covered by major contracts not have decreased, it should have shown an increase of some 919,000, according to the table. Thus, during 1972-79, unions lost the representation of almost 1.7 million workers. These were workers who would have been represented had unions held on to their 1972 representation rates in each industry.[7]

---

[7]Major union contracts covered 10.2 million workers in the private sector in 1972. The figure fell to 9.4 million in 1979 and to 7.9

Table 6

Change in Major Union Contract Coverage,
1972-1979

	Number (000s)	As percent of Production and Nonsupervisory Workers, 1979
Decrease in workers covered by major union contracts, 1972-1979	-734	-1.2
Explained by industrial employment shifts	+919	+1.5
Unexplained by industrial employment shifts	-1,653	-2.7
Construction	+16	*
Manufacturing	-681	-1.1
Transport and utilities	-566	-0.9
Wholesale and retail trade	-100	-0.2
Extractive industries	+24	*
Services and other	-346	-0.6

*Absolute value less than 0.05 percent.

Source: **Monthly Labor Review, Employment and Earnings,** various issues.

The situation became much grimmer from the union viewpoint during the 1979-83 period. Table 7 shows that about 1.5 million workers disappeared from the major contract sector in those years. Since employment was declining, some decrease in representation could have been expected. The table indicates that about half of the decline - 764,000 workers - can be explained by detailed industry employment trends. However, the remaining loss (740,000) cannot be explained by reference to changing employment levels.

These figures are by no means precise. However, they point to an interesting similarity between the two periods. At an annual rate, the unexplained loss of union representation in the two periods, 1972-79 and 1979-83, averaged roughly 200,000 per year. This unexplained loss can be viewed as an ongoing erosion of the union sector. Unions did not react to the erosion in the earlier period because it was largely masked by rising employment. During 1972-79, industry-level employment growth offset the underlying erosion by about 100,000

---

million by 1983. It might be noted that the BLS updates its estimates of the number of workers covered by particular contracts as they expire. Hence, during periods of declining employment, the numbers may be overstated, since not all contracts expire in a given year. For that reason, the loss of union represented workers during 1979-83 may be understated in Table 7. Finally, it should be noted that the estimates of Tables 6 and 7 would vary with the industry classification scheme used. Estimates described in the text used the most detailed industry code available from the published data. For the period 1972-79, it was necessary to interpolate certain industry estimates in construction, transportation, and retailing due to more limited detailed information.

Table 7

Change in Major Union Contract Coverage,
1979-1983

	Number (000s)	As percent of Production and Nonsupervisory Workers, 1983
Decrease in workers covered by major union contracts, 1979-1983	-1,504	-2.4
Explained by industrial employment shifts	-764	-1.2
Unexplained by industrial employment shifts	-740	-1.2
Construction	-144	-0.2
Manufacturing	-314	-0.5
Transport and utilities	+4	*
Wholesale and retail trade	-206	-0.3
Extractive industries	-101	-0.2
Services and other	+21	*

*Absolute value less than 0.05 percent.

Source: **Monthly Labor Review, Employment and Earnings,** various
   issues.

per year. That is, generally favorable economic conditions cut the observed erosion by approximately one half of the underlying erosion. A gradual employment decline could be accommodated by unions in their periodic wage negotiations. Senior workers were not threatened by job loss; decline could be met through attrition and turnover of junior level individuals.

But, during 1979-83, the underlying erosion was not masked. Rather, it was reinforced by general employment trends. Declining employment added roughly 200,000 lost workers at an annual rate on top of the underlying erosion. The observed erosion was approximately double the underlying rate. Under those conditions, senior workers were threatened. Mass layoffs, plant, and company shutdowns became a real threat. This threat to core union workers triggered the wage concession movement.

V. Bargaining Outcomes

There has been debate over whether the wage settlements reached during the concession era will have a "permanent" effect on future collective bargaining. The question usually posed is whether bargaining will eventually return to "normal." Unfortunately, different notions of "normality" are possible and no meaningful answer to the question can be given unless precise definitions are used.

"Normal" should not be identified with a specific magnitude of wage settlement. The high wage increases of the late 1970s were no more normal than the previous lower settlements were abnormal. Different economic conditions will produce different sized settlements. Price inflation is a key determinant of the rate of wage inflation. Ten percent wage increases in the face of the very low inflation rates of the early 1960s would have been abnormal. But ten percent settlements in the late 1970s were not.

It is possible that as the economy recovers, there may be demands for wage catch-up by unions and workers who previously made concessions. In that sense, wage settlements for a time might exceed normally expected levels but would be reflecting abnormally low bargains earlier. But even in that limited case, not all demands will be translated into actual outcomes. Management resistance is likely to be strong where changes in the competitive environment have occurred. Sometimes management resistance may fail, as it seemed to do in the Eastern Airlines settlement with the Machinists in early 1983. However, that contract illustrates the difficulty of ignoring permanent changes in the economic environment (deregulation in the airlines case). Within a few months after the contract began, a new concession bargain had to be reached which overrode it.[8]

Increases in Real Wages

Since "normal" settlements cannot be defined without reference to price inflation, it may be useful to consider settlements in real terms. Table 8 summarizes union wage settlements during the 1981-83 period. As can be

---

[8]The original contract called for 21 percent on January 1, 1983 (following an extended wage freeze) with subsequent increases bringing the wage rise to 32.4 percent over its three-year term. By late 1983, however, the contract was interrupted and pay cuts were imposed.

Table 8

Union Contract Characteristics
1981-83

	All Contracts			Contracts Excluding Wage Freezes and Cuts	
	1981	1982	1983	1982	1983
Median first-year wage increase(%)	9.6[a]	7.0	4.5	7.9[b]	6.3[b]
Proportion of contracts with COLA in effect (%)	24	17	23	14	22
Mean contract duration (months)	32	29	32	29	33
Proportion of contracts containing wage freezes or cuts(%)					
Manufacturing	5	11	24	—	—
Nonmanufacturing excluding construction	3	11	16	—	—
Construction	0	13	62	—	—
All contracts	3	12	29	—	—

[a] If this figure were adjusted to exclude wage cuts and freezes in 1981, it would be 9.9 percent.

[b] Medians have been treated as if they were means to make these estimates.

Source: Daily Labor Report, various issues.

seen from the table, the proportion of contracts with wage freezes or cuts steadily rose during these years. To determine what "normal" bargainers were doing, the table presents a revised tabulation excluding the freeze-and-cut contracts. By 1983, wage settlements in the first year had fallen to 4.5 percent. But when the wage freezes and cuts are omitted, the typical settlement was a little over 6 percent.

Bargainers in 1983 were looking at price inflation rates over 1982-83 in the 3 to 5 percent range. They might well have assumed an ongoing price inflation rate of 4 percent or so. Thus, a 6 percent bargain would have been perceived as a real wage gain of roughly 2 percent. Extrapolating this experience suggests that when the concession fever runs its course, wage bargains running roughly 2 percent above the increase in consumer prices might be expected. Such a rate of real wage gain is consistent with productivity trends through the mid-1990s as forecast by a number of economists.[9] Thus, there is no evidence that an in-

---

[9] For example, see "Brookings Economist Optimistic about Trend in Productivity Growth," **Daily Labor Report**, January 10, 1984, pp. A6-A7, in which Martin Baily of the Brookings Institution suggests that a pattern similar to the productivity improvement of the 1960s could be expected (slightly above 2 percent per year); "Economist Kendrick Projects Healthy Productivity Gains over the Next Decade," **Daily Labor Report**, November 22, 1983, pp. A12-A13, in which John Kendrick of the American Enterprise Institute and George Washington University predicts average gains in the 1980s and 1990s of 2.7 percent and 2.3 percent, respectively. The BLS is projecting private, nonfarm productivity gains of about 1.6 percent for the period 1982-95. See Arthur J. Andreassen, Norman C. Saun-

flationary wage push is awaiting the U.S. economy. Renewed inflation may come, but not because of some alleged, built-in union sector wage pressures.

Long-duration Agreements and Escalators

Collective bargaining contracts prior to the concession era had two prominent features: multiyear duration and - particularly in contracts covering large numbers of workers - escalator clauses providing cost-of-living adjustments (COLAs) indexed to the CPI. Especially during the late 1970s and early 1980s, many in management circles felt that they had been "burned" by COLA clauses. In the automobile case, for example, a leaked memo from General Motors early in 1984 suggested a push by that company to eliminate COLA in its upcoming negotiations.[10]

It is useful to ask initially why management felt that its experience with COLA was undesirable. Table 9 shows the pattern of wage increases experienced under contracts expiring from 1976 to 1984. As is clear from the table, contracts with COLA clauses in retrospect provided larger wage increases than non-COLA contracts up through those contracts expiring in 1983. Only in the case of contracts expiring in 1984 did the pattern reverse.

---

ders, and Betty W. Su, "Economic Outlook for the 1990's: Three Scenarios for Economic Growth, **Monthly Labor Review,** Vol. 106 (November 1983), p. 17.

[10] See "GM Has Plan to Cut 80,000 Workers, Eliminate Wage Increases, Document Shows," **Los Angeles Times,** February 19, 1984, Part 1, p. 22.

Table 9

Annualized Rate of Wage Change Experienced by Contract Expiration Date

Contracts Expiring in:	COLA Contracts[a]	Non-COLA Contracts
1976	7.8	6.6
1977	8.8	8.6
1978	8.1	7.2
1979	8.4	7.3
1980	8.4	7.5
1981	8.6	7.7
1982	8.8	7.4
1983	8.1	9.6
1984	3.9	7.4

Annual Wage Change Experienced (%)

[a] Increases are slightly understated since final COLA adjustments may be omitted.

Source: **Monthly Labor Review,** various issues.

dropped more rapidly than the proportion of workers covered by such contracts. It appears that what COLA abandonment occurred was concentrated in smaller agreements, i.e., those covering relatively small numbers of employees.

Table 11 indicates that some COLA eliminations did occur under new settlements reached in 1981. However, 1981 was a "light" bargaining year and relatively few workers were involved. In 1982, in contrast, virtually all workers who had COLA clauses under previous agreements kept them in their new contracts. And, indeed, 30 percent of workers who did not have COLA clauses in 1982 under previous agreements received new COLAs under their 1982 settlements.

An analysis of the reduction in COLA coverage that occurred for workers under major private contracts during 1979-83 is provided in Table 12. The table shows that the number of workers under COLA contracts fell by just over 1 million in 1979-83 and the number of COLA contracts declined by 243. Some of this decline can be explained by the decline in the number of union represented workers in the various industries in which COLA applied in 1979. If COLA coverage of union workers had remained constant, industry by industry, at the 1979 rates, a decline of 866,000 COLA-covered workers and 194 COLA contracts could have been expected by 1983. Put another way, 86 percent of the decline in COLA-covered workers and 80 percent of the decline in COLA contracts can be explained by changes in union employment patterns.

Table 11

Changes in Escalator Coverage in New Major
Contracts, 1981-1982
(percent of workers)

	Had COLA in Prior Contract		
	Kept COLA in New Contract	Dropped COLA from New Contract	Total
1981	69.5	30.5	100.0
1982	94.1	5.9	100.0

	Did Not Have COLA in Prior Contract		
	Added COLA to New Contract	Did Not Add COLA to New Contract	Total
1981	3.6	96.4	100.0
1982	30.0	70.0	100.0

Source: **Current Wage Developments,** various issues.

Table 12

Change in COLA Coverage in Major Union Contracts, 1979-1983

	Number of Workers (000s)	Number of Contracts
Decrease in workers or contracts with escalators, 1979-1983	-1,008	-243
Explained by industrial shifts in union workers and contracts	-866	-194
Unexplained by industrial employment shifts	-142	-49
Construction	+23	+2
Manufacturing	+218	+20
Transport and utilities	-149	-24
Wholesale and retail trade	-246	-42
Extractive industries	-5	-2
Services and other	+17	-3

Source: **Monthly Labor Review,** various issues.

Since there is not a great deal of unexplained decline in COLA coverage, the residual can be plausibly attributed to the decline in the observed rate of price inflation. Historical evidence suggests that COLA clauses rise in popularity during periods of high inflation and fall in periods of low inflation. The falling inflation rate, rather than a concerted management push, combined with shrinkage of the union sector, accounts for the drop off in COLA coverage during 1979-83.

However, the "quality" of COLA coverage may have been influenced by a management push. Table 13 presents a tabulation based on wage cut and freeze contracts negotiated in 1983. As can be seen on the table, 27 percent of these contracts contained an "active" COLA clause, i.e., one that could potentially provide a pay adjustment during the life of the contract. Only a handful of COLA clauses were either "frozen" (kept in the contract, but suspended from operation) or eliminated. But 61 percent of the active COLA clauses were encumbered by some type of limitation. These limitations involved such devices as "caps" (limits on the absolute amount of COLA wage increase, regardless of inflation), "corridors" (minimum amounts of inflation required to occur before the COLA clause activated), diversion of COLA money to pay for fringes, or some type of degradation (from the worker viewpoint) of the COLA formula. Restriction, not elimination, appears to have been the typical COLA story.

One of the advantages of COLA from the management perspective is that it provides incentive to unions to sign multiyear agreements. The historical evidence suggests that multiyear agreements were a management-side demand. Man-

Table 13

COLA Status and Duration of Contracts Containing First-Year Wage Freezes and Cuts, 1983

	Contracts with Wage Freezes and Cuts	
	All	Contracts with Active COLA
Proportion with active COLA (%)	27	–
Proportion with frozen COLA (%)	1	–
Proportion eliminating COLA (%)	2	–
Mean contract duration (months)	29	35

Source: Calculated from data drawn from **Daily Labor Report,** various issues.

agement wanted to have a guarantee of an extended period of industrial peace. Recent evidence suggests that management still feels strongly about retaining multiyear agreements.[11] Thus, a push to eliminate COLA altogether might not be in management's interest. Moreover, an informed manager would have known that the CPI housing methodology problem was slated to be eliminated from CPI-W (the version of the CPI generally used for escalators) in 1985. Hence, a repeat of the experience with COLA of the late 1970s and early 1980s has become less likely.

Contract duration held up substantially during the concession era. Table 8 showed that contract duration averaged about two and a half years during 1981-83. Concession contracts were slightly shorter than others in 1983, twenty-nine months versus thirty-three months. But some of this discrepancy is due to the heavier weight of construction in concession settlements than in other settlements. Agreements in construction tend to be shorter in duration, even apart from concession agreements, partly because COLA is unusual in construction.

Provisions for Job and Income Security

Wage concession negotiations were not exclusively union givebacks to management. In some instances, in exchange for wage relief, management gave assurances to the union involving job security and plant closings. Sometimes

---

[11]Sanford M. Jacoby and Daniel J.B. Mitchell, "Employer Preferences for Long-Term Union Contracts," **Journal of Labor Research,** Vol. 5 (Summer 1984), pp. 215-228.

these assurances involved guarantees not to close particular plants for some specified period or to provide advance notification for any future shutdowns. Probably the most elaborate schemes were developed in the 1982 auto negotiations. Ford and General Motors provided income protection for long-service workers in case of layoff and agreed to experiment with Japanese style lifetime job guarantees in a few plants.[12]

Obviously, there is a clear-cut benefit to long-service workers in such guarantees. But there are potential costs to management if workers who are idle due to general business conditions must be retained on the payroll. There may be a tendency for management to be more cautious about hiring new workers during business upturns. Management may seek to use subcontractors to handle production peaks and to encourage turnover of junior employees to prevent too many workers from acquiring "tenure." All of these problems will have to be resolved in future negotiations.

Nevertheless, there may be benefits to employers who provide employment guarantees. With workers less nervous about displacement,

---

[12]At a Ford plant where an agreement containing the lifetime employment provisions was put to a worker vote, it was rejected. However, it appears that the rejection was due to other provisions contained in the agreement and local union politics. See "Agreement on First Lifetime Employment Plan Overwhelmingly Rejected by UAW at Ford Plant," **Daily Labor Report,** March 21, 1983, pp. A14-A15. After the rejection, cautious negotiations were reported at both GM and Ford with both parties trying to avoid a repetition of the rejection. See "Training and Job Placement Highlights Gains Under Auto Security Pacts," **Daily Labor Report,** June 1, 1983, pp. A4-A8.

management may find it has a freer hand to introduce new technology, work rules, or even re-site plants. Given the competitive climate in industries such as autos, such freedom could be more valuable than the direct costs of the guarantees.

It is difficult to estimate the scope of the job and income security arrangements which have been negotiated. The Bureau of National Affairs, Inc. (BNA) reported that 23 percent of the contracts it defined as concessions included "implicit" employment security guarantees in 1982.[13] Explicit guarantees - those appearing in the contract and spelling out in detail promises to keep plants open or provide advance warning of shutdowns - were found in 25 percent of the concession contracts. For the first half of 1983, the percentages of contracts including implicit or explicit guarantees were, respectively, 17 and 19 percent.

Two-tier Pay Plans

Use of two-tier pay plans seemed to become more popular - at least with employers - during 1983. Under these plans, wages and/or benefits are reduced for newly hired workers - those who are hired after the plan becomes effective - while members of the existing work force suffer no reductions in pay. Unfortunately, good data on the frequency of such plans do not exist. A rough estimate would be that about 5 percent of new settlements in 1983 had some type of

---

[13]See Bureau of National Affairs, Inc., **BNA's Labor Economic Report: First Half 1983** (Washington: BNA, 1983), p. 13.

two-tier plan.[14] According to the BNA, about 9 percent of concession contracts had "grading" provisions affecting entry level employees in 1982.[15] Approximately 8 percent of the concession contracts surveyed had such provisions during the first half of 1983.

If an employer meets resistance to the idea of a general wage cut, there is an obvious attractiveness in asking instead for a reduction in entry level pay. The individuals who will be hired at the lower rates - by definition - do not take part in the union's ratification process. And the existing work force would rather see someone else's pay cut than their own. But existing workers and their union representatives may be concerned about the future implications of two-tier pay plans. At some future date, management may be tempted to substitute the new, cheaper workers for the more highly paid senior employees.

Some two-tier plans merely stretch out the period during which new workers receive below standard pay, or widen the starting differential. But eventually new workers catch up with the standard rates of pay. Such plans are unlikely to cause substantial future frictions. It is the plans which provide for a "permanent"

---

[14]The BNA reported this estimate, based on its 1983 contract files as of late December 1983. See "Two-Tier Wage Plans: Will They Save Jobs and Money or Just Create Added Problems?", **Daily Labor Report,** December 19, 1983, pp. C1-C3.

[15]Bureau of National Affairs, Inc., **BNA's Labor Economic Report: First Half 1983,** p. 13.

second tier of wage earners that have the potential to spark eventual conflict. They raise the specter of individuals working side by side at identical jobs but earning different rates of pay indefinitely.

Permanent two-tier pay plans were resisted in several well-publicized negotiations. These include disputes at Greyhound Bus Lines, Louisiana-Pacific Corp., Phelps-Dodge, Union Oil, and McDonnell-Douglas. In some cases the union resistance was successful; in other instances it was not.

Probably the most prominent defeat of a two-tier pay plan came in the case of a proposed "rider" to the Teamsters' National Master Freight Agreement covering intercity truck drivers. The union's president negotiated a plan that would have permitted laid-off truck drivers to be recalled at below standard pay rates. But the plan was overwhelmingly defeated in a membership vote. In contrast, one of the more prominent implementations of a two-tier plan came in a settlement involving flight attendants at American Airlines. The union approved an entry level pay reduction of 30 percent in that negotiation.

While the morale and equity issue inherent in two-tier pay plans is obvious, there may be other complications. For example, an employer with an affirmative action plan may find that over a period of time it is paying newly hired women and minorities less than white males in the same jobs. Legal problems for the employer could arise from such a situation. Difficulties for the union could also arise if the new hires raise questions about the fairness of the union representing them in legal forums or through the union's own political mechanism.

Negotiators of two-tier pay plans were undoubtedly aware of their inherent complications. But the complications would arise in the future and the priority was to settle a dispute today. However, even if both sides understood that a problem would eventually arise, they may not have consistent expectations concerning its likely resolution.

The two-tier pay problem can be resolved in the future if pay is again equalized. However, equalization can occur only if the lower pay rates are raised (presumably the union's preferred solution) or if higher pay rates are lowered (the management solution). As the proportion of new hires grows within the work force, the pressure to pick one of those options will also grow. Hence, a future bargaining conflict may have been built into the two-tier pay plans.

Participation and Gain-sharing Arrangements

Quality of work life and issues related to worker participation in management were attracting interest in labor and management circles before the concession era began. Indeed, experiments in labor-management cooperation can be traced back to at least the 1920s.[16] In modern times, American interest in this area was stimulated by examples from Europe and Japan, particularly as concerns mounted about

---

[16] See Sanford M. Jacoby, "Union-Management Cooperation: An Historical Perspective," in Eric G. Flamholtz, ed., **Human Resource Productivity in the 1980s** (Los Angeles: UCLA Institute of Industrial Relations, 1982), pp. 173-215.

U.S. economic performance.

During the concession era, however, the negotiation of cooperative arrangements had an added attraction. From the union perspective, obtaining some kind of greater role in management could be presented to members as a "gain" extracted from management in exchange for a wage concession. The negotiation's outcome would not appear as a one-way giveback, as long as management also conceded something. From the management viewpoint, such arrangements held out the possibility of increasing productivity and efficiency by enlisting or co-opting the union and the work force in the effort.

Probably the most publicized case of union involvement in management came in the Chrysler case in which Douglas Fraser, president of the Autoworkers Union, was placed on the corporation's board of directors. Fraser continued to serve after retiring as president; there appeared to be reluctance on the part of Chrysler management to recommend Owen Bieber, the new union president, as his successor on the board.

There are obvious conflicts of role for a union leader/board director. In 1982, Fraser suspended his board membership during a labor dispute at Chrysler and did not participate in discussions explicitly relating to collective bargaining. Nevertheless, the potential for charges from both sides - union members and management officials - of improper action is always present. Despite this problem, the Autoworkers were interested in establishing a similar arrangement at American Motors, although progress at that firm was stymied by the antitrust complications of representation on two competing enterprises.

In spite of the prominence of the Chrysler case, there were few imitators in other industries. Board representation was extended to unions at Eastern Airlines. But it appears that the cooperative mode was mainly advanced during the concession era through "quality circles" (under various names) and labor-management committees. Unfortunately, the frequency with which these approaches were negotiated - and their effectiveness - is unknown.

In some cases, worker participation arrangements were linked to gain-sharing plans such as profit sharing. Under these plans, worker pay would reflect the economic conditions of the employer. There appeared to be management reluctance to consider such arrangements.[17] During the first half of 1983, the BNA reported that about 5 percent of the concession contracts it surveyed contained profit-sharing or stock-ownership schemes.[18]

Use of profit sharing and other forms of gain sharing has a long history. A government survey of profit sharing was undertaken as early as 1916; some plans go back before the turn of the century.[19] The original motivation for establishing such plans was not concession bargaining but a combination of idealistic objec-

---

[17]"A Management Split Over Labor Relations," **Business Week,** June 14, 1982, p. 19.

[18]Bureau of National Affairs, Inc., **BNA's Labor Economic Report: First Half 1983,** p. 13.

[19]Boris Emmet, **Profit Sharing in the United States,** Bulletin 208 (Washington: Government Printing Office, 1917). The report is dated December 1916, but was published in 1917.

tives of enlisting worker support for the employer and boosting morale. In more recent times, tax benefits have encouraged gain-sharing arrangements. There is much to be said in favor of gain sharing from an economic viewpoint.[20] However, in the context of concession bargaining - particularly when combined with schemes to enable a measure of worker participation in management - gain sharing makes a good deal of sense.

If workers are to participate in management decisions, it can be argued that they should share in the fruits (bitter or sweet) of those decisions. Moreover, the concessions on wages in benefits can be viewed as "investments" in the employer by the workers involved. To the extent the investment has a payoff, there is a logic in sharing the returns.

One of the most interesting attempts to establish a gain-sharing plan - in its extreme form of a complete worker takeover - developed at Conrail. Conrail was formed and operated by the federal government out of the ruins of several bankrupt railroads in the northeastern states. Significant wage concessions were granted to Conrail by the unions with which it bargains. Eventually, the unions submitted an offer to buy the railroad from the federal government. However, at this writing the Reagan administration appeared to be unhappy with the offer and was soliciting bids from other sources.

---

[20] Daniel J.B. Mitchell, "Gain-Sharing: An Anti-Inflation Reform, **Challenge,** Vol. 25 (July-August 1982), pp. 18-25.

VI. The Management Hard-line Approach

During the concession era, there were several disputes which were widely interpreted as representing a new hard-line management approach to collective bargaining. These situations typically involved the announcement that management was prepared to replace strikers with nonunion personnel in the event that the union resisted a demand for concessions. In some instances, Chapter 11 bankruptcy was used to abrogate existing union contracts, a tactic the U.S. Supreme Court upheld for employers in economic distress in early 1984.

In evaluating the hard line, it must be remembered that American management has never welcomed unionization. With limited exceptions the attitude has varied from hostility to grudging acceptance in situations where the costs of union avoidance were more than management wanted to pay. On a day-to-day basis, management and labor might well have carried on an amicable relationship. But management would still have preferred to operate without a union if it could have done so. Thus, it would be wrong to interpret hard-line management tactics of the concession era as heralding a fundamental change in U.S. management ideology.

A more reasonable interpretation is economics. The economic developments of the concession era strengthened the management side. When the labor market is buoyant, workers are more willing to strike than when jobs are scarce. If jobs are available, other family members are likely to be able to bring in income during a strike. And if the worst happens and the striker is replaced, he or she can always find another job. The concession era was marked by a depressed labor market; workers were more likely to accept management demands rather than risk their jobs by striking. And if they did not, replacements were easier to find among the unemployed.

The shift in labor-market conditions can be seen in the available data on strikes. Due to budget cuts, the U.S. Bureau of Labor Statistics now keeps data only on strikes involving 1,000 or more workers. There were 235 such strikes in 1979, 187 in 1980, 145 in 1981, 96 in 1982, and 77 in 1983. It is clear from these data that the climate for militant worker resistance to management demands was unfavorable.

Adoption of a hard-line approach seemed to be as much a matter of personalities as opportunities. Some managements sought labor cooperation in the face of economic distress, rather than take a hard line. This polarizing effect was most apparent in the airline industry. The hard-line approach was epitomized by the decision of Continental Airlines to break its existing union contracts through a bankruptcy filing and then to operate on a nonunion basis in the face of the ensuing strike. At the same time, Eastern Airlines - although operating in the same industry and under similar economic duress - brought in an independent auditor in cooperation with its unions to examine its financial status. The result was a successful concession bargain and a variety of cooperative efforts.

During the early 1960s, economic circumstances resembled those of the early 1980s. In both periods, there were two back-to-back recessions, high unemployment, and declining inflation. Both periods produced a pronounced moderation of wage settlements. And in both, there was discussion of an emerging management hard line, while at the same time there were innovative examples of labor-management cooperation.[21]

In fact, management objectives - whether implemented by a hard-line or soft-line approach - can be linked to a combination of immediate economic circumstances and the prior history of wage determination. Both the concession era which began in 1979 and its counterpart in the early 1960s followed periods in which union wage adjustments had outrun nonunion. While good data were not kept for the early period, beginning in 1976, annual data are available on union and nonunion wage adjustments in the private economy. Table 14 summarizes those changes for the period 1976-83. On a wage and salary basis, union wages outpaced nonunion wages prior to the concession era and even through 1982. Only in 1983 did nonunion wage increases exceed union. And on a total compensation basis, union wage and benefit increases slightly exceeded nonunion, even in 1983. The effect of concession bargaining was therefore a halt (or almost a halt) in the upward creep of the union/nonunion pay ratio. A similar phenomenon was also noted in the early 1960s.[22]

---

[21] I have explored the history of these developments in my paper, "Recent Union Contract Concessions," **Brookings Papers on Economic Activity** (1:1982), pp. 165-201.

[22] Ibid., pp. 174-175.

Table 14

Union and Nonunion Pay Increases, Private Sector, 1976-1983
(percentages)

Year	Wages and Salaries Union	Wages and Salaries Nonunion	Total Compensation[a] Union	Total Compensation[a] Nonunion
1976	8.1	6.8	—	—
1977	7.6	6.6	—	—
1978	8.0	7.6	—	—
1979	9.0	8.5	—	—
1980	10.9	8.0	—	—
1981	9.6	8.5	10.7	9.4
1982	6.5	6.1	7.2	6.0
1983	4.6	5.2	5.8	5.7

— = not available.

[a]Includes private and legally required fringe benefits.

Source: **Current Wage Developments**, various issues.

It appears that concession-prone industries were especially likely to have experienced above-average wage increases during the period leading up to the concession era. Table 15 shows movements in average hourly earnings which have been identified previously as centers of concession bargaining. Hourly earnings data were available on a consistent basis for fifteen two-digit Standard Industrial Classifications. In one industry (air transport) an alternative data source had to be used. Where the two-digit classification did not appear to well represent the highly unionized sectors of the industry, more detailed industry classifications or data specific to union wage rates are used.

During the period 1972-79, hourly earnings in all private, nonfarm industries rose at an annual rate of 7.7 percent. Only two sectors appear to have experienced wage increases below the average rate: the various components of construction and of printing and publishing. In the construction sector a wage explosion occurred in the late 1960s and again - after mandatory controls on wages were lifted - in 1974. However, the initial wage explosion set in motion a movement toward nonunion construction contractors. This movement was severe enough to produce wage moderation in the late 1970s and - when combined with economic recession - wage freezes and cuts during the concession era. In short, the concession story in construction is intimately connected with prior wage movements, but the timing is different from other industries.

Printing and publishing were affected by difficulties in the economic health of newspapers in a number of cities and a revolution

Table 15

Wage Trends in Concession-prone Industries, 1972-1979

	Industry	Annual Rate of Wage Change, 1972-1979[a] (%)
a)	General building construction (15)	6.3
b)	Heavy construction contractors (16)	6.3
c)	Special trade contractors (17)	6.1
	Union wage rates: building trades[b]	6.6*
d)	Food and kindred products (20)	8.5
	Meatpacking plants (2011)	8.3
e)	Lumber and wood products (24)	8.8
f)	Paper and allied products (26)	9.1
g)	Printing and publishing (27)	6.4
	Union wage rates: printing trades[c]	7.4*
h)	Rubber and miscellaneous plastics products (30)	7.7
	Tires and inner tubes (301)	8.6
i)	Primary metal industries (33)	9.9
	Blast furnace and basic steel (331)	11.0
	Primary aluminum (3334)	10.7
j)	Fabricated metal products (34)	8.6
	Metal cans (3411)	10.4
k)	Machinery, except electrical (35)	7.8
	Farm machinery and equipment (3523)	8.6
l)	Transportation equipment (37)	8.4
	Motor vehicle and car bodies (3711)	8.7
	Aircraft (3721)	9.0
m)	Local and interurban passenger transit (41)	9.0
	Union wage rates: local transit operators	8.3
n)	Trucking and warehousing (42)	8.2
	Union wage rates: Chicago, general freight[d]	9.1*
o)	Transport by air (45)	N.A.
	Wages and salaries per full-time employee[e]	7.6*
p)	Food stores (54)	8.5
	Grocery stores (541)	8.9

Note: Average hourly earnings; private nonfarm economy   7.7
Hourly earnings index; private, nonfarm economy   7.7
Wages and salaries per full-time employee[f]   7.5*

Table 15 (continued)

Note: SIC code shown in parentheses.

*Indicates that a series other than average hourly earnings has been used.

[a] November-to-November basis unless otherwise noted.

[b] July-to-July basis.

[c] July 1972 to September 1979. September 1979 figure estimated as average of September 1978 and September 1980.

[d] Drivers' lowest wage rate, July 1972 to September 1979.

[e] Year-to-year basis.

[f] Year-to-year basis, private sector.

Source: **Employment and Earnings, Union Wages and Benefits, Current Wage Developments, Survey of Current Business**, various issues.

in printing technology made possible by computerization. Union wages in the printing trades represented levels of skill which were no longer required. The upshot of these forces was that concession bargaining and the management hard line had an earlier history in printing than elsewhere. A dispute at the **Washington Post** in 1975 foreshadowed strikes at Continental Airlines, Greyhound, and other employers in the 1980s. In the **Post** dispute, management trained supervisory personnel to operate during a strike, subcontracted its printing, and so on. A violent reaction in which presses were damaged ultimately led to permanent replacement of the strikers.

Hourly earnings data for airlines were not available, but an alternative measure - wages and salaries per full-time equivalent employee - suggests that wages in that sector were rising at roughly the average rate for the economy. The story in the airlines industry is largely one of deregulation. Wages in the industry may not have been out of line with the regulated environment in which competition among carriers was restricted. But once deregulation permitted the entry of low-cost, non-union carriers, preexisting cost levels were suddenly excessive. Since airlines have little control over fuel prices and equipment costs, competition centered heavily on wages.

It appears that collective bargainers have difficulty in projecting the long-term implications of their actions, or foreseeing the consequences of changing markets, technology, and public policies such as deregulation. The available data suggest an unfortunate pattern in which short-term considerations dominate until a crunch arrives. At that time, an unwinding of past mistakes occurs through a mix of concession bargaining, management hard-line tactics, or - in some cases - through innovative labor-management experiments.

Correcting this tendency will not be easy. Higher level union officials are better able to comprehend long-run economic consequences than the rank and file. In the short term, unless the employer is verging on bankruptcy, wage pressures have little effect on employment. A manufacturing firm might typically have a ratio of labor costs to sales of, say, 20 to 40 percent. A 10 percent wage increase adds only 2 to 4 percent to unit costs. Employers may gradually respond to cost increases - perhaps by siting new plants in nonunion areas or subcontracting to nonunion or foreign suppliers. Or new competition may slowly penetrate the marketplace. These adjustments probably explain a significant part of the "unexplained" erosion of union membership discussed in Section IV. Slow erosion can be absorbed without much effect on wage determination in a generally expanding economy because its effects are largely masked.

VII. Public Policy Changes

The concession era was not marked by significant changes in basic labor law. Any shifts in public policy which did occur came through administrative changes, appointments to regulatory bodies, and court decisions. An example of an administrative change was a reinterpretation of the procedures for determining prevailing wages under the Davis-Bacon Act by the Reagan administration Labor Department.

Davis-Bacon requires that contractors on federally funded construction projects pay prevailing wages to their workers. In the past it was charged that the Labor Department tended to pick union wage rates as its definition of "prevailing," thus depriving nonunion, lower-wage contractors of their competitive advantage. In fact, Davis-Bacon procedures were more complex than simply picking the union wage. But the Act did limit competition from nonunion contractors and was strongly supported by the building trades unions.

The Reagan administration did not seek repeal of Davis-Bacon, but it did interpret its requirements in such a way as to give contractors more latitude. These changes probably did not have much direct effect on bargaining up through 1983, since they were delayed by court challenges. However, they will undoubtedly have an effect in the future, if retained.[23]

There has been considerable controversy surrounding Reagan administration appointments to the National Labor Relations Board (NLRB). The NLRB conducts union representation elections and hears unfair labor practice charges against employers and unions. However, the Board does not mediate disputes or directly set wages and working conditions.

---

[23]See "Labor Department Issues Davis-Bacon Rules Minus Provisions Voided by District Court," D**aily Labor Report,** May 2, 1983, pp. A9-A10. The new rules took effect on June 28, 1983 and could conceivably have influenced some construction negotiations. It might also be noted that the Reagan administration modified procedures under the Service Contract Act. These changes were upheld in an initial court challenge. See "AFL-CIO Appeals District Court Decision Upholding DOL Service Contract Act Rules, **Daily Labor Report,** February 6, 1984, pp. A11-A13.

NLRB decisions contribute to the overall climate of bargaining over an extended period of time rather than to the short-run outcomes of specific negotiations. As such, the NLRB had little to do with concession bargaining. However, in the future, its attitudes may influence the outcomes of union organizing campaigns. The Board's 1984 **Milwaukee Spring** decision, discussed earlier, could contribute to future union membership erosion to the extent that it makes employer decisions to resite plants to nonunion locations easier.

Finally, court decisions can have a long-term impact on the practice of collective bargaining. The main case of substantial importance during the concession era was the already mentioned bankruptcy case (**Bildisco**) decided by the U.S. Supreme Court in early 1984. It is true that **Bildisco** could give employers more leverage in bargaining about possible concessions with unions during the life of a contract. But most concession bargaining has occurred after contracts have expired. Moreover, to the extent that **Bildisco** undermines the confidence that unions have in long-term contracts, it could provide a future incentive to negotiate short-duration contracts with employers in economic difficulties. Since management has historically preferred long-term contracts, the **Bildisco** case has some unfavorable aspects from the employer viewpoint.

The Reagan administration has generally remained aloof from specific contract negotiations. It did not follow the Carter administration's approach, which included the enunciation of wage guidelines. The main exception to this laissez-faire stance was in the aerospace industry where the federal government is a major consumer of the industry's output. Prior to the 1983 negotiations in aerospace, there were some communications from the Defense Department to employers suggesting the need to hold down labor costs.[24]

Probably, the most dramatic development involving collective bargaining and the Reagan administration came in the air traffic controllers dispute where the federal government was the direct employer. After threatening to fire strikers - striking against the federal government is illegal - the administration carried out its threat and operated the air traffic control system with replacements and those union members who crossed the picket line. It appears that the administration had prepared for a strike situation in advance, if one occurred.[25] However, it is often forgotten that the union and the government initially reached

---

[24]The Reagan administration committed itself to noninvolvement in specific negotiations during its first year or so in office. See Leonard Silk, "Reagan Goals and Labor," **New York Times,** September 18, 1981, p. D2; "Donovan Rejects Government Interference in 1982 Contract Talks, Outlines 1982 Goals," **Daily Labor Report,** January 12, 1982, pp. A3-A5; "Administration Sticking to Principle of Collective Bargaining Noninvolvement," **Daily Labor Report,** February 8, 1982, pp. A5-A7. On the aerospace exception to this policy, see "Air Force Trying to Impose Wage Cap, Aerospace Unions Maintain," **Daily Labor Report,** August 1, 1983, pp. A2-A4; and "Aerospace Unions, Air Force Meet on Alleged Bargaining Interference," **Daily Labor Report,** February 10, 1984, pp. A2-A3.

[25]Attitudes of the Reagan administration toward strikes were spelled out in an article by the director of the U.S. Office of Personnel Management written before the air traffic controllers strike. See Donald J. Devine, "The Chal-

a tentative agreement; i.e., it does not appear that the government deliberately triggered the strike by refusing to negotiate. Rejection of the proposed agreement by union members led to the walkout and firing.

While some view the air traffic controllers dispute as the model for the management hard line which later appeared in the private sector, this interpretation is dubious. The dispute involved an illegal strike in the public sector. To the extent that there were lessons for employers in the outcome of the dispute, those lessons were mainly applicable to government. The administration did not appear to lose public support by taking a tough stance. Public managers and politicians might well have taken note of that fact. The bottom line in government is, after all, voters rather than dollars.

Obviously, the public policy climate during the first term of the Reagan administration became decidedly less favorable from the union viewpoint. Over an extended period of time, such a climate cannot be helpful to unions. However, most of the changes came late in the concession era and had little effect on the concessions of 1979-83. The adverse economic

---

lenge to Federal Employees Today," **Labor Law Journal**, Vol. 32 (July 1981), pp. 387-394, especially pp. 391-392. It might be noted that a Postal Service negotiation was under way while the air traffic controllers were bargaining. The Reagan administration may have been anticipating strike action in the Postal Service, which employed substantially more workers, when it made plans for federal strikes. As it turned out, there was no postal strike and the air traffic controllers may simply have blundered into a strategy which had been designed for another group of employees.

climate dominated the scene. Paul Volcker, chairman of the Federal Reserve Board, had much more to do with concession bargaining than Ronald Reagan.

VIII. The Longer Term

An unfriendly public policy climate for unions will probably take its toll more in terms of organizing and membership than in lower wage settlements. But even if it does, the effect of public policy changes on membership trends may well be substantially less than the membership effects which already accrued from the economic adversity felt during 1979-83.

Suppose the longer term is defined as the period 1984-95. There were 9.4 million workers in 1979 covered by major union agreements in the private sector. The Bureau of Labor Statistics has made employment projections for the year 1995. Using these projections, it is possible to estimate the number of workers who will fall under major private agreements in that year. [26]

---

[26] The projections made by BLS cover all employees, not just production and nonsupervisory workers. Hence, it was necessary to make the calculations described in the text on an all-employee basis. If the proportion of production and nonsupervisory workers in total employment falls during this period, the union representation gains could be overstated. Note that, in any case, the projections make no allowance for the unexplained erosion of unionization of earlier periods. For the BLS projections, see Valerie A. Personick, "The Job Outlook Through 1995: Industry Output and Employment Projections," **Monthly Labor Review**, Vol. 106 (November 1983), pp. 24-36.

One useful tabulation is to pretend that the adversity of 1979-83 never occurred, and to project the number of union represented workers under that assumption. If unions had been able to hang on to their unionization rates on an industry-by-industry basis after 1979, the number of unionized workers by 1995 would rise to almost 11 million, due simply to employment growth. But unionization rates in fact fell between 1979 and 1983. Using 1983 rates to make the projection for 1995 yields only 10.1 million members. Thus, the slippage in unionization between 1979 and 1983 suggests that there will be about 900,000 fewer workers under major contracts by 1995 in the private sector.

The drops in unionization between 1979 and 1983 were heavily influenced by industry economic conditions, plus the continuing underlying erosion effect discussed previously. It is difficult to imagine a single change in public policy which would lead to a loss of 900,000 union represented workers by 1995. Hence, the economic forces which operated during 1979-83 may prove to have had a larger effect on future unionization than the various public policy shifts which occurred during the first term of the Reagan administration.